Understanding
the Male Hustler

HAWORTH Gay & Lesbian Studies
John P. De Cecco, PhD
Editor-in-Chief

New, Recent, and Forthcoming Titles:

Gay Relationships edited by John De Cecco

Perverts by Official Order: The Campaign Against Homosexuals by the United States Navy by Lawrence R. Murphy

Bad Boys and Tough Tattoos: A Social History of the Tattoo with Gangs, Sailors, and Street-Corner Punks by Samuel M. Steward

Growing Up Gay in the South: Race, Gender, and Journeys of the Spirit by James T. Sears

Homosexuality and Sexuality: Dialogues of the Sexual Revolution, Volume I by Lawrence D. Mass

Homosexuality as Behavior and Identity: Dialogues of the Sexual Revolution, Volume II by Lawrence D. Mass

Understanding the Male Hustler by Samuel M. Steward

Sexuality and Eroticism Among Males in Moslem Societies edited by Arno Schmitt and Jehoeda Sofer

Men Who Beat the Men Who Love Them: Battered Gay Men and Domestic Violence by David Island and Patrick Letellier

Understanding the Male Hustler

Samuel M. Steward, PhD

Harrington Park Press
New York • London • Sydney

ISBN 0-918393-96-5

Published by

Harrington Park Press, 10 Alice Street, Binghamton, NY 13904-1580
EUROSPAN/Harrington, 3 Henrietta Street, London WC2E 8LU England
ASTAM/Haworth, 162-168 Parramatta Road, Stanmore (Sydney), N.S.W. 2048 Australia

Harrington Park Press is a subsidiary of The Haworth Press, Inc., 10 Alice Street, Binghamton, NY 13904-1580.

Cover design by Marshall Andrews.

Library of Congress Cataloging-in-Publication Data

Steward, Samuel M.
　　Understanding the male hustler / Samuel M. Steward.
　　　　p.　cm.
　　Includes bibliographical references.
　　ISBN 0-918393-96-5 (pbk.)
　　1. Prostitution, Male — United States.
HQ144.S76　1991b
306.74′3 — dc20
　　　　　　　　　　　　　　　　　　　　　　　　　　　90-27226
　　　　　　　　　　　　　　　　　　　　　　　　　　　CIP

CONTENTS

The author learns that Phil Andros, a well-known and famous hustler, has recently retired. He travels to the hustler's house to hold Phil Andros to a long-standing promise of a lengthy interview on the subject of male prostitution. The two prepare to examine their extended notes on understanding the male hustler and his clients.

They agree to avoid certain sociological and academic mistakes about hustling. Andros describes his early life and first sexual experiences for profit. Both of them briefly consider the beginnings of hustling in classical eras, and an early view of hustling in America is quoted at length. The author shows Phil a list of titles of porno books.

They consider the best ages and characteristics for success in hustling, and discuss some cautions about truth in advertising. They talk about the desirability of weightlifters, cops, and certain other types as hustlers; and rate gyms and bars as hunting preserves.

The lures of money and power are strong, with even laziness seen as a motivating force. They conclude that many hustlers are strongly exhibitionistic and narcissistic, and briefly speak of the skills necessary for the post-hustling period.

The novice eventually becomes the expert in hustling. Their discussion turns to the uses of photography, and the pleasures of the Polaroid camera. The hazardous route of hitchhiking, and the techniques of truckdrivers are surveyed. A mastery of sports-talk is necessary for the hustlers who frequent straight bars. What to do when the fleet's in.

meyer's terminology. Phil attains expert status on the matter of homosexual lovemaking. They discuss various techniques, from the Hindu *auparishtaka* to the listing of the body's most sensitive areas and erogenous zones, and reveal methods of easily stimulating erotic response.

ABOUT THE AUTHOR

Samuel M. Steward, PhD, was a tattoo artist in Chicago and Oakland — under the name of Phil Sparrow — for 18 years. In that capacity he was both confidante and father-confessor to scores of hustlers, absorbing their accounts of the pains and pleasures of hustling, its advantages and drawbacks, and its profits, perils, and dangers. Prior to that, he was a university professor of English for 20 years. A contributor to *World Book Encyclopedia* and the author of several hundred stories that have appeared in European magazines, Dr. Steward has also published many books, including *The Caravaggio Shawl* (Alyson, 1989), *Murder Is Murder Is Murder* (Alyson, 1984), *Parisian Lives* (St. Martin's, 1984), *Chapters From an Autobiography* (Grey Fox, 1981), *Dear Sammy: Letters From Gertrude Stein and Alice B. Toklas, With a Memoir* (Houghton, 1977), and *Bad Boys and Tough Tattoos: A Social History of the Tattoo with Gangs, Sailors, and Street-Corner Punks* (The Haworth Press, 1990). He has also written several erotic novels under the pseudonym Phil Andros, including *Different Strokes* (Perineum, 1984), *The Boys in Blue* (Perineum, 1984), and *Below the Belt and Other Stories* (Perineum, 1981).

Introduction:
Investigating Hustlers

John P. De Cecco, PhD
Editor-in-Chief
HAWORTH Gay & Lesbian Studies

It may be mildly surprising to many that male hustling is probably as common, though perhaps less visible, than female prostitution. The streets and bars and arcades where hookers can be found are often right next to the "meat racks" where the hustlers hang out. The advertisements for call girls and boys often appear side by side in the underground newspapers of metropolitan areas. In big city night-places, while some men are watching women dance, strip, and perform erotically on a dime-sized stage, other men are groping hustlers in the privacy of the video cubicles, or copping a feel of the buns and basket of the guy sitting on the next bar stool.

The social science literature on female prostitutes is abundant at present and growing still larger as feminist contributions swell the number of papers. The investigation of male hustlers, however, has lagged far behind. Hardly more than a dozen empirical studies have been produced in the last 30 years, and most of those have only superficially surveyed the male hustler. The paucity of studies can be partly attributed to a never-ending and persistent homophobia in the academic world — perhaps occasioned by the reluctance of many researchers to paw through the clutter in their own closets.

But the meager attention that has been given to male prostitution is also the result of the implicit taboos that exist to guard the integrity of male sexuality. In the group mind, men are not supposed to be the objects of lust but rather the dynamic agents of lust — to be the active providers of sex rather than the passive receptors. The inexperienced researcher becomes slightly confused when confronted with a man—the male hustler—who must perform equally well both as provider and receptor.

Still another barrier exists to help explain the lack of research on male hustling. The male is supposed to be—according to the tradition of the western world—all-powerful, potent, and macho when it comes to sex. For a man to buy sex from another man, or to sell it to him, threatens the concept of male domination from both sides of the equation, although it might well delight feminists.

Finally, male hustling quite frequently—although not invariably—involves an older man having sex with a younger one. Such a concept once again runs counter to the idea that sexual encounters that cross between generations are inevitably exploitive, coercive, and abusive for the younger partner. In innumerable instances, it is the younger male who uses the older one for his own selfish advantage and becomes the contemptuous and bullying conqueror.

The studies on hustling most frequently cited or recently published have certain characteristics and findings. Almost all have been done from demographic perspectives. They have been made by sociologists, clinical psychologists, and social workers, and sometimes by psychiatrists; and their investigative attention has been concentrated on the surface features of hustlers rather than on the relationships between hustlers and their customers.

In the published research the hustlers are usually described as adolescents and young men, between the ages of 15 and 25. The younger ones are the street hustlers; the older hustlers sometimes avoid the streets altogether and confine their hunting and affairs to the gay bars that are known and recognized as hustler bars, but are not the popular meeting or cruising establishments in gay communities. Some of the particularly handsome men are known as "call boys," often older and more experienced than the street hustlers; they present themselves through newspaper ads, gay strip shows, houses of prostitution, and modeling or escort services. Some of them are former models and performers who have appeared in the gay media and porn films. A few, the "kept boys," find rich "sugar daddies," older men who dazzle them with money, cars, clothes, swimming pools, travel, and more money.

A few exceptional hustlers, like Phil Andros in the pages that follow, survive into middle age through enduring good looks and charm as well as a shrewd understanding of their patrons. According to the research, however, the livelihood of most hustlers vanishes with their youth for it seems to be youth and new faces that kindle the fire in the gonads of their clients and propel the clients to do the horizontal dance. As a group, hustlers compose a homeless, migratory, urban underclass. Few of them have anything more than the most tenuous ties with their families; many have been raised in foster homes and have less than a high school education. They lack marketable skills or job experience and interest in steady work. They have a record of at least minor crimes such as loitering, marijuana use, petty theft, and solicitation. Many of them have had or are currently experiencing some sexually transmitted diseases contracted through either heterosexual or homosexual intercourse.

Although all hustlers, of course, are engaged in homosexual behavior, not all of them call themselves gay. Those who are feminized in dress and behavior or androgynous in appearance may do so. Those who appear masculine — often to the point of caricature — call themselves straight, although in sophisticated urban environments some "straights" will acknowledge a little bisexuality. Such labels are intended to reveal more about which sexual behaviors they will and will not engage in than about any immutable psychical state of sexual preference. The straight or butch ones are generally the insertors in oral and anal intercourse, and that is what their clients pay them for. The androgynous ones are more "international" in performance but may charge more for their artful pliability. Since there have been no extended follow-up studies of hustlers, it is difficult to know how many of the straight or bisexual — or, for that matter, gay — prostitutes end up in heterosexual marriages.

Hustlers are great liars when it comes to the question of the fees they charge, and whether money is the only material medium of exchange. None of them wants to appear cheap, and the ones who present a straight persona want to ward off any impression that they are engaging in sex for any reason other than money. In actual practice, many will settle for drugs or even a roof over their heads, a temporary respite from streets and bars. It is generally reported that the high-grade call boys currently charge the most money — from a low of $50 to an unlimited high — with $150 not being unusual. Street hustlers charge the least—perhaps as low as $20 or $25 at current levels of the economy, although those working the streets may easily turn up more customers. The income of the bar hustlers probably falls in between that of the call boys and street hustlers since they sometimes get paid for their social and sexual time as well as their drinks and occasionally a meal. Many members of the street and bar groups often have a little extra added as a tip for catering to some idiosyncrasy of a grateful client.

Dr. Steward's examination of hustling from an interior perspective has turned up three theories about hustler-client relationships, which it is hoped will attract serious research attention. First, there is his theory about the hustler's fantasy—that he has at last found his "great dark man" who will be his eternal lover and keeper. This fantasy is sometimes recycled by the client, who hopes that the hustler will fall in love with him—that their crass business relationship will be metamorphosed into a high romance.

Second, there is the power exchange between the hustler and the client, with the client holding the authority of the purse over the hustler's sexual performance, and the latter holding the authority of his physical attractiveness over the frenzied and feverish desires of the client. The movement of each in any direction is a gain or loss in power for the other.

Third, there is sometimes a subtle double-forked fantasy of the client: that in bedding with the hustler he is also bedding with a long line of all the hustler's past clients, among whom certainly is his long-sought ideal. The other branch of his fantasy lies in the satisfaction that—if the hustler is handsome and widely desired—the client has beaten out the competition for his services.

What Dr. Steward provides us with then, in his inimitable style that artfully blends information, insight, and mordant humor, is an *inside* look at hustling, largely from the hustler's point of view. He has already promised to revisit this topic for us from the vantage point of the client. This approach—which may be disturbing to some—has never before appeared in the social science literature on hustling, which, with few exceptions, has described hustlers from the *outside* and at a sanitized (called "objective") distance between them and the investigators.

By this time all the world must now know that Dr. Steward is a.k.a. Phil Andros, the eponymous author of classic gay erotica/ porn. Speaking on behalf of the publisher of The Haworth Press, Bill Cohen, I feel indeed fortunate to have attracted his talent and fame to our Gay and Lesbian Studies program.

Selected References

Allen, D. M. (1980). Young male prostitutes: A psychosocial study. *Archives of Sexual Behavior, 9*(5), 399-426. From 1974-1977 in Massachusetts, 98 males were interviewed, most of whom were street or bar hustlers about 17 years of age.

Boyer, D. (1989). Male prostitution and homosexual identity. *Journal of Homosexuality, 17*(1/2), 151-184. Based on 49 street hustlers in Seattle, between the ages of 16 and 17.

Caukins, S. E., & Coombs, N. R. (1976). The psychodynamics of male prostitution. *American Journal of Psychotherapy, 30,* 441-451. A study of the relationship of 33 hustlers and 20 customers in southern California. Concludes that both groups deeply resent their mutual dependency.

Coleman, E. (1989). The development of male prostitution activity among gay and bisexual adolescents. *Journal of Homosexuality, 17*(1/2), 131-149. A review article that attributes hustling to faulty psychosexual and psychosocial development.

Coombs, N. R. (1974). Male prostitution: A psychosocial view of behavior. *American Journal of Orthopsychiatry, 44*(5), 782-789. A study of the background of 41 street and bar hustlers from the ages of 12 to 28, probably in Los Angeles.

Deisher, R. W., Eisner, V., & Sulzbacher, S. I. (1969). *Pediatrics, 43*(6), 936-941. Sixty-three hustlers from 15 to 23 were interviewed in Seattle and San Francisco for purposes of "rehabilitation."

Fisher, B., Weisberg, D. K., & Marotta, T. (1982). *Report on adolescent male prostitution*. San Francisco, CA: Urban and Rural Systems Associates [URSA]. A study of male "sex workers" in large urban environments. *See* Johnson, *below*.

Ginsburg, K. N. (1967). The "meat rack": A study of the male homosexual prostitute. *American Journal of Psychotherapy, 21,* 170-185. Interviews with 26 street hustlers in San Francisco.

Johnson, E. C. (1983). *In search of god in the sexual underworld*. New York: William Morrow, 1983. Describes some of the findings in the URSA study cited in Fisher, *above*. The study was based in San Francisco but included Boston, Charleston (SC), Los Angeles, Minneapolis, Muncie (IN), and Seattle. It included interviews with hustlers, customers, police, social workers, hotel managers, cafe owners, business people, city officials, and residents of hustling locales. No comprehensive report has been published.

Pleak, R. L. & Meyer-Bahlburg, H.F.L. (1990). Sexual behavior and AIDS knowledge of young male prostitutes in Manhattan. *Journal of Sex Research,* 27(4), 557-587. A study of 50 men between the ages of 14 and 27, describing their use of condoms with male customers and lack of use with female and male friends. Contains reference list of related AIDS studies.

Reiss, A. J. (1961). The social integration of queers and peers. *Social Problems,* 9, 102-120. About 48 boys in prison in Nashville, Tennessee, between the ages of 12 and 17. Describes the boys' rules restricting their relationships and sexual conduct with their customers.

Ross, L.H. (1959). The "hustler" in Chicago. *Journal of Student Research, 1,* 113-119. An early study of rough trade among street and bar hustlers and also a study of call boys.

Visano, L. A. (1990). The impact of age on paid sexual encounters. *Journal of Homosexuality, 20(3/4), in press.* Street hustlers (120) in Canada and the USA and their unflattering view of their customers.

Chapter I

Genesis

"Phil Andros has retired!"

That's what Doug Martin called from Chicago to tell me. Even though Phil and I both lived on the west coast, in these days of cheap long-distance telephoning and fax machines, of the global village, there's never any guarantee that you can learn what goes on in your own backyard before it's already known by someone a thousand miles away.

Within a week of Doug's call, three others came in on the tele-queen network, each relaying the same information; and I knew — from Lewis Carroll's formula in snark-hunting — that if you heard a thing three times from the snark, it was true.

In the past, Phil and I had been collaborators of sorts, jointly working to produce his series of short stories and novels about hustling. The only things that I could add to his narratives were occasional commas and semicolons, and a few anecdotes about the hustlers who had frequented my tattoo shop in Chicago. People who knew him as an author were continually asking whether his stories were true, and his answer was always the same — about eighty-five percent, he'd say, with a slow wink and his tongue poked into his cheek.

The novels themselves were erotic enough, but with Phil I always had the feeling that they had been put through a literary sieve of some kind — that perhaps they had been prettied up for the general reader. He had really never tried to write an honest autobiography — said he was too lazy and moreover tired of writing. Two or three years ago I had threatened to write his autobiography myself — as Gertrude Stein actually did for Alice B. Toklas — and he

1

had laughed and told me just to wait, halfway promising that he'd cooperate with me when he retired from hustling.

So . . . that day had come. After I got the phone calls, I telephoned him to verify what I'd heard.

"Yup," he said.

"I thought you'd go on forever."

He laughed. "Not me."

"Why not?"

"For one thing," he said, "I'm nearly fifty. For another, the demand for my services has fallen off."

"The plague?"

"Yeah. It works both ways. Clients are afraid. And just as important — so am I. I've been lucky so far . . ."

I made some indeterminate telephone noise.

". . . I hope," he added.

"We've gotta get used to the Damoclean sword," I said.

Then I hit him with my proposition. "Your biography. Or some kind of book about you. Or about hustling. Do you remember that a coupla years ago you promised to let me try it when you retired?"

"Yeah," he said. "But I'm not sure you'd really want to. The early years were dull as hell. Just the usual knockabout adolescence, up through college."

"I'm not interested in that anyway," I said. "It's the hustler I want to know about. The *real* one."

"You plannin' to do another thing such as Gide did in *Corydon*?"

"Lord no. That was more philosophical than anything I could manage. Besides, he wrote it in 1911, and it even *sounds* like 1911. This is the *last* decade of the century. Things have changed."

"Not too much," he said. I could hear his grin even over the phone. "At least not sex-wise."

"Well, can I come up and talk to you for a few days?"

He seemed a bit reluctant. "I can't put you up," he said. "Sorry. Not enough room in my little *pied à terre*."

"I thought that meant a temporary lodging."

"Yeah — it belongs to Ward Stames. I'm just house-sitting. Anyway, who can tell what the future holds?" he said piously.

"Oh, hell."

But in the end he said yes, he wasn't doing anything for the next week. He told me that there was a good motel only a block away from his house in Berkeley, and since once in the past he'd been with the young stud manager, he thought he might be able to get me some bargain rates. I told him to go ahead, and we settled on dates.

But that meant I'd have to take the plane from Del Mar, and leave my bonsai tree with my sister, who wouldn't be too happy with such an arrangement. And god, how I hated to fly! I guess my writer's imagination plus my empathetic projection coupled with all the news stories about air tragedies really did a job on me. Flying gave me a horrid vision of those last thirty seconds when the plane headed straight down — passengers shrieking and tumbling everywhere, the cabin filled with the stench and liquids of all opened sphincters — and the final obliterating crash — or death by flames — that awaited us all.

I knocked myself nearly senseless with a coupla tranquilizers, however, and took the plane to Oakland, and a taxi to Berkeley, arriving there about mid-afternoon on a pleasant day in August. I had lived in northern California for a long time, and it was good to feel the paradisiacal cool weather once more instead of the muggy heat of Del Mar.

Phil lived in a rear cottage in the "flatlands" section of Berkeley — the part the snobs called the ghetto, and those who lived there called the "meadows" — in what James Purdy, visiting him once, had christened "Invisible House" since it was so well-concealed from view. It was equally sheltered from noise — existed, indeed, in a small island of silence; although University Avenue was only a half-block away, there were so many trees and bushes between it and the house that no traffic noise reached your ears.

Phil was in his yard when I got there. From a short distance away, as I stood at the gate trying to remember how you opened the "secretary's lock," he looked mighty fine.

"Press up on the bottom edge, dummy," he called, flashing me one of his hundred-dollar smiles.

He was dressed in black slacks and a white tee shirt that showed his still-impressive biceps and the swelling plateau of his chest — tanned and healthy, with the best and strongest forearms I had always liked to look at. His face seemed a bit more rugged, but the

Greek nose was still there, and all of the curly black hair full and heavy and low on his neck. And—how wonderful!—he had no paunch at all, probably vanquished by the gym, and by the horizontal dances just recently abandoned. I could not avoid looking at what the French call *une bourse lourde*, a heavy purse, which is their charming term for "basket"—the genital bulge. It was still there, making him look for all the world like one of the wonderful Tom of Finland sketches that had adorned the covers of Phil's novels—and (as I teased him continually) probably accounted for three-fourths of their sales in adult bookstores. He had not recently trimmed the space between his heavy eyebrows; they grew together in a straight line which he could somehow mysteriously manipulate parts of—making either end fly upwards like a startled bird, or putting a peaked wave over one eye or the other.

His two long-haired dachshunds—one black and tan, the other a color called "red"—barked at me wildly until Phil quieted them with a word. Then he came towards me, hand outstretched, as I closed the gate. But when I extended my hand he grabbed it and yanked me towards him, enfolding me in those great arms, where for just a second (without his being aware of it) I turned my head to nuzzle against his broad chest, just to smell the fresh laundered fabric of the tee shirt, and the oh-so-slight male odor of his skin. I might as well confess it at the beginning, and get it off my mind: I had always adored this minor Greek god, but aside from a dalliance or two twenty years before, there had been nothing to complicate the alliance between us—that of the "maker" and his amanuensis.

"How ya been, ole cock?" he asked, releasing me and grinning. Oh, that black black hair, that smile, those lips . . . The charisma still dripped from him, his magnetism was almost tangible, the curve of his flanks as strong and vibrant and visible as in the days when he wore the light chinos to show off his musculature better—to sell his goods.

"Great. I've missed you, these past years."

"And me you," he said, putting his arm around my shoulders. "I always had a kind of yen for you."

"Now he tells me," I said ruefully.

"But I always thought you didn't care much for sex. Sort of virginal, like Chaucer's Prioress. More interested in our literary partnership than in playing at two-backed beast, as they used to call it.''

"For all your perceptiveness in most things," I said wryly, "you're blind as a noonday bat."

He laughed, and squeezed my shoulder. "Maybe we can do something about that . . . later," he said. His eyes were smoky, and I had a flash of rumpled sheets . . .

"I'm here to do a job on you," I said. "To work. I intend to peel you apart, layer by layer like an artichoke, to see if all those things in your novels were true, or were just pretenses created to hoodwink a reading public."

He looked at me, amused. "Lotsa luck, ole buddy," he said.

Chapter II

Backwards,
Turn Backwards, O Time . . .

It was too late in the day for us to begin an interview that afternoon, so we did nothing except talk about old times, old friends, old tricks, and all the old things that rise to the surface when people meet after a three-year absence. Memory in such cases feeds upon itself, and grows in length and volume accordingly. Recalling one incident or person invariably triggers the lead to another close by, and reminiscence becomes a kind of game, the sort that one used to play with the dictionary: you looked up one word, which referred you to another, and after a few moments landed you far afield from your starting point.

The next morning, armed with notebook and pen, and with fresh audio cassettes for the tape recorder, we settled ourselves in his cluttered living room to begin.

"Messy, ain't it?" Phil asked, looking around. "Luckily, my mind is in order. I really couldn't live in a neatnik's environment — that would turn my mental processes into chaos."

"Paradox," I murmured. "I strongly suspect your brain is as chaotic as your life has been. You're just trying a cover-up for your disorder."

He laughed. "Guess you know me pretty well already."

"I ought to, after all we've done together — the books, the short stories."

He settled himself in his leather chair. "Just what the hell is it you really want?" he asked, not annoyed, just interested.

"Actually, I'm not sure," I said. "I hope to get into the hustler mind, I suppose. I know you're not an ordinary one by any means, and I would like to think you have enough sense and experience and knowledge of others in the same line of work to help me understand what makes them tick. Why they start doing what they do."

"I hope I'm not going to appear in this thing as patriarchal, or avuncular, or as being in my anecdotage."

"Absolutely not," I said. "I'd be pleased if you came across as somewhat authoritative."

"That would please me too, if I didn't sound like Moses with the tablets."

"I promise you won't."

"The 'why' business bothers me a little," he said. "Why they got into it. Why *we* got into it, I mean . . . I suppose. There are as many reasons as there are hustlers, I imagine."

"We can cut out the 'broken-home syndrome,' I think. Don't need to discuss it. Most of the academic writers fall back on that."

"Yeah," he said. "It may be the cause in some instances, but not exactly in mine."

"What *was* it in yours?" I said, rather coyly.

He grinned. "Trappin' me, ain'tcha? Or tryin' to?"

"No way. I'd really like to know."

He cleared his throat. "Well, in the first place — it wasn't a broken home. It was no home at all. I was a bastard. My mother was only seventeen when I was born in Athens. Father — a Greek soldier, I guess. When I was about four years old I was sent to live with Aunt Elena in Columbus, Ohio. Fourteenth Avenue, right across from the University. I went to grade school and then North High School, and when it came time I went to the University. Aunt Elena took in male students as roomers."

I grinned. "Kinda convenient, wasn't it? All the sex you wanted without having to go out on the street at all."

He laughed. "Later, bud," he said. "I had to work my way through college. In the library. That kept me busy enough."

"What was the first time you had sex for money?"

"Not money, exactly. More like barter. I knew a guy who worked at the old Hartman theatre, and there was a young feller there in a revival of Ibsen's *Ghosts* — well, I had a case on him, and the usher got me his autograph. But I had to let the usher screw me."

His eyes got dreamy all of a sudden, and he sighed. "Behind the schoolhouse, bent over a wooden sawhorse. It's a wonder someone didn't see us. Henry—Wadsworth, I think his name was. Had a monster big birthmark on his right shoulder.''

"Tsk,'' I said. "How could you know that, if all this happened out in the open? Did he take all his clothes off?''

Phil laughed. "Got me, didn't you? I guess I'll have to confess. I saw him several times after that, under somewhat more comfortable conditions. His room. Or mine.''

"How about the first time . . . for real money?''

"That was a cash register vice-president from Dayton by the name of Art. Art Ugle. I called him 'Ugly.' Gave me ten bucks. Not bad for those days. It suddenly occurred to me that I could pick up quite a bit of extra cash with what I had. I was pretty good lookin' back then.''

"Hah!'' I said. "Still are. Your peacock period has been extended beyond all reasonable limits.''

"Tell me again,'' he said. "Flattery in the right amount gets anyone a freebie.''

"I wonder just how ancient the business of hustling is,'' I said after a moment. "Is it as old as female prostitution?''

"Dunno. Maybe older. At least just as old.''

He got up from his chair. "Just a minute,'' he said, and went into his bedroom where Ward Stames's books completely lined one wall to the ceiling and overflowed into three other bookcases. He came back in a few moments carrying several volumes.

"I'm not really interested in the background all that much,'' I protested. "I ain't about to do a history of male prostitution. I just want to get inside you.''

"Watch your language,'' he said, grinning.

"You know what I mean.''

"One can never be sure with you.'' He held up a small red book. "This is Sir Richard Burton's 'Terminal Essay' to his translation of *The Arabian Nights*. Special printing, quite old. But the essay itself is more easily available in Donald Webster Cory's *Homosexuality: A Cross-Cultural Approach*.''

"I read the Burton thing once, a long time ago,'' I said. "Quite a strange theory, wasn't it? Something about homosexuality being permissible, or at least tolerated, in a band of latitudes around the world."

"Yeah," Phil said, leafing through the book. "John Addington Symonds attacked the theory immediately. There's a little in it about early hustling among the Greeks."

"Interesting . . . but a little off what I'm interested in. Didn't the Greeks take away certain rights of a citizen if he took money for sex?"

"Yes," Phil said, "but I don't know which rights were lost and I was never concerned enough to look the matter up. But Burton has some fascinating facts. The city of Uranopolis, for instance, allowed public male brothels staffed by adults as well as boys down to seven years of age. Catullus complained about the many young men who haunted the public baths of Greece, selling sex. Citizens cruising the Roman streets for hustlers used the hand sign of closing the fist — to represent the scrotum — with the middle finger raised, same as our 'giving the finger' sign. Juvenal described another Roman sign — scratching the head with the little finger . . ."

"People seem to be more realistic today," I said. "Or more obvious and direct. They just grab the genital bulge and jut the hips forward."

"Yeah," Phil said. "No more romance." He turned a few more pages. "Domitian was perhaps the first to forbid the prostitution of boys, I think."

"I would have thought it to be Saint Paul," I said. "Early Christianity needed all the supporters and converts it could get, and male prostitutes certainly didn't contribute any new noses to count."

"Or any other body parts," Phil said, poking his tongue against his cheek. "But on the other hand, as Burton says, Mohammed seems to have regarded pederasty with philosophic indifference."

"His modern adherents seem to believe that if you 'sin' with another man, you are forgiven if you drop a few coins on the first beggar you see the following morning."

"Easier than a trip to the confessional," Phil said. He picked up another volume — the poems of Martial. "Here's someone complaining about the high prices charged in Roman times for a blow-job: 'Informer you are and blackmailer, swindler and trickster, fellator and bully. The wonder is you have no money when your charges are so high.' ''

"Could have been written yesterday," I said.

"Or here's another by Martial: 'You sold your three little pastures, Labienus? And you've bought three pretty little slave boys, Labienus? You still own three little pastures, Labienus.' ''

"Tsk," I said. "The old pimp."

"I like Catullus," Phil said. "Short and dirty things. Such as — " he turned through another book — " ' 'You see a pretty boy out walking arm in arm with a pimp, And you suspect that this young man has an eye for trade, And sells himself.' ''

"Is the one there about Vibennius the thief and his son?"

"Yeah . . . 'Vibennius steals napkins and clothes, and everyone fucks his son's ass. Since you are both so well known, you ought to go elsewhere to find a place where you can sell your hairy buttocks itching with desire.' ''

"When I was a lot younger," I said reminiscently, "I used to spend many a pleasant rainy afternoon searching through Suetonius's *Lives of the Twelve Caesars* looking for tidbits. Did you know that the Deified Octavius Augustus sold himself early in life to Aulus Hirtius in Spain for three hundred thousand sesterces, that Caligula was a male whore and loved drag, and that Nero and Tiberius were not far behind?"

"Yup," said Phil, "and I also found the Caesar who dressed like a woman and exchanged places with a female prostitute so he could have the gladiators screw him — and collect their money, too."

"I always sort of admired Caracalla," I said, "building those great public baths just so he could find the Romans with the biggest dingdongs."

"The most sensational Roman emperor I found — " Phil began.

"I know — you're going to say Heliogabalus!"

"Yes," Phil said. "Lampridius's life of him in the *Historiae Scriptores Augustae*. He dressed up like a wild beast and chewed up the privates of men bound to stakes in the arena . . . ''

" . . . and he preferred only the lower classes — masseurs, gladiators, wagon drivers, bricklayers, actors, locksmiths, even a latrine-cleaner . . .''

"Each of whom," Phil said, "grew rich with the money he got from old Helio . . ."

"Coming just a little closer to the present," I said, "how about the house of the Vetti brothers uncovered in Pompeii? All the historical accounts tell you is that they were merchants. But what did they sell?"

"Is that the place with the louvered window at the entrance? The one you have to bribe the guard to unlock?"

"Yes. It's a wall painting of a well-dressed young Roman man, weighing his cock on one balance-tray of a pair of scales. There's a bag of gold on the other balance . . . "

"Well, I've got a coupla more books here," Phil said. But he seemed to be getting a little restless.

"I'd sort of like to get on with the main business," I said. "You."

"In just a minute." Phil held up a battered volume. "This is *The Sins of the Cities of the Plains* by Jack Saul. London, 1881," he said, looking at the title page. "Or, *Recollections of a Mary-Ann*. Early pornography. It's about a bisexual hustler who recounts his adventures to a wealthy man who picks him up and then pays him for his tales. It's got a lot of hetero episodes in the beginning, but then it gets down to the real stuff — homosexual encounters with hustlers in drag. Uses the word 'gay' in its modern sense, too."

"You sure?"

"Yup." Phil put the book down and picked up another. "And then there's John Rechy's *City of Night*."

"About 1963, wasn't it?"

"Right on the head. It was the first serious account of a homosexual hustler's experiences in this country's night cities — New York, Chicago, Los Angeles."

"But wasn't it a sort of waffling thing? I'm not sure he ever admitted being a hustler."

"It was as unvarnished as the times permitted," Phil said. "No, of course there wasn't any *absolute* honesty of expression; the times wouldn't allow it. But it's a landmark achievement."

"And still a milestone after a quarter century or more."

"The last thing is this," Phil said, holding up a slender magazine with a stylized 'lamp of learning' in blue on a grey cover. It was a copy of *Der Kreis*, a small trilingual homosexual magazine which had been published in Zurich from the 1940s to 1967. I had often seen it. Phil's copy was that of June, 1961.

"I've just got to go up to the post office to mail this letter," Phil said. "Why don't you read the article on hustling in this issue? I'll be back in twenty minutes."

He was gone out the door before I had a chance to say anything, or I would have told him who Donald Bishop was. But I turned to the English section anyway to read the thing, which was called "The Bull Market in America." It had been many years since I had seen it, and it was not unpleasant to refresh my memory. It began:

> You find the handsome young male peacocks on the street corners of every large city in the United States—preening themselves self-consciously, fingering their duck's-ass hairdos or standing scowling in their skin-tight levis with legs apart and thumbs hooked into their broad leather belts, wearing their leather jackets; or even sitting in their funny little Ivy League suits in fashionable bars. They swagger along the sidewalks always alert for the "eye" from a passing queer, their own eyes darting right and left under narrowed lids, much as do the eternally questing glances of the genuine homosexual. For these are the new "hustlers," the boys who sell their bodies during the prime-time of their lives, when their muscles are stronger, their hips smaller, and their complexions fresher—and they have discovered that these assets are marketable, at least for a while.
>
> New, we say? The male whore is not new. It is just that at present, with more persons aware of homosexuality as an actuality rather than as the subject for a nightclub joke, the hustler is increasing rapidly in numbers, technique, and prices. It used to be, in the days when a homosexual had to be obviously effeminate in order to make a pick-up, that the occasional hustler was referred to as "being out for pennies," or sometimes "rough trade" if a beating accompanied his request for money; or—worst of all—if only the prelude of sex had been accomplished before the knuckles hit the jaw and the rough hands found the wallet, he was simply called a "jack-roller."

Today much of this has changed. Large numbers of young men are making either a partial living—and some an entire one—by selling themselves. The professional hustler of today is really a small businessman in a sense: he has his regular clientele, and visits them weekly or every other week, as their inclinations and pocketbooks allow. The part-time ones perhaps do not have regular customers—the young hoodlums, the sailors, the weightlifters, the boys who have experimentally dipped into this seemingly inexhaustible source of wealth, but have not yet decided to devote their entire energies to the business. But the full-time hustlers—and there are many—have well-set in their heads their memorized lists of phone numbers, days of the week to call, how often, and the fee expected, just the way a competent call-girl does. The best ones never write anything down.

The types of hustlers in London have been discussed by Simon Raven in a recent publication [*Encounter*, November 1960, pp. 19-24]. Though his classifications, as he says, tend to melt into each other, there is no essential difference between his groupings and those in America. There is the part-time soldier or sailor who uses his extra money to buy stockings for his girl; the true homosexuals with "refined" jobs like those of hairdresser or ribbon-clerk; the dull quasi-moron who feels the world owes him a living, and that but for his bad luck he would be as well off as any other; the small criminal, given to any shady enterprise as long as it brings in money; and the intelligent, witty, and urbane full-time male "whore" who is completely homosexual and moves in the best circles.

The American hustler is usually more business-like than any of his British fellows, save perhaps the last-named type. He lives by a code. The main tenet of it is: Silence. He never talks about his clients, save to give a fellow-hustler the name and phone number of a new mark—but he does this only when a customer has asked him to furnish a new body for the old bed; he never talks unless his client wants someone new. The second tenet is: Have the financial arrangement clearly understood before you go with the customer; settle for two or five or ten dollars, and then stick to it. Again, never steal anything from a customer — for the hustler realizes that the homosexual world is a kind of large and formless Mafia, a "telequeen" network; word of a theft or jack-rolling would be flashed as if by magic everywhere. And then — no more clients! And finally, the grade-A hustler never blackmails, nor makes any suggestion of it — again, for the reason that to do so would reduce his clientele. And why kill the goose that lays those lovely eggs?

America is greatly different from Britain. We are, if possible, even more hypocritical; we have not yet reached the stage of having a Wolfenden committee. It is only with the greatest anguish that American authorities can bring themselves to recognize homosexuality officially, and this despite all of Kinsey's efforts at education. Only recently has the Post Office taken note of the "painful fact" of homosexuality and begun to censor body-building magazines and photographs, instead of merely delivering the mail as it is supposed to do. Many police officials are aware of the "problem" of homosexuality in America — especially prison officials — but most of them prefer to minimize the prevalence of the male whore. In the United States, where the vital force has decayed to the extent of endangering the country as a republic, where one loudly preaches freedom in principle and yet hypocritically denies it to citizens in actual practice, and where the basic puritanism has turned every bigot into a self-appointed professional reformer, it is only to be expected that (to a heterosexual) such a loathsome practice as a young man whoring with men for pay is so against the "normal healthy American way of life" that he will do his damnedest to refuse to recognize its existence at all.

But the major point is this: there would be no hustlers unless there were a demand for them. And the demand is growing. It is a bull market in more ways than one, for the prices are steadily rising. Ten years ago you could buy a "heterosexual" boy for two or three dollars; at present, the going price is five, or more likely ten. Approximately half of these boys are still just "trade" — that is, they submit to manual or oral sex passively; but after a few years' experience with hustling, plus the attractiveness of higher fees for more co-operation, many of them will — at first tentatively, and then with growing frequency, ease, and even pleasure — take a more active role, until finally they are doing "everything" if their customers pay them well. It is only the naif and beginning hustler who sets his price extremely high and remains untouchable or uncooperative. A little experience brings his prices down, and makes him take a hand in things himself, and generally become less finicky in choice of clients and limitation of his actions.

There are currently so many hustlers in America that we can say also of the bull market that it has become a buyers' market as well; there are hardly enough clients to go around. But there would be no hustlers here, as we have said, unless there were people to purchase their services. And these clients — what of them?

They seem to fall into three classes, two of which overlap. The first is made up of the older ones, who can no longer have love without paying for it. Though these may retain some bloom of youth far beyond the age at which the heterosexual, with his family worries, can keep his, there must come a day when it grows obvious that he is no longer attractive to anyone under his own age. Pity the poor soul, thus aging, who retains his passion for young men in their twenties! There are three possibilities for him: the fruitless evenings making the rounds of the bars, and going home alone; or the questionable miasmic shadows of the Turkish baths with its slimy floors; or the hiring of a hustler, and grasping with a feeble clutch at a pretense of happiness. For no matter how ancient and toothless and bald the client, the only face the hustler sees on him is that of Lincoln or Hamilton; and the only wrinkles are those that pocket-wear in a wallet has put into the money that pays him.

The second — and perhaps the largest group of clients, overlapping the first — is that composed of homosexuals who must, by reason of their professional status, keep their homosexuality secret. What is such a one to do? If he is a doctor or dentist, for example, he cannot in America afford to let his inclinations become known. He turns to the hustlers to answer the howl within him. You will find in the hustler's mental lists the names of bankers, doctors, lawyers, a judge or even a couple of legislators, dentists, school teachers, university professors, ministers, musicians, corporation executives, movie stars, newspaper men—you name the profession and you will find some member of it, somewhere, listed in a hustler's head, some "Andy," or "Frank," or "Pete." Not every hustler knows an impressive array of professional persons, of course, but you can wager that every calling is represented somewhere.

The third group is small. Its members are those homosexuals who have lived hard and fast. Though still comparatively young, in their late twenties or thirties, they have become so jaded with the succession of thighs threshing under or above them that they turn to hustlers for new thrills. With homosexual activity in America reaching new highs, and the average homosexual having hundreds of "contacts" before he is thirty, it is small wonder that many of this group (especially if they like one-night-stands) increase their number of conquests by means of hustlers. This same group often tires of the endless hours it is necessary to spend in cruising, or in bars trying to find a bed partner for the evening, and turns to hustlers simply to keep from wasting time.

Thousands of goodhearted dull Americans would be inexpressibly shocked to learn that such a thing as the male whore exists in their midst. Their immediate reaction, were they to learn of it, would be "Make a law against it! Wipe it out!"

Dear J. Edgar, dear governor of every state, dear city commissioner of every police force, dear dull square Americans—you can't stop it, and you never will. The law of supply and demand is incontrovertible. You can never be in every bar, on every street corner, in every bus and movie house, to keep these sweet little arrangements from being made. You have legislated against the homosexual, harried him and hounded him with a persecution more virulent and unending than that against the Jews, permitted him by your laws and repressions to be blackmailed, sterilized him, laughed at him, kicked him, beaten him—but you cannot change his inclinations, and chances are he would not let you if you could. Is it any wonder that you have made him defiant, and made him sneer at your attempted restrictions? If he wants to buy the pleasure of a hustler's company for an evening, or ten minutes, how can you stop him?

Go to the ruins of Pompeii, dear reformer. Find your way to the house of the Vetti brothers. Pay the guard a few lira and ask him to show you the small shuttered painting in the outer vestibule. It is of a stalwart young man, exposed, standing next to a pair of scales, and resting a part of himself on one of the balances, whilst on the other — outweighted — stands a pot of gold. You cannot but realize that for many hundreds of years a high value has been put upon such things, whether by men or women. You will also realize that such things have been marketable for a long, long time.

And can anyone in America — by city ordinance or state law — undo a world tradition that is centuries old?

I was still in a rather dreamy mood when Phil returned, thinking of the old days visiting the *Kreis* people in Zurich — especially Rudolf Jung, now dead, who had begged and cajoled me into writing for his magazine, and so in a fashion launched me on my delayed "career" as a writer of sorts.

"A very perceptive essay," I said, dangling the magazine from two fingers. "I had no idea it would hold up as well as it has, when I wrote it."

"What?!" Phil yelled. *"You* wrote it?"

I nodded. "Yes. In those days the United States circulation for *Der Kreis* was only about two hundred, and the stable of contributor-writers was very small. I had about six or seven pen names. Thomas Cave was my philosophical one, and Donald Bishop my sociological one. When I started to write for the Copenhagen magazines, I invented even more pseudonyms. A total of eleven or twelve."

"That's spreading yourself pretty thin," Phil said. "You'd find it difficult to make a name for yourself in any one name."

"Right. Maybe that's the way I wanted it — not to have my comfortable obscurity interrupted."

Phil just looked at me. Finally he said, softly: "Bullshit."

I laughed. "At least I don't pant for *la gloire*," I said. "Let's get on with it."

"Okay," Phil said. "But since you wrote that essay, a few changes have taken place."

"Such as . . .?"

"Well, the United States never had anything approaching the British Wolfenden committee, which had been formed expressly to study and recommend the abolition of the harsh laws about homosexuality. On the other hand, you wrote that essay only one year before the law was passed in Illinois legalizing sexual encounters between consenting adults. Again—fees of two, five, and ten bucks have given way to a hundred or two hundred bucks an hour. Moreover, the Postal Service no longer censors magazines produced inside the United States. And you didn't include televangelists in your list of those who employed hustlers . . ."

He was grinning.

"In 1961," I said defensively, "we didn't know anything about televangelists' hanky-panky at all."

"And you've mentioned the Vetti brothers twice," Phil said.

"Hell," I said. "I had just been to Pompeii in 1960."

"There's been a bunch of studies about male prostitution. Professional investigations as well as popular. I hear that some government agency recently gave a guy a million dollar grant for a study about male whores . . ."

"That should keep him quiet for quite a while," I said.

"And there's a flood of novels and short stories. Reminiscences. Diatribes. Sermons. Attacks by orange juice ladies and congressmen . . ."

"Don't you understand why? At the moment, wouldn't you consider yourself a Compleat Male Homosexual?"

"At the moment, yes," Phil said, grinning.

"Would you then ever engage in cunnilingus?"

Phil shuddered. "No way," he said.

"Then imagine what a heterosexual thinks about what we do," I said. "Fellatio, amongst other things. Point of view makes for an entirely new set of prejudices and dislikes."

"Let's get off this topic," Phil said.

"All right. We were talking about studies. Ever notice how many porno books have been written about male hustling?"

"I've noticed a lot of 'em, occasionally even produced a few of 'em myself from time to time," he added sardonically.

"I've got a friend who's trying to make a computer list of *all* the dirty porno books that have appeared since the Supreme Court in 1966 opened the floodgates for the cheapie publishers."

"A gargantuan task," Phil said. "Or does he think of it as a cleansing of the Augean stables?"

"Don't ask me. No one can ever really get into another person's brain. He's collected over three thousand books physically, and has another thousand titles. I asked him about hustling books and he pushed one of his magic buttons to give me a listing. Here it is."

I handed it to Phil.

"The author's name is in brackets," I said. "Several titles are repeated; you can't copyright titles. If there's nothing but a date in the brackets, it means no name was on the book."

"Very impressive," Phil said. "Got a coupla mine here."

"The list will be part of my notes," I said.

B & D HUSTLERS [1981]
BIG HUSTLE [Chaney. 1986]
BLACK PUNK HUSTLER [1984]
BOY HUSTLER [Cummings. 1982]
CHICKEN HUSTLER [Kiva. 1982]
COME HUSTLER COME [Hoffman. 1981]
DIARY OF A GAY LOVE HUSTLER [Ricky. 1970]
GLORY HOLE HUSTLER [Dixon. 1967]
HAPPY HUSTLER [Forbes. 1974]
HAPPY HUSTLER [Saxon. 1975]
HARD CORE HUSTLER [1983]
HAZARDS OF HUSTLING [1981]
HIGHWAY HUSTLER [Brunner. n.d.]
HOLLYWOOD HUSTLER [1983]
HOMO HUSTLER [Bradbury. 1973]
HOT HOLE HUSTLER [Boysen. 1975]
HOTEL HUSTLERS [Wilhelm. 1977]
HUMPING HUSTLERS [Wilson. n.d.]
HUNG HUSTLER [Michaels. 1984]
HUSTLE [Miller. 1970]
HUSTLE WITH MUSCLE [Love. 1976]
HUSTLER [Cannon. 1975]

HUSTLER BAR [Shaft. 1978]
HUSTLER MAN [1979]
HUSTLERS, THE [Stevens. 1981]
HUSTLIN' LIKE DAD [Starrem. 1975/1978]
HUSTLING HACKIE [Case. 1971]
HUSTLING HOMO [1968]
HUSTLING PLACE [Corley. 1970]
HUSTLING STUD [1982]
HUSTLING STUD [Brace. n.d.]
LEATHER HUSTLER [1980]
LIGHTS OUT, LITTLE HUSTLER [Lester. 1968]
MALE HUSTLER [Shearer. 1966]
MIDNIGHT HUSTLER [Wilhelm. 1981]
MY BROTHER THE HUSTLER [Andros. 1970]
PUNK HUSTLER [1983]
QUEER HUSTLER [Culver. 1967/70]
QUEER HUSTLER [Caruso. 1965]
RENEGADE HUSTLER [Andros. 1972]
SAN FRANCISCO HUSTLER [Andros. 1970]
STREET HUSTLER [Brooks. 1982]
STREET HUSTLER [1979]
$TUD [Andros. 1966]
STUD HUSTLER [Garcin. 1969]
TEENAGE HUSTLER [Loring. 1972]
TENDERLOIN HUSTLER [1982]
WELL HUNG HUSTLER
WELL HUNG HUSTLERS [1981]
YOUNG HUSTLERS [Kell. 1973]
BOY BODY FOR SALE [Cleaver. 1970]
BOY FOR SALE [Styles. 1973]
BOYS FOR SALE [McBride. 1973]
SAILOR FOR SALE OR RENT [James. 1968]
SALESMAN AND THE HITCHHIKER [Travis. 1969]
SIDEWALK SALESMAN [Dean. 1971]
STUD FOR SALE [Richards. 1982]
STUDS FOR SALE [Stroth. 1978]
PRICE OF PANSIES [Dale. 1968]
PRICE OF PRIDE [Moore. 1977]
PRICE PER INCH [Weeks. 1969]
10 1/2! [Stevens. 1975]
HE BOUGHT HIS BOYS YOUNG [Lamarr]
BOY BUYER [Harper. 1977]
BOY FOR HIRE [Guy]
COLT FOR HIRE [Forbes. 1972]
HARD COCK FOR HIRE [1984]

STUD FOR HIRE [Baxter. 1983]
THIS MAN FOR HIRE [Peters. 1985]
UNCLE'S HIRED HAND [Cooper. 1978]

"Sheez," said Phil. "That's quite a list."

"There's lots more," I said, "where 'hustler' doesn't appear in the title. Like *Different Strokes*, *The Boys in Blue*, *$tud*, *Below the Belt*, *Roman Conquests*, *Greek Ways*, *My Brother My Self*, *Shuttlecock*, and others."

I looked at him. The ones I'd mentioned were all titles of his books.

"You might coin a phrase," he said wryly. "Where there's smoke there's fire."

"Yea," I said, "and folks for hire."

Chapter III

Portrait of the Hustler
as a Young Man

1. A THING OF BEAUTY: THE LILY GILDED

"What do you think should be the qualifications of an ideal hustler?" I asked Phil. "I have my own ideas, but of course they are slanted in the directions of my own sexual preferences."

"I think most people would say that youth is one of the prime requirements," Phil said, "unless you happen to find yourself in a specialized category, such as sado-masochism, and are looking for a mature middle-aged 'daddy.' You called it the peacock period a while ago, as good a name as any for it. The years between eighteen and about twenty-eight or nine."

"Just when a person's beginning to rot," I said. "That used to be my preference."

Phil laughed. "Yeah, well—eighteen to twenty-eight is about the limits. The belly's still flat, the muscles firm. The zits are gone along with the chin fuzz. The hair hasn't begun to thin. Most clients prefer that period."

"But don't the younger ones have more disadvantages? They may be inexperienced. Nothing ruins a good encounter like having to gasp physiological instructions in the middle of it—'Higher! Lower! *There!*'"

"Negligible," Phil said. "It's amazing how quickly a beginner can pick up on all that."

"In certain countries," I said, "like maybe Thailand, or Greece, even young kids—down to eight or ten—are hustling. Pedophile heaven."

"Not exactly one of my preferences."

"Nor mine. But at the other end of the scale — lots of masochists, whether guilt-ridden or not, go chasing after the 'daddy' types — unshaven, cigar-smoking, unwashed and smelly tattooed macho jocks in motorcycle boots . . ."

"Let's drop the special categories for the moment," Phil said. "Both pedophiles and gerontophiles . . . or middle-age-ophiles, if you'll accept that."

"With difficulty," I said. "I'll grant the peacock period is best, but perhaps a successful hustler might be favored in other ways. He really wouldn't need to have a surfer's body or a boxer's or weightlifter's density, or a football hero's reputation, or the looks of a young movie star — *if* Dame Genetics had endowed him with a . . . er . . . sizable appendage. Then he could be the ultimate goal of the night-stalker."

"Ah, he really wouldn't even need that," Phil said. "In Chicago I once met up with the scrawniest ugliest bespectacled young man possible — bowlegged, small, with a sloping forehead, buck teeth, eyes too close together, and a receding chin. His arms were pipe-stem and hairless — he probably had Froelich's syndrome. He wanted to be a hustler."

"With all that against him?"

"Yay. I tried to talk him out of it, but couldn't. He went on trying to be one. And then I ran into him a coupla years later. He was with a prosperous-looking pot-bellied businessman, both of them in expensive silk suits. The businessman was equally as ugly and unattractive as the young hustler. But they were happier to-gether, even after two years, than any hetero married couple that I had ever known."

"De gustibus — " I began.

"No accounting for taste," Phil said.

"So then, physical perfection isn't really necessary."

"Oh, it helps a lot. But even if it is lacking and a guy has a good charismatic personality, he'll get along. And if he's also willing to play any sort of game that isn't too much of a clash with his image or appearance — that's another plus. Or he might be a winner just for his body language — a languorous stretch at the right moment, a spreading of his trousered legs, a movement of his neck, a certain tigerish rising from a chair. A lot can depend on a very little."

"I'll say it can," I said. "Me — I hate to see anyone tap a cigarette before lighting it . . ."

"Or even to light one," Phil said.

I nodded. "Or smoothing one's hair. Or talking about the novels of Firbank if he's with a bank president who's looking for a blue-collar guy."

"Hustlers carry the burden of human selfishness to a new high, in a way," Phil said. "They are selling *themselves*, and that means for the period of the transaction they have to tailor all their words, gestures, and opinions to suit those of their buyers. You mustn't be a Democrat if you're with a Republican, or argue the merits of atheism if you're with a televangelist. You've got to watch every word, because the goose that produces the gold egg mustn't be lifted off the nest."

"That means you've gotta be like an actor — an empty vessel until you see what you have to be to satisfy your . . . 'employer.'"

"Involves being a class-A hypocrite from time to time," Phil said.

"A first-class liar?"

"Yup. No client — and really no hustler — can ever be expected to be entirely truthful about anything at all."

"Baron Munchausen and son."

"Any hustler who takes the promise of a Caribbean vacation or a trip to Paris seriously, without a certain nonchalance, is very likely to be an innocent. A beginner. Anonymous and impersonal sex is just that and no more. The hustler may see the john again, or he may not. But you've really got the Camille complex if you believe everything that's said because of a hot hole or a long stiff."

There was a pause of a few moments. I turned over some notes to see if I'd forgotten anything.

"How about signs and portents?" I said. "Such as advertising you're a hustler and what you want."

"Like the handkerchief codes, hanging out the back pocket?"

"Yea. Did they ever really catch on?"

"Not really," Phil said. "Too complicated to remember."

"There's a great many 'bitch badges,' as they used to be called. In the 1920s slave bracelets for a while indicated you were gay. All because of Valentino wearing one, and the powder-puff episode about him in Chicago. You're much too young to remember how hard it was to introduce wrist-watches to the American male. Big full-page advertisements of a husky hairy forearm in the Saturday Evening Post, with the watch nearly completely buried in the underbrush.''

"Things like the lambda pin today, or the pink triangle, don't indicate anything about hustling—just that you're gay."

"And the ear-ring doesn't even indicate that, today," I said. "But in the 1920s and 1930s the red necktie, the large amethyst ring, and the slave bracelet were giveaways."

"Didn't the ear-ring for males originate with the Navy?" Phil asked. "If a swabbie had a sub sunk underneath him, wasn't that supposed to allow him to wear one ear-ring?"

"Right. Or sometimes, just if his ship had crossed the equator. Things got sort of blurred during World War II."

"All the gender confusions of the 1960s left things in a heluva mess," Phil said. "Tattoos used to be for he-men. Then for the s/m crowd. Then for gals. Finally for everybody. The lily is gilded."

"I still have the small gold lapel pin with the *Kreis* lamp-of-learning symbol which told people in Europe that you were gay. Like the lambda pins."

Phil laughed. "I used to tell people that when my left elbow tingled, I knew the guy was queer. And when my right one tingled, I knew he wanted to hire me."

"True?"

Phil looked at me. "You're the one who mentioned Baron Munchausen in connection with hustlers."

"Yea," I said. "But I'm beyond blushing with embarrassment." I looked back over the few notes. "This peacock decade—how many people tell the truth when they're talking about age?"

"Hardly anyone on either side of the fence," Phil said. "You can expect five to ten years to be shaved off a hustler's age when he runs an ad anywhere under the 'Models, Masseurs, and Escorts' sections of a gay newspaper. And if he includes a picture of himself, you can be reasonably sure it's an old one, taken when the bloom was on."

"I suppose the same thing happens when the john who's looking for a hustler runs his ad."

"Better believe it, bub," Phil said. "But the guy who hires the hustler is generally in a position of power and money. And he never runs *his* picture. If he's rich enough, it really doesn't matter if he's too old or looks like Caliban. The hustler never really sees him anyway; no matter how withered the guy might be, he still looks like the picture on the bigger bills. On the other hand, only a beginning hustler would require that the john be within certain age limits."

"Would even the experienced ones put up with someone who was really ugly or repulsive?"

Phil nodded. "It's hard sometimes, but you've gotta do it. Wasn't it Tennyson who said that the 'jingling of the guinea helps the hurt that honor feels'? It's all too true that a hustler's self-esteem is eroded rapidly on the grindstone of need. A coupla hundred bucks makes a swell ointment for a wounded ego and the humiliation that a fellator might feel as he forces himself to go down on an unattractive guy."

"I don't suppose," I said, "that the hustler ever complains about a client's being *too* young."

There was a short explosive laugh from Phil. "A guy I knew in Chicago was once asked for a dollar by a young black kid in a lonely subway station at night. The kid was about eight years old. My friend said, 'I don't have it.' And the youngster eyed him coldly and said, 'If you-all don't gimme it, I'se gonna find me a cop and tell him you-all moh-lested me.' My friend said that he ripped the edge of his pants pocket in his hurry to produce a dollar bill."

"I suppose then that the conclusions from all this are that one simply ought not to expect too much from the printed ad or photograph when it comes to the matter of age—for both hustler and john."

"Right," Phil said. "The actual appearance of either the hustler or the score can often be an astonishment. It's really like a blind date. The poke sometimes has a pig in it, and only rarely an angel. And 'thirty-something' could really be closer to 'pushing-fifty.'"

"How about all those handsome weightlifters in gyms? What's really going on in gyms today?"

"Not as much as there used to be in the past," Phil said. "In Chicago there was one really notorious gym down at the south end of the Loop, back in the 1950s and 1960s. It was first run by a homosexual, and then sold to another gay guy who was quite an entrepreneur. Actually—the second one was more like a pimp. He managed to get a few of the best-looking body-builders on his string, and then he'd arrange with many of his gay friends to hire the guys out. Mostly these kids were just trade—not real hustlers, just trade . . . or tricks. All they'd do would be 'make the plank,' as the French say. Lie flat on their backs, hands behind the head, and let the gay one do all the work. One of the handsomest went on to become a Chicago cop later. I've often wondered just how he handled that.''

"Don't I seem to recall that one of your short stories in *Stud* was concerned with that? Wasn't it called 'A Collar for Achilles'? And didn't that same guy reappear in a novel called *The Boys in Blue*?''

"Yup . . . on both counts," Phil said. He paused for a moment and then went on. "I wonder what kind of hi-jinks went on in the gymnasia of ancient Greece. Must have been something happening now and then, since all the athletes were stark naked. It must have been necessary even then for the young Phaedrus—if he were to be admired by Socrates—''

"—and immortalized in a Platonic dialogue," I added.

"—to be well-constructed in body as well as mind," Phil finished.

"Mens sana in corpore sano," I said. "The only Latin I can remember. A healthy mind in a healthy body."

"Yeah," Phil said.

"I guess any intelligent hustler today must realize that he's gotta preserve the commodity that's been given to him for a few years. His body has to be taken care of. If he develops a paunch or even love-handles, he can't charge so much."

"You're right," Phil said. "You don't really have to be Mr. Universe, or talk all the time about the merits of blackstrap molasses or brewers' yeast or protein powders. And certainly you don't have to conserve your . . . er . . . vital fluids for fear you'll weaken your stamina by spilling your . . . vesicular reserves, the great bugaboo of dedicated weightlifters. But . . . it *is* necessary to maintain yourself reasonably well."

"And that means, I suppose, a more or less faithful following of a program in a gym that'll keep you well-toned, ready for almost anything.''

"Yes," Phil said. "But the really upper-class hustler has got other places to go as well. There's the hair stylist, the manicurist, and maybe the podiatrist . . . and who knows just what kind of fetishist he may meet along the way?"

"Years ago in the 1930s and 1940s many arrangements were made in bars, but in the ordinary gay bar, or even the s/m bar, there aren't many hustlers at present."

"Hardly," Phil said. "Most gays are outraged or annoyed if an evening's pickup brings up the subject of money."

"But don't hustlers have their own bars where making dates is taken for granted?"

"Sure do. The 'hunter' knows which ones they are, and what to expect if he goes to one. But the arrangements that are made in gyms, where the presence of an occasional hustler is a tolerated if not exactly approved fact, are somehow mysteriously considered to be more stamped with favor than pickups arranged in an alley or at a meat-rack."

"Very odd," I said.

"Oh, I don't know," Phil said. "The American tradition favors finding your wife-to-be at a church social or a bingo game rather than under a street-light."

Chapter IV

Little Lamb [or Tyger]:
What Made Thee [Start It]?

It had been a hot afternoon—hot for Berkeley, that is—which meant that the temperature had climbed to seventy-five or thereabouts. At some point Phil had removed his tee shirt, and watching his musculature and seeing once again the almost-tailored look of the fan of black hair on his chest, the sculptured pectorals and the excellently defined arms and large-veined hands, was sometimes so disturbing that I found it hard to concentrate. Even sitting as relaxed as he was in his black leather chair, his belly retained its ridging, and did not fold in upon itself. The power of memory and the fascination of a good body to my eye and imagination were things that I had always found difficult to resist, and occasionally to control. But I was with him for a purpose, and anything else would have to wait.

About six o'clock he rose, and said that he was hungry and how about dinner?

"Fine," I said. I watched the play of his muscles as he put his tee shirt back on, the movement in his strong neck as he thrust his head through the neckband, twisting it just a little from side to side, and grinning at me as his face again appeared.

"Dinner's on me," I said.

"Are you outa your head? You're my guest."

"Then tomorrow."

"We'll see." He put on a dark blue cashmere jacket, said goodbye to the dogs, and admonished them to bark at burglars. Out front we got into his black Jaguar and drove a bit north, to eat at Christopher's Cafe, a small restaurant with a faintly European ambience and arrangement—open kitchen at the rear so you could watch the flames spring up occasionally, good prints on the wall, a small bar for light liquids and wine . . . and one of the most excellently savory meals I'd had in quite a while, with many small flavors surprising the palate, and textural astonishments such as tiny cubes of pineapple and water chestnuts mixed together, with scorching salsa to accompany the "blackened" pork chops.

Afterwards as we were driving back, I asked him if he wanted to continue, or wait until the next day.

"Oh, let's go on for a coupla hours," he said. "Bad night for television, and I don't feel like reading."

That was agreeable to me, and after we were settled, I said, "Just what do you think makes a person start hustling? I know you've told me how you think you got started, but let me hear a few generalizations about the whole profession."

He smiled. "So now it's a profession, is it? Very dignified, and quite generous of you to name it so."

"World's oldest," I said. "Or maybe second oldest."

"Whatever." He settled comfortably in his chair. The dogs slept at his feet, and the only sounds in the room were the tickings of the several clocks.

"That's easy," he went on. "Only two or three reasons for getting into it. Easy money. Love of luxury. Fundamental laziness and reluctance to face the nine-to-five day. Or as Aldous Huxley described the American work week: routine interrupted by orgy."

"No others?"

"Maybe," he said. "Maybe as in my case."

"And what might that be?"

"Hooked on sex. I just plain liked it."

"Years ago," I said, "Ben Hecht in *Fantazius Mallare* spoke of 'the feeble tickle of the orgasm.'"

"Not for me," he said. "Sheez! It's a rip-roarin' tornado when it tears through my system. For nearly a minute sometimes I've got the rush, the tingle everywhere — tunnel vision, fishmouth, gasping, sweating, blood pressure up, heart pounding, toes curled under, the calves of my legs are aching, and every damned muscle in my body is tensed up. Whee! Feeble tickle, my ass. It's a bodyquake, and so violent I sometimes think I'm gonna shake apart. And I'm noisy — which most customers like."

"You're evidently one of the lucky ones who really do enjoy sex," I said. "You're very fortunate."

"You fill me with admiration," he said ironically.

"Some persons just sigh and shut their eyes. Or look cross-eyed."

"To go back to your question and try to answer it seriously," he said, "I suppose there are as many differing motivations as there are types of hustlers — no two *exactly* the same. Always some slight differences to make unique combinations of reasons for everyone."

"I think that most of the professional sociological or psychiatric studies of hustlers mention the 'broken-home-syndrome' as one of the most heavily weighted reasons. At least, that seems to be what the runaways mention most."

"It's a little annoying," Phil said. "The 'broken-home-syndrome' seems to be blamed for everything that's wrong with the American male — his greed, hypocrisy, racism, lack of ethics, selfishness, and all of his male chauvinist piggottry. A kind of catch-all for everything which it's hard to find the real blame for."

I shook my head. "It may contribute to many of the difficulties of the American male," I said, "but only that. I couldn't accept it as the major factor in many cases, simply because I've known too many hustlers who came from perfectly well-adjusted and reasonably happy homes — middle-class, maybe, but good solid ones. And I could name a few notable cases where a wealthy son from an impeccable family turned out to be a hustler."

"I agree," Phil said, "and I suppose when you get right down to it I've known even more hustlers than you have. They don't fit any kind of pattern or pigeonhole."

"Then we both feel that the motives can be quite complex and that any attempt to simplify or to find one formula to explain all is quite impossible. But what would you say is the most heavily weighted possibility?"

"Envy of the observed lifestyle," Phil said. "The financial rewards of call-boys — as separate from the street hustlers or runaway juveniles — are quite impressive. And the high-toned lifestyle is made possible only through money . . ."

". . . Enabling one to buy real estate . . . and Jaguars," I said.

"Yea," said Phil, with a ministerial inflection and a worshipful look ceilingward.

"But doesn't it take quite a while to work up to such big bucks?"

"Unless you happen to be tops in the field," said Phil, doing an imaginary buff-and-inspection of his fingernails. "Takes quite a while for some to climb that ladder to a reputation. Often when a hustler reaches his goal, it's been so long that his charms have faded, and demands for his services or his company have begun to diminish."

"Then he's just left with a sad little catch-22 situation."

"Yes." Phil was silent for a moment. "But there are other impelling forces . . ."

"Such as — ?"

"Hard to find them because they're so deeply hidden. They are mostly unrealized because they're way down in the psyche under lots of layers of cotton wool. But I think one of them is power."

"Sounds very subtle. Power from whom? I can maybe sense its effect on the hustler — maybe it simply comes from the fact that his john holds the money, and that's a kind of invisible radiation that's bound to affect him."

"True enough," Phil said. "I was very conscious of that when I was beginning. Made me turn on all the charm I could produce, and even do everything I could physically, try all the techniques I could dream up, just to overwhelm my score physically."

"To increase the tip, I suppose," I said sardonically.

"Why not? All's fair in sex. And big tips often kept the landlord happy . . ."

"Just how does . . .?" I asked, mystified.

"He got paid the rent on time," Phil said. "But there's also another kind of power that's even more mysterious and arcane than the strength of the fee, and that's the power the hustler has over the purchaser of his services."

"What's that? What kind of power? Where from?"

"The client is after all as susceptible to the power of sexual ecstasy within himself as any Armand is to the lady with camellias. If a hustler really knows how to make love, knows all of the refinements and ways to bring his customer to unfamiliar heights, to prolong the electric explosion of the orgasm, and all the tingling everywhere — then how's about the addiction of the patron to that particular hustler? To his power? Many people are really addicted to sex, lots of it, and the agent of physical rapture is quite likely to create a real *habit* of himself . . . as strong as cocaine or heroin . . ."

"But hardly as debilitating," I said. "And maybe not quite as expensive. So — we're back to your earlier statement, and more proof that some people are simply hooked on sex."

"There may be one or two other motivations behind the hustler."

"I'm running dry on ideas," I said. "We've already gone farther than I've ever been in the past."

"Suppose you have a hustler who's a real exhibitionist. Or a gen-you-wine narcissist. Many of the types in gyms are one or the other, even if they are not body-builders or weightlifters with *their* obvious love of their own persons. So then the possibilities for pleasurable satisfaction become another incentive for their hustling."

"How so?"

"Well, I had a friend in Chicago who for many years enjoyed the handsomest weightlifter-hustler in the business in those years. The guy could never ejaculate unless he was able to watch himself in a full-length mirror while he was being serviced. And there was another one who, while standing behind his client bending over the bed-edge, exclaimed: "Chee! I like to look down and see it goin' in and out!" And there was one Midwestern hustler from Kansas who particularly appreciated a pair of prism spectacles one patron had — the kind that enable invalids to watch television without raising the head. The hustler while lying flat on his back to let the client work on him could observe every movement from a strange and novel perspective. And finally, there is the small pleasure the exhibitionist can have if he is endowed more generously than most — the murmured tribute that 'enriches the sensory enjoyment and response,' as D. H. Lawrence once wrote."

"Such a small sweet statement can be murmured either for the hustler's or his client's equipment and enjoyment, I imagine?"

"Of course," he said, grinning. "I've even heard it myself."

"Naturally," I said.

"I knew another guy in Chicago," Phil said. "He wasn't very far from being a sociopath — or maybe he was just guilt-ridden for some reason or other, maybe from a religious background. It might even have been possible that he just had a curious kind of sympathy for poverty-stricken street people. But he could never enjoy their favors without paying for them, even if they had not yet embarked on a career of whoring. He would insist on their taking money.''

"Very odd, I'd say.''

"Just how many might have been turned to hustling as a result of his generosity, no one could ever know. If any were.''

"You mentioned laziness as one motivation.''

"I suppose that was wrong,'' he said. "Laziness is a passive state — certainly 'motivation' as a term suggests some little output of energy. So a state of inertia or laziness could hardly ever be counted as a moving force.''

"Perhaps we should invent a term from the new physics,'' I said. "We might call it dynamic laziness.''

"Contradiction in terms,'' Phil said, grinning. "Like the new 'fuzzy logic.'''

"And there's the beautiful but dumb ones. Are they to be included under laziness?''

"They're really unlucky. Beautiful but lazy. With nothing to fall back on, no second job, after the peacock period's over.''

"How about you? If you've really retired from hustling, what are you going to do now? Have you got a second job to fall back on?''

"Damn betcha.''

"I knew a Scotsman once who said he wanted to be the mirror inspector at a Scot military barracks, to check when they went out in full kilt on evening permission. Regulations required them to wear nothing underneath the kilt.''

Phil laughed. "Yeah, that'd be for me,'' he said. "Except some of them might never get past the mirror. But I'd never be lucky enough to find something like that.''

"Just what is your fall-back skill?''

"I've kept up an Ohio license for about twenty years,'' he said. "As a pharmacist. Then maybe I can prescribe for what ails you.''

"Such as — ?''

He came as close to twinkling as a he-man could. "Penis normalis,'' he said, and grinned. "*Pro re nata* — as need arises.''

Chapter V

How Do I Get
to the Primrose Path
from Here?

1. SOME GENERALIZATIONS

The next morning when I arrived at Phil's cottage he seemed a little distraught, and his hair even more windblown than ever. He had a hammer and trowel in his hands.

"Come on in and sit down," he said. "I've gotta fix the fence so's the dogs can't get into the neighbor's yard. They dig underneath it, and this morning I had to chase them a full block to corral 'em. Trouble is, they've been mostly house dogs, and haven't got enough gumption to avoid cars on the street. I'll be back in a minute."

I went into the living room and sat down. Phil had "inherited" the house from an older friend of his, Ward Stames, who had disappeared somewhere along the way, perhaps at the moment living in Europe. I had never inquired about their relationship, feeling that if it were at all important, Phil might tell me at some time or other just what the details of the situation were.

There was an abundance of clocks around the room—several kinds, including a wooden facsimile of the type that Dante had mentioned in the *Inferno*—one with a slowly swinging horizontal escapement, called a verge or foliot, and with only one hand. I had once, long ago, asked Phil why he was so interested in clocks, and he said that he had been fascinated with the visible passage of time ever since he had read Thomas Mann's *The Magic Mountain*, which contained many interesting little side-bar essays on time. At one period there had been about thirty clocks in the house, most of them collected by Ward Stames. They did not include electric clocks, which were looked upon scornfully by Stames as being about as worthy of interest as electric meters.

Phil was back in a few moments, looking still more disheveled. "So . . . do you know anyone who might be interested in having a coupla dogs?" he said. "There are times when I feel they own me, not the other way around."

I laughed. "You know very well you wouldn't part with either of them for any reason. And they'll mean more to you as you grow older. And lonelier. Have you trained them yet to bring your slippers?"

"Don't wear slippers yet," he said. "Go barefoot."

"Think you'll run into a member of the Foot Fraternity now and then?"

"Who can tell?" he said, somewhat dreamily.

"I suppose you're thinking of a story you once wrote called 'The Green Monkey,'" I murmured. "About foot fetishism."

"Could be."

"One of only two times you wrote about someone dying," I said.

"I've forgotten the other one."

"The cop at the end of *Greek Ways*."

"Ah yes." He let his breath out in a forcible exhalation. "Where were we when we stopped talking yesterday?"

"We'd been trying to find the motivations for being a hustler."

"Which oughta lead us," he said, "into the specific ways or paths for becoming one."

"Yea," I said.

"Whence cometh the oh-so-biblical 'yea'?"

"I'm temporarily tired of yeah, yoh, and yup," I said.

"There's *Ja, Da, Si and Oui.* And even 'Yes.'"

"Oui," I said.

"Well, there's lots of roads to it, yellow brick and gravel and cobblestone. Maybe the candidate's got a friend who's already hustling, and can give him some hints about beginning. Or mebbe an evening's pickup, out of wild gratitude for a good lay, gives the guy a reward—a dinner, a bottle of booze, a big hundred-dollar bill, or a trip to Paris. You don't have to be extra smart to realize — either immediately or else on the following day — that you may have something to sell, and maybe it might be possible to turn your body into a money-machine."

"A reasonable deduction."

"And then sooner or later you will be struck with an entrepreneurial thought: how can I best inform the world of the great treasure I possess? You will then abandon street cruising, the 'pave' or the 'meat-rack' or even the neighborhood bar, and decide that it pays to advertise."

I sighed. "I kinda miss the picture of our young rookie leaning against the lamp-post like Lilli Marlene."

Phil paid no attention. "The new kid on the block may then think of the wonderful world of newsprint that's available to him, with its gross exaggerations and fraudulent claims and hyperbole. He is ready to leave the turf of catch-as-catch-can and move up to the next level — the landed gentry. There's still a long way to go, but below him is the random chancey tricking that he can leave forever."

"I know," I said, almost tempted to wave my hand like a student eager to answer a question; "he can now have a twenty-four-hour secretary."

Phil looked annoyed. "What're you talking about?"

"A telephone and an answering machine."

He smirked. "I was getting to that," he said.

"I yield the floor," I said, "and I will alert the media."

"Back in the '50s and '60s," he continued "before the Supreme Court decided that community standards should govern obscenity, you might say that the United States was in its posing-strap period."

"Yea," I said, with an evangelist's minor third inflection.

"The Athletic Model Guild in LaLa Land, like lots of other studios all over the country — the Kris Studio in Chicago, for instance — employed hundreds of handsome young studs, put them in posing straps and suggestive situations or positions and made five-by-seven photos of them, which they then sold at outrageous prices to panting homosexuals everywhere."

"I think I remember reading one of your stories about that route to hustling," I said. "Wasn't it in *$tud* — 'Once in a Blue Moon'?"

"Yes, but there were several body-builders who became success-ful hustlers that way — one of the handsomest weightlifters got to be one of the most popular hustlers in the Chicago area."

"The one who later became a cop?"

"Yes."

"You called him Rudolf Dax, didn't you? In the story called 'A Collar for Achilles,' and later in *The Boys in Blue* you wrote about him again."

"Lord, you seem to have a steel-trap mind," Phil said.

"I was the collaborator, remember? Or rather, amanuensis. But I think the best 'treatment' you gave this path to primroses was in 'Once in a Blue Moon,' in *$tud*."

"Kenny was a nice kid," Phil said reminiscently.

"I wouldn't recommend such a way to become a hustler for just anyone. First of all, many couldn't — you have to be damned good-looking and have a great body. And there seem also to be some hidden hazards to that method."

"Such as?"

"Well, the Kris Studio in Chicago also had as models the two hustler brothers who bludgeoned Ramon Navarro to death in Holly-wood, and occasionally a policeman father scared the hell out of the Krissies by appearing at their door to inquire just what they were doing with his good-looking son."

"But sometimes one of the photographed models got really suc-cessful," Phil said. "Nationwide popularity. It was actually just a small beginning, sort of, for such yet-to-be-made inventions as video tapes and X-rated sex movies in general. But the rates of pay for the models in the '60s were usually very low — five to ten dollar range, just the same as for sex. Not many got rich on those scales. But there were occasional exceptions. Some even got as high as a hundred bucks for posing."

"And aren't we forgetting the greatest single blessing to pictorial pornography and hustling ever made?"

Phil looked puzzled.

"I mean the Land Polaroid camera," I said. "When it came along in the early 1950s, it created thousands of amateur pornogra-phers almost overnight. The *modus operandi* was quite simple: you saw a handsome kid and approached him with a story of wanting to hire a good model and would he like to earn a few bucks posing for you. If you were a skillful salesman and a convincing talker, then — bingo! — you had him made. You settled for ten bucks, say, and if sex were later involved, maybe ten more. And then *he* would discover that he could sell himself, and might go on from there to hustle.''

"It used to happen quite often like that," Phil said. "I knew several. And one Chicago hustler carried a small book of Polaroids of his genitals around with him. Said it saved a lot of time with his customers."

"Well, our rookie is now on the way up the ladder, not so? The photographer at the studio usually acted as pimp . . .''

" . . . matchmaker . . .''

"Whatever. He'd tell his friends that a new body was available. Or if it was an amateur with his Polaroid, he would tell *his* friends, and the same advancement would take place."

"But on a smaller scale," Phil added.

"The hustling business really began to grow in the 1960s. There were even more male whorehouses. Did you ever read Kenneth Marlowe's *Mr. Madam*? It was the 'confession' of a male hustler who had a stable of boys in Los Angeles, and wrote his memoirs in 1964.''

"I think I read it years ago," Phil said.

"Then there was J. Brian," I said, "who called himself the 'porno king' of northern California. He made lots of porno films, and was a really ambitious entrepreneur. Had a house on Mason Street in San Francisco with several handsome young men living on the premises . . . as you know only too well. I think *Greek Ways* was one of your best novels, and you certainly laid Mr. Brian's enterprise wide open in that one."

"It was really a rendezvous spot for many celebrities," Phil said. "There was one rough-and-tumble motorcycle stud who never came to San Francisco without going to J. Brian's house. He died of lung cancer without ever having his cover blown in the Rock Hudson manner."

"There were lots of escort services in San Francisco in the 1960s. They advertised in the *Berkeley Barb* and then later in the homosexual *Advocate*. Early on, they were all politely called 'Models' or 'Masseurs' or 'Escorts' . . .''

"Still are, aren't they?"

" 'Escorts' as a term seems to be more or less disappearing," I said. "I haven't seen it in a coon's age. Most of the euphemisms have been discarded — sometimes in favor of the initials: 'WS' for water sports, 'B&D' for bondage and discipline. And lots of other specialties involving rubber garments, sado-masochism or 's/m,' feet, enemas and such like — they all developed their own arcane references and abbreviations."

"Things changed rather fast," Phil said.

"I've heard that for the top-grade hustler there was only one final level he could achieve. The telephone was no longer necessary, nor any printed advertisement. Word-of-mouth now carried him from one wealthy patron to another, and a golden Nirvana was there for the taking . . . at least for his few last years, until the 'sad grey hairs' took over. Is this all true?"

"More or less," Phil said.

"How about fees?" I asked. "We've already talked about fees in the '50s and '60s — two to ten bucks. But it's the 1990s now, and everything's more expensive. I've heard that an hour or an evening with the really top-grade stuff ranges from a hundred to two-fifty, and occasionally even more."

"That's about right," Phil said.

"Heluva time for you to stop hustling, wasn't it?"

"Not if you've got something tucked away," he said with a grin.

"Want to lend me about twenty-five grand?" I said.

"What have you got for collateral?"

"Never mind," I said. "Perhaps today's fees don't equal those of a surgeon or specialist, but certainly the hustler now approaches the money an ordinary doctor makes, or what a lawyer or dentist takes home — tax-free, too. I'll wager the century's last decade will certainly be a prime one for decadence and overload, and specialists like Warhol and Mapplethorpe may well be known as the last brilliant representatives of the penultimate period before the apocalypse."

"Jaysus," Phil said. "You really are a weird one."

"Look who's talkin'," I said with a grin. "A pot is calling a kettle names."

2. THE USES OF THE THUMB

"Is there any real connection between hustling and hitchhiking?" I asked Phil.

"Perhaps," Phil said. "Trouble is, you can't ever find any kind of statistics about a link. But there's enough anecdotal information to suspect there is one."

"There's a short program on television called 'The Hitchhiker,'" I said, "which has one of the most erotic introductions — at least for homosexuals — that I ever saw."

"I don't remember the introduction especially," he said. "I *do* remember that there was always an obligatory nude scene or a 'romantic encounter' in it along the way. What was the introduction like?"

"Well, it started off with some rather dissonant strains of slow, thudding electronic music, and then you saw the backside of a tall and handsome hitchhiker slowly walking down a road against a desolate ocher-colored landscape. Backpack high on his shoulders, and the faded jeans visible beneath his scarred old leather jacket. The little half-moons of his lower buttocks slowly working up and down below the jacket edge as he walks. His left arm hangs straight down, his hand angled slightly away from his body, thumb up. He is viewed against four different landscapes, all desolate, with three or four color screens shifting from orange through an angry red to icy blue. Sometimes you're looking at his face as he approaches the camera — a very well-made face with a dark beard-mark, strong jawline, and curly dark hair falling in a carefully disarranged forelock over piercing eyes . . ."

"Sheez!" said Phil. "Somebody's caught on the flypaper!"

"You're absolutely right," I said. "He is *the* hitchhiker — the quintessential romantic wanderer."

"I suppose," Phil said, "that in this automotive age you'd say that the hitchhiker is the real force that takes the gay hunter out on the road on Sunday afternoons."

"An unjustified conclusion," I said, "but it may be true in some cases. But how is any of this connected with hustling?"

"It just so happens some time ago I knew a soldier stationed at Ford Ord, who frequently hitchhiked up to San Francisco, and three times out of four he got propositioned by the one who picked him up. So he developed a little habit of poor-mouthing about his army pay, and almost every time he collected a sawbuck or two for unzipping his fly."

"So he became a hustler?"

"Well—yes. But hardly one of the more successful ones."

"I wouldn't expect the high-class and well-established hustler to take to the open road if he could fly from one job . . . er . . . contact to the next."

"Sometimes," Phil said, "he might do it just for fun. To see if he still had the common touch."

"I would think it all might be somewhat dangerous," I said, remembering several violent movies about hitchhiking.

"Yup," Phil said. "Both parties really ought to have a little frank discussion about money and expectations before the event takes place."

"Might keep the driver from losing his wallet or his car—hey?"

"—or maybe his life," Phil added.

"Is hitchhiking *within* a city any different from hitching *between* cities?"

"Much the same, I think," Phil said. "Sections of the larger night-cities are known to be pick-up-for-pay areas, and the kids who wait around on those corners know all the devices, wordings, and little tricks that go along with the event. Down in LaLa Land—"

"Los Angeles?"

"Where else?—they like to go shirtless. One of the old hands at hustling down there says the reason he never moved to San Francisco was that it was too cold to go without a shirt."

"Proving," I said, "that even climate has something to do with hustling. Maybe Burton was right about the 'sotadic zone.'"

"I was in Colorado one summer for a few weeks," Phil said. "The young airman going back to base at the Air Force Academy really expected to pay for the ride there by letting someone blow him."

"And why not?" I said. "It usually does no harm to anyone, it feels good and it saves bus fare, and hell no, I ain't gay but I sure as hell could use some cigarette money . . ."

" — and no, I ain't a hustler, I'm just one of the 37% of American males who have had a homosexual encounter to the point of orgasm, as Doctor Kinsey pointed out back in 1948," Phil ended, laughing.

"I guess that around all the military bases in the country there's a big Sunday evening traffic back from liberty, or weekend passes or whatever."

"The roads out of Chicago to Fort Sheridan and Great Lakes Naval Training Station were always full of traffic on Sunday evenings and nights," Phil said.

"But if the sailors or soldiers were traveling in groups, no one would want to pick them up. A bit dangerous."

"Yeah, but the rookie hustler always went back alone. He could usually find a friendly motorist willing even to go a bit out of his way to deliver a guy to home base."

"How nice," I said. "Such cooperation is a hallmark of the true American spirit of neighborliness."

"Or privates enterprise."

"Good grief," I said. "That is the most forced and leaden quip I ever heard you make. You ought to be ashamed."

"I am," said Phil. "I stand with bowed head, naked and abashed before my tattered Muse."

"And that statement doesn't help your case a damned bit," I said, glad to have the last word at least once.

3. TRUCKS STOP . . . ANYWHERE

"I've heard," I said, "that in the past, a lot of truckdrivers took up a kind of hustling as a sideline."

"Yeah," Phil said, readjusting his legs as he sat in the black leather chair. "Damn," he said, "these jeans are too tight in the crotch. They squeeze the hell out of me when I sit down."

"The better to make one drool, grandmaw," I said.

"Once upon a time," Phil said, "we were both looking for the

French slang word for 'basket,' and I don't mean 'panier.' Did you ever remember it?''

"Finally," I said. "It's 'bourse.'"

"Ah," he said, "a purse."

"Yes, but they attach the word for 'heavy' to it if it's a good-sized one . . . 'lourde.'"

"Very nice," he said. "A heavy purse . . . or a loaded one."

"Well, just how could a truckdriver be considered a hustler? As it is, it seems to me they make enough money driving. The extra that they might take in by hustling would seem insignificant."

"I think they'd just consider it fun to make a little that way. Might seem adventurous. Or even romantic. Or keep them being real heteros in their own mind . . . just people who like blowjobs. A little harmless diversion before the plague arrived from Mother Africa."

"I can hardly analyze why truckdrivers have acquired such a romantic reputation amongst today's crop of gays," I said.

"It's that old open road syndrome," Phil said. "Started with Whitman. Same as for hitchhikers. Here's a stalwart he-man barrelin' along in his eighteen-wheeler cab, with bulging biceps hanging out the window of his high perch, shirt sleeves rolled up to show his latest tattoo, and along comes some little pipsqueak car beside the behemoth, with a friendly face smiling up at him. At least he thinks it's friendly; it's twilight and he can't see all that clearly. But the car passes and once it gets ahead, its lights flick twice in the up-and-down mode, high and low . . ."

"Ah *ha*!" I said.

"So our trucker is full of juices and anticipando . . ." Phil said.

"Like the lady of Shalott," I added.

". . . whatever. And he answers with a double high-low flick of his own lights. Same response. A mile goes by. We presume the first flickerer is deciding what to do. Finally he makes another double flick, pulls to the shoulder of the road and stops."

"The welcome mat is out."

Phil nodded. "There's a big *whoosh*! from the air-brakes and the monster comes to a monumental halt. And from the little car — whether Lamborghini or plain ole Toyota — there descends an exquisite of a certain age who walks back to the truck. The cab door opens, he climbs up and disappears into the darkness . . ."

"Let us draw the congressional curtain over the events of the next twenty minutes," I said.

"Beware the monsters Helms and Dannemeyer," Phil said darkly.

"Does the truckdriver join the hustler ranks thereafter?"

"Strictly amateur status," Phil said, "if even that. You must certainly know that straight men like to have their dingdongs engulfed . . . "

"Of course," I said.

"And even reciprocate from time to time," Phil added. "Makes them feel they're just having he-man sex, they ain't really queer. Maybe they ask for money just so they can go on feeling straight."

"Sounds logical," I said.

"If everyone who gave a blowjob for money was to be considered a hustler, I think the ranks would get overcrowded real soon. Anyway, truckdrivers are a little like sailors."

"How so?"

"They've got a reputation to uphold," Phil said. "A girl—or a guy—in every port."

"Any old receptacle in a storm, as Fanny Hill said."

"I don't think the hustlers' union has anything to fear from the truckdrivers in the long run," Phil said. "Or even in the short run. They're just what you might call dilettantes."

I guffawed, very unladylike. "Dilettante truckdrivers," I said. "It's a contradiction devoutly to be unwished."

We were both silent for a moment. Phil moved restlessly in his chair.

"Damn," he said finally, "every once in a while I still want a cigarette."

"How long you been off?"

"About a year," he said. "And you?"

"Three," I said, "and I've got a little sad news for you. You're never going to get over wanting one."

"It's as bad an addiction as heroin, I'm told," he said.

"Some say worse."

He indicated with a nod of his head the four-foot high steel cylinder with a brown plastic top which was sitting in one corner of the room. I had not commented on it, thinking it some kind of space heater.

"There," he said. "That's what Ward Stames had to have eventually."

I was somewhat mystified. "A space heater?"

"No way," said Phil. "Liquid oxygen. He really doesn't need it very often, he says — but it's a kind of security blanket for him, in case he does. Says a person can't smoke for as many years as he did without paying for it."

"How long was he at it?"

"Dunno exactly," Phil said. "Once he told me that when he began, cigarettes were fifteen cents a package."

"Sounds about the right price for the 1920s," I said. I pointed to a black leather zippered case standing in another corner of the room. It was about three feet long.

"What's that thing?" I asked.

Phil chuckled briefly. "That," he said, "is the famous pool cue that young Clint left behind. I gave it to Jimmy, and it came back to me when he died."

"Seems a little short for a pool cue," I said.

"Comes in two pieces. Screws together."

I sighed. "Lucky pool cue. Self-sufficient. That's the story you told in *Different Strokes*, ain't it?"

"What a brilliant deduction," Phil said sardonically.

"I didn't know we could look on you as a pool hustler as well as a . . . er . . . as the real thing."

"There's all kinds of hustlers," he said. "There's even a guy, an astronomer on PBS, who calls himself a star hustler. Every salesman's a hustler. A workaholic is a hustler about his job. A man hustles a woman when he gets her to marry him."

"And a woman hustles when she traps her husband?"

"Sure," Phil said. "Hustling's a universal occupation."

"Are you any good as a poolroom shark? A pool hustler?"

"I betcha I could beat you with one hand tied behind me."

"You could beat me with *both* hands tied behind you," I said.

"I forgot you love to be beaten," Phil said slyly. "In the face with . . . things."

"Hey," I said, "let's get on with it. Are there any loose ends to what we've already said about the more stabilized forms of hustling and the localities for them? We've been over bars and gyms, streets and meat-racks, and parks and highways."

"Tearooms," Phil said.

"Yeah," I said, "but we'd just be repeating all the stuff that Laud Humphreys covered so well in *Tearoom Trade* some years ago. Ever read it?"

Phil nodded. "I guess it was his doctoral dissertation, wasn't it? Heluva catchy title for one of those."

"The title did it," I said. "It went through several editions and was widely sold . . . even read."

"I always found tearooms a bad place for hustling," Phil said. "Lots of things against it . . . mainly audiences. You can't strike a serious financial bargain with a half-dozen eavesdroppers hanging on every word."

"Of course," I said, "I suppose a hustler could pick up a score anywhere, or vice versa — a trick might pick up a hustler — even in the ruins of Beirut — "

"Or the Vatican library," Phil said with a grin. "I did once. Maybe even the sacred halls of Congress . . ."

"Or the dark alleys of Chicago's Loop," I said. "But I've heard from several hustlers that there's one place that's not usually thought of as good for pickups — and that's the straight bar, frequented by hetero men and women."

"It's a dandy place for the one type of homosexual hustler who depends solely on the kindness of hetero males."

"Is there such an animal?"

"Sure," Phil said. "Lots of 'em. Many gays will have absolutely nothing to do with other gays. All they want is the 'real' man, whatever that is. And many hustlers are just the same. The hustler who's out for straights is usually pretty skillful at man-talk — about baseball, football, and all the other masculine sports such as fishing and fucking females. Or else he's a real feminine type so that the he-men can easily recognize him and know what he has to offer."

"Do the butch-talking ones make out all right?"

"Well, I don't like to generalize," Phil said, "but they do. They also have, however, one big drawback — they're inclined to be the one type of hustler who's almost always dishonest. They depend mostly on one-night stands, usually after getting the john so drunk he can't stand up, much less perform in bed.''

"Tsk," I said. "And then—?"

"The score passes out, and then his cash and credit cards are lifted along with his Philippe-Patek wristwatch, and our hustler flees, never to be seen again in that neighborhood."

"A point I was about to make," I said. "He has to move around quite a lot, doesn't he?"

"Yup. And he's the type that gives hustlers the bad name in the majority mind."

"Doesn't the amateur truckdriver-hustler sometimes also try the shakedown or even the robbery?"

Phil nodded. "But he can usually be outsmarted even by the dumbest and most inexperienced gay guy, who can be really devious if he's pressed into it."

"Many gays have had lots of training in outsmarting heteros since they've been fooling them all along by acting straight."

"There's one more chance for the occasional hustler—or better call him the 'jack-roller,' since he's not at all interested in sex, only in robbing. And that's when a ship with foreign sailors gets into any west or east coast port. A lot of guys are after the foreign stuff . . . the money, that is."

"I see that a 'tall ship' from France, a training ship, is due in San Francisco next week."

"Ah yes," said Phil. "So the opportunists will sharpen their claws, put on the welcome front, and go out to practice their French . . .''

I pretended to shudder, but I really do love word-games.

Chapter VI

I Will. I Won't. Maybe.
I'm a Specialist

"How about a game of chess?" Phil said after dinner.

I eyed the very *moderne*-looking chess set in a dark woodcase perched above the large living-room window. The pieces seemed to be of brushed aluminum or some silvery metal and were sleeping in a wooden display case behind a sliding blue-tinted plastic panel. I could just barely see that the black ones merely had one side surface darkened. They'd be hard to tell from the "whites."

I shook my head. "I'd need all my wits about me for chess," I said. "It's been years since I played, and I'm no longer capable of doing two things at once."

"Can't walk and chew gum at the same time?"

"Possibly. But if I were jacking off, I'd probably have to move my jaws in the same tempo."

He grinned.

"Anyway," I went on, "you'd probably trip me up with some sort of fool's mate or scholar's mate, and it'd be over before it began, and then you'd gloat."

"Not me," he said. "My compassion wouldn't let me. I'd just pity you."

It was my turn to grin. Then I said, "Did you ever play chess with any of your scores?"

"Lord no," he said. "If anybody's laying out a hundred bucks for an hour, he's hardly going to spend forty-five minutes of it trying for a checkmate. Tain't profitable."

"Would there be any types of hustlers who *would* be willing to play chess with their scores?"

"Maybe the very top-notch ones," Phil said, "or those wealthy enough not to care about the time spent . . . either the score himself, or the hustler. I suppose that those who look on themselves as 'escorts' or 'companions' would be willing.''

"Just how many types of hustlers do you think there are?'' I asked.

"Perhaps as many as there are dingdongs at all the meat-racks of the world,'' he said. "Or maybe really only about a half-dozen basics, with thousands of variations added here and there.''

"I've got a few notes somewhere about the attempts of some earlier writers to do some classifying,'' I said, busying myself with scanning some loose papers in one of my notebooks. I must confess that I have little of the ideal scholar's reverence for order and systematizing. As part of my rationale about such things, I have always said that the truly creative mind deliberately *creates* the clutter around himself, and leaves it to the plodding research assistant to tidy up. Admittedly not universally accepted reasoning.

"Here are some scribbles,'' I said, finding the proper piece of paper. "Back in 1961 a guy named A. J. Riess, in something called *Social Problems*, divided Chicago hustlers into a three-stage hierarchy—the lowest being the street-hustlers, and next up the ladder, the bar hustlers, with the topmost being the call-boys. Let us, he said, think of these guys as being sufficiently career-minded to be classed as professional groups. Thus he turned hustlers into a sociological concern.''

"Hell,'' said Phil. "Weren't there any opinions earlier than that?''

"Oh sure,'' I said. "There was a G. W. Henry who as early as 1935 had named two types of hustlers—'trade hustlers,' who allowed fellatio on themselves for money; and 'drag queen hustlers,' who dressed like ladies of the evening and performed fellatio on bucks for bucks.''

"We are all co-workers in the vineyard,'' said Phil with mock solemnity. "Any other notables?''

"That same guy in 1955 in his book, *All the Sexes*, classified hustlers into three groups—the orderly, by which he meant the professionals or the middle-class ones; the hoodlum, or the drifter/cruiser mercenary type; and the fairy—the sissy counterpart of the hoodlum.''

"Doesn't sound especially friendly or brilliant to me," Phil said.

"Right on," I agreed. "And there were several other preliminary studies, none with new ideas. Investigators like Lemert, Benjamin, and Masters, to one degree or other suggested that all hustlers were victims of the 'B.S.'"

"What's the 'B.S.'?"

"Short for the 'broken-home syndrome,'" I said. "Because of that, and through additional valiant efforts of their own, the hustlers achieved sociopathy, psychopathy, demoralization, anomia, or feeble-mindedness."

"You're sure that society's low opinion of them wasn't really founded on their not having the right kind of haircut?" Phil asked sardonically.

"I've had a really limited acquaintance with the early and current 'scholarship' in the field of hustling," I said. "I prefer not to be infected with the virus that's kept most of the commentators at 'harm's length' away from direct involvement with the hustling scene."

Phil was somewhat astonished. "I don't see how you can say that," he said, "since you operated a tattoo shop in Chicago and Oakland for at least eighteen years. That must have put you in close contact—"

"Really close, some times," I murmured.

"I'll bet," he said, grinning, " —with scores if not hundreds of hustlers who must have frequently used your shop for making arrangements with their tricks."

"Well, you're right again. But mine was a one-man operation and I had to overlook the hustling angle for the most part, except when I was . . . er . . . intimately concerned. Or wanted some temporary diversion from the arduous and confining work of . . . ah . . . dermagraphics."

"Is that your new ten-dollar word for tattoodling?" Phil demanded.

"Yea," I said. "Gotta do my best to elevate the art."

"After ripping it apart in *Bad Boys and Tough Tattoos*."

I waggled my hand at him. "Not by any means. According to some opinions, it's the most important book on the topic in the last fifty years."

"Oh, I don't disagree with that," Phil said impatiently. "It's just that you blew away the only bit of romantic fog around one of the last erotic and earthy folk arts."

"I had no idea you were such a sentimentalist," I said.

"I've got one on my shoulder, remember?"

"Uh . . ."

"Got it from ole Pete Swallow in Chicago," he said. "A dicky-bird. With whip and rose."

"Oh yeah, I remember. To show your soft center."

"Which in the passing years has somewhat hardened."

"We all grow up," I said, matter-of-fact.

"I still go to pieces over the death of a dog," he said, reaching down to scratch the ears of the black-and-tan dachshund lying on his foot.

"Who doesn't?" I added.

"I certainly wouldn't want to know any sonofabitch who doesn't," Phil said with a frown.

"Well," I said. "Forward."

"What next?"

"You may think me a Johnny-come-lately into the field of hustling . . ." I said.

"Hardly."

". . . but maybe we can find a new approach to help identify the different types."

"That's the damned academic sediment in you," Phil said. "Always have to classify . . . pigeonhole. And I did mean sediment."

"I classify just for the sake of convenience. Maybe to clarify. Or remember."

"Or just give things a name," he said, "so they'll have an identity. Isn't that what Gertrude Stein did all the time?"

"Perhaps. Anyway—"

"We might try," Phil said. "We could arrange them as to what they will or won't do—if they are paid accordingly. Or if they think they won't lose face—or reputation—by taking a little side-trip into another field."

"I'm thinking of that old joke," I said. "Someone is asked if he would blow a guy for ten dollars, and if he says no, then the fee is gradually raised until he says yes. At which point you say: 'Now that we've determined what you really are, will you do it for nothing?'"

Phil sighed. "I suppose we'll never get to the end of discovering into how many parts the human psyche is divisible."

"Along with many others Kinsey felt that most persons were a mixture of the two elements of male and female. That the exclusively heterosexual and the entirely homosexual were rare."

"And everyone agrees except the bible thumpers—*they* believe that the perfect man is completely heterosexual," Phil said.

"Even those who deny the mixing," I said, "still have their fishing buddies, their good-ole-boy drinking companions, their male bondings in sports and battles, and their camping chums."

"Of whom Hemingway is the perfect example," Phil said.

"Kinkier than you'd think," I said. "That posthumous novel of his called *The Garden of Eden* has the wife and the husband reversing roles—even to haircuts and clothes. Very strange. If all his life he was struggling against being homosexual, it's not surprising he blew his brains out at the end. As in most of the gay novels of the 1930s and '40s."

"Ward Stames told me that Alice Toklas said Hemingway met Sir Francis Rose once in the Penthièvre Baths, in those years the most notorious homosexual meeting place in Paris, and that they had a little fling together. But as soon as each of them found out who the other was, they were both horrified—and never saw each other again. Afraid Gertrude Stein would find out. But Alice said she had no proof, that it was just gossip."

"I guess no one will ever know for certain," I said. "It's widely known, however, that Hemingway punched out Robert McAlmon in Paris—knocked him flat, accusing him of spreading the rumor that Hemingway was gay . . . a real closet queen."

Phil had been engaged with a black marker and a piece of paper for a few moments. He held it up for me to see. It was a rough approximation of Kinsey's rating scale from zero to six, looking something like this:

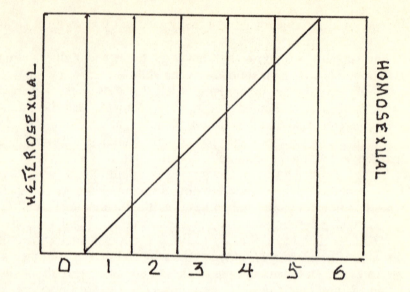

"I think I've got this right," Phil said. "Column zero is the completely heterosexual one, and number six the entirely homosexual one."

"Yes," I said, "and then everyone not in zero or six falls somewhere along the slant line, his position determined by the number of straight and gay contacts he's had. Bisexual would be column three."

"I think Kinsey himself wouldn't mind," Phil said, "if we just borrow this scale for our own use. We could classify hustlers — since you seem to insist on 'order' — according to the degree that they cooperate with the client's desires or whims . . ."

"A good idea," I said. "The zero column would be those who were 'trade' in the strictest sense — lying with arms crossed behind the head while being fellated, making no movements at all — "

" — Or looking at the ceiling, or eating an apple," Phil said. "Or in our French phrase, *'faire la planche'* — 'making the plank' — which originally meant to float on one's back."

"We could draw up a brief description of the six types," I said. "Zero could be your strict trade . . . plank-makers. The ones who claim to be entirely hetero, and allow blowjobs only."

Phil grinned. "The next column could make a few little pelvic movements — or put his hands on your head, or maybe groan a little or give out with a few dirty words during his 'ordeal' . . ."

"And column two would let you put it between his legs, from the front. Maybe he'd sodomize you if you asked him pretty enough, or grab you with his arms . . . or even his legs! Heavenly!"

That got a chuckle from Phil. "And then column three might let you really inside, or get inside you — or if you beg, even lower his head to . . . well, he'd be very reluctant about *that*, but he just might."

"He would not, however," I said, "allow deep French kissing. But I think column four would be very acceptable. He'll have a slightly aggressive attitude in bed, and will match almost anything his score does . . . even deep kissing. But no rimming," I added as an afterthought.

"You're correct about that," Phil said. "Then column five would take control without any urging. He enjoys sex — rimming, blowjobs, sodomy — the whole works. But not the specialties."

"And that will be column six," I said. "S/m, bondage and discipline, rimming, golden showers . . . anything goes. You might call him a jack-off all trades. And he'll be expensive."

"The most," Phil said.

"And just where would Mr. Andros fit into this scheme of things?"

Phil winked. "As if you wouldn't know."

"I think," I said, "it would finally depend on what you thought of the score. But I'd say four . . . five, if everything is right."

"A good guess," Phil said.

"If we can come to this much agreement about the extent of what hustlers do, perhaps you're the one to carry it all just a little farther."

"How so?" Phil asked.

"Well, out of a cast of thousands of cases you've known," I said, "perhaps you could select one or two who might best illustrate each of the columns. That is, of course, if your much-celebrated experience can furnish us with an example. If your reputation is genuine, and not merely imagined."

"You jealous?" Phil said, smirking a bit.

"Nope," I said, "just eager to be enlightened, O Master."

"Then make a notation," Phil said. "Put down a big fat zero."

"What shall we call this one?"

Phil thought a moment. "How about the 'Reluctant Nutcracker'?"

"Shades of Tchaikovsky," I muttered.

"He's a very familiar type," Phil said, "a member of any attractive group of young men — surfer with a good tan, young athlete, swimmer, boxer, football or tennis star — closer to eighteen than thirty, because after twenty-four it's real hard to claim to be a novice in the game."

"Granted all that," I said. "Who's this specifically?"

"Johnny in Chicago," Phil said. "He wasn't fond of any particular sport, unless you count bongo-thumping as one. Or bodybuilding. He was Puerto Rican, small of stature, his only imperfect feature a somewhat prognathous jaw."

I tapped my pencil against the clipboard. "I suppose now you're going to say that the huge lumpish hand on Michelangelo's David performed the same aesthetic function as Johnny's jaw."

Phil looked puzzled. "What *are* you talking about?"

"Well, the aestheticians would call it the 'glory of the imperfect.' That puts me one up on you," I added smugly.

"Maybe not," Phil said slyly. "You mean a detail that distracts the eye only momentarily, so allowing it to roam all the more admiringly over the whole."

"Damn," I said.

"You weren't the only one to take Dorn's course in the Renaissance at Ohio State, buddy."

"So I see."

"Well, anyway, Johnny had a flawless body — really classical. Praxiteles would have seized him for the ideal model. Most of his leisure time was spent combing his hair — it was the kind that would have really thinned out by the time he was thirty. He was essentially hetero, but from the age of twelve on, he had submitted to the adoration of his uncle Carlo, who subjected him to innumerable 'releases,' as Kinsey might have said."

"So Johnny fell in love with fellatio."

"Yeah," said Phil, "but he wouldn't allow anything else. If you coaxed and directed him, he'd avoid making the plank, and straddle the john—even whop him in the face with whatever might be at hand. Kinda playful—''

"I suppose the straddling got him the nickname of 'nutcracker','' I said.

"Yup,'' Phil said. "Well, that's the zero column.''

"What happened to him?''

"Oh, the usual. Marriage. Eight kids. Such hot Latin blood he never took the time to put on a condom. *If* he even knew such things existed.''

"How long did he hustle before getting married?''

"The two overlapped,'' Phil said. "Johnny was very faithful to his more generous tricks. If he found a 'regular' who would put up with his hair-combing and his compulsive bongo-drumming on any hard surface, little by little he would skillfully up his fees. In one case he was so successful that his nutcracking got him a new car.''

"I finally recognize him,'' I said. "He's the leading character in one of your stories—'Jungle Cat' in *$tud*.''

Phil nodded.

"And now,'' I went on. "Who is behind Column One?''

"I've been thinking,'' Phil said. "I guess we might call this one 'Narcissus in Illinois.' Ralph was Austrian, and had come to America when he was about twelve. He still had an accent—a rather faint one. And very early he began to be a body-builder, going to a gym run by a notorious, middle-aged, bug-eyed queen who—as a pimp—supplied a great many hustlers to gay clients.''

"That particular gym in Chicago seemed to pass from one gay pimp to the next. Three owners in a row were farming out their good-looking members,'' I said.

"I guess they did it just for love,'' Phil said. "They never got any of the money their stable-boys made . . . just the satisfaction of scattering a little joy and sunshine around town. But before he began hustling seriously, Ralph had been a waiter at a German beer-garden, wearing lederhosen and singing drinking songs with and for the customers. By the age of twenty-two he'd developed a massive body and won several titles as a weightlifter.''

"I've seen pictures of him which that same studio sold all over the country,'' I said. "Damn, he was handsome—a real blond god, cornflower blue eyes, radiant coloring . . . And that casually tousled sun-streaked hair and classic profile . . .''

"Whoa," said Phil. "Let's not go overboard. But I'll admit he was damned good-looking, and one of the best ever to be shot by that physique photographer."

"Did he have a lot of clients?"

"No, not many. But fairly wealthy ones. He was selective, and saw them regularly. And because he knew each of them for long periods of time, he felt he could afford to make a few little pelvic movements whilst being fellated, maybe even lay hands on the bobbing head—or groan a bit or whisper 'Dat's good' during the workout, even let them occasionally put their head on his chest—a sort of prickly pillow because he was continually shaving his hair in order to win points in contests."

"How did the 'Narcissus' part come in?"

"There was one client who wanted Ralph to stand over him and put his foot on his face while they both masturbated, and Ralph could never come unless he had a full-length mirror standing beside him so he could watch himself jack off."

"Now I remember. That story in *$tud*—what was the name of it?—was about him, wasn't it?"

"Yoh," Phil said. "It was 'A Collar for Achilles.' Later on he became a Chicago cop."

"I wonder what he did if he passed a former client on the street— or had to give one of them a traffic ticket. Who might be blackmailing who?"

"Whom," said Phil. "Not our problem."

"True enough," I said. "Now *whom* is to fill Column Two?"

Phil thought a moment. "I guess we could pick Larry, one of a trio of identical triplets—"

"Who's being careless now?" I said. "Trio and triplets is just a teensy bit redundant."

"Well, anyway . . .'' Phil said with a smile, "there's lotsa folklore about identicals. Lester was gay, Louie was straight, and Larry 'doubled in brass,' the phrase that was used for 'bisexual' before it was called 'AC-DC.'"

"Do we spell 'bisexual' with 'b-u-y' instead of 'b-i'?"

"Oh, ain't we smart," Phil said. "Well, Larry became a hustler almost by accident. He heard about a college professor who was using a lot of hustlers, and so he showed up at the guy's door without knowing him or even calling, and said that so-and-so had told him the professor was looking for newer bodies, hotter blood, etc. He was eighteen with absolutely no experience except what he had learned while at Boys' Town. And this time his sexual confusion really *was* partly caused by the 'broken-home' deal.''

"A real novice, then.''

"Yes. After that first encounter was over and Larry got his ten bucks or whatever and was dressing, a small toy meat-cleaver — weighing all of three ounces, with a dull blade that wouldn't cut butter — fell out of his trousers, much to the john's amusement.''

"Larry doesn't sound too bright. Or sophisticated.''

"I guess he was almost corpse-like in bed,'' Phil said. "But warm. He'd permit intercrural sex, liked blowjobs, and with insistent begging would maybe grab the client in his arms or legs.''

"Sounds as if he wouldn't have grown rich for his services.''

"Nope. He never set his fees. Just depended on the generosity — or stinginess — of the score. He was married two or three times, and after the first one he learned how to screw his johns with a kind of rabbity speed and intensity. At one point he thought he was completely homosexual, but was talked out of it.''

"By whom?''

"Dunno. Haven't you recognized him yet? He was the young thief in 'The Pool Cue,' and was also in *Shuttlecock* and *Greek Ways.*''

"Sorry,'' I said. "It's my cognitive slippage. The neurotransmitters are flaking off more rapidly than I thought. Who's next — for Column Three?''

"We might call this one 'Anything for a Buck,' '' Phil said. "His name was Joe Bob. Reddish-brown hair. His neck was red in a different way.''

"Sounds about right for a name like Joe Bob.''

"He had a kind of lanky, almost a swimmer's body which never seemed to change much as he grew older — didn't get fat or paunchy or grow love-handles. At forty-five — when I knew him — he still had the frame of a twenty-year old, although his face had aged considerably.''

"I hate people like that."

"Doesn't everybody? Joe Bob was the prototypical Drifter/Hustler. But he'd never admit to being a hustler. For about twenty years he lived off a man who screwed him occasionally, but who finally got tired of his drinking, doping, and general lack of cooperation, despite the food and lodging provided for half a lifetime. Joe Bob could hold a job for about six months, and then his desire to be the Big Shot Know-It-All always got him in trouble . . . and fired. Even from a second Navy hitch."

"The great drawback of the Me generation," I said.

"But sexually," Phil went on, "it was 'anything goes' with him — except deep French kissing and rimming. He even liked to be screwed — and when he was the active agent, screwing was his favorite method of release. He would also — and at times even enthusiastically — give head, and suck male nipples. And his hetero side seemed just as strong. You might say that everything was useful — even knotholes in a fence . . ."

"With or without a mouth on the other side?"

"Yeah. When he jacked off — not caring who was watching — he even liked to have a dog lick the semen-covered glans. He liked the voyeuristic aspects of sex. He was the one with a client who had a pair of those prism spectacles — you know, the kind that let sick people lie prone to watch television. Man, did he like them! Nothing that was sexual was strange to him — if you want to change the old Latin motto a little."

"He sounds to me like a template for the Compleat Hustler," I said slyly. "Maybe more so than you, hey?"

"Except for one small detail," Phil said. "He had absolutely no aggressiveness. He had to be coaxed. As for the pay — well, money was okay, but he'd accept valuables, especially of the hockable sort. His AC-DC balance was pretty equal. He left several children scattered over California, but at last got married to a Polynesian bride and had two more kids. Then he got tired of her and moved back to the mainland from Hawaii."

"So — that's that, for Column Three," I said, making the hand-dusting gesture. "Who's for the next number?"

"I guess I'd have to pick a cop," Phil said.

"Oh really?" I said, sardonic. "I had no idea you liked 'em."

Which was not at all true. He often liked to surprise a listener by saying something high-flown about Lycurgus and the beauty of law, going on to point out that the cop was the single point at which the majesty of the law touched the individual — and then startle his audience by saying 'And now you can believe that if you want to.' He had written a full novel about his own brief time as a cop, *The Boys in Blue*; and one of his short stories — which many readers found to be one of the most erotic things he ever wrote — was called "The Peachiest Fuzz" and appeared in *$tud*.

I happened to know that story was about a cop named Jim B. How he had ever become a policeman was a small mystery; he had actually been in prison for a while for some unspecified felony, perhaps involving his hustling. He had probably managed to conceal the prison background by exerting pressure on a high-placed official with enough clout to alter records or hide facts.

I met him once. He had the kind of face and figure that belonged with a cop's uniform. It was very male. The shadow of his cap brim brought out the height of his cheekbones by darkening the flat planes beneath, and likewise highlighted the cleft in his chin. The carving of the dark full lips was subtle and precise. His hair was black, short, and curly; his eyes dark and humor-filled beneath straight black eyebrows.

"Real yummy," I said.

"Yup," Phil said.

"Was he doing the hustling as a cop? while in uniform?"

"Yes. A simple and effective *modus operandi*. In full cop drag he'd drive his black unmarked sports car around the city streets until he spotted a homosexual hunting for a trick to pick up. He'd drive up to him, pause, and call the guy to his car. Then he'd startle him by suggesting sex, tell him his rates — which were high, and invite the man into the car. Many were frightened away by the uniform, but many succumbed. They were overwhelmed by the kind of crackling charisma and almost tangible animal magnetism that surrounded him . . ."

"I also imagine that some of them were afraid of what might happen if they refused his proposal . . . proposition."

"Probably had something to do with it," Phil said. "At any rate, he was successful, and a 'romantic encounter' with him was one of the high points of one's sexual life. It involved as many releases as the john was capable of, because Jim's attitude was slightly aggressive. And then he always arranged the stage setting — he managed to leave his uniform in full sight, draped over a chair, and his extra-long night stick sticking up out of one of his boots, with his cap on top of it. Everything worked together to give the customer a completely sensual hour, and leave him gasping over the greatest event of his experience — at least for that week.''

"It sounds to me as if it was also one of *your* great experiences," I said.

"How did you ever guess?" Phil said. "He would match everything you would do, and sometimes did things first."

"Did he have many clients?"

"No — he was pretty selective. But the contact always wanted to see him again, and often became a regular. Then Jim's aggressiveness would continue to increase, as well as the money demands. Oddly enough, he never lost a customer because of his requests — which sometimes came close to the edge of extortion . . . or maybe a vague sort of blackmail. He was one of the most successful operators in the whole damned town."

"I guess I never knew where he lived," I said.

"Would you believe Milwaukee?" Phil laughed.

"No, I wouldn't."

"Well, that's where he operated. I'll grant you it was an unlikely place for such a dazzling entrepreneur. But for the next colyum I can name an even more unlikely place to find a hustler."

"The straight man will dutifully say 'Where?'"

Phil was astonished. "A straight man? You?"

"For the immediate purpose, you nut."

"Well — the desolate wind-swept dunes at the south tip of Lake Michigan, just above Gary, Indiana."

"You win," I said. "Hustling is for the dark alleys, the night cities. You won't find too many hunters amongst the lonely Indiana dunes . . . or even wild Arabian sheiks riding around on wilder steeds."

"But they did offer Wally. He was a tall raw-boned gangling sort of ex-Marine with a broken nose and a flat-top haircut. And he'd come barging along the sand and water behind the prow of a *big genital bulge.*"

"Why am I getting a maritime image—old windjammer with sails, and a maiden figurehead?"

"All wrong in this case. Wally's approach and general technique were a lot like hurricanes or tornadoes. He'd spot his prey with an eye that made absolutely no diagnostic mistakes. Then he'd advance, and without a word seize and kiss, and just like a wrestler throw the guy to the sand and begin. Absolutely no hint of foreplay or talk. If it had been a female, it would have been called rape—violent rape."

"But since it was only two males, what was it?"

"A playful cavorting on the beach," Phil said. "Or just two guys wrestling. And really, since Wally's way answered the deep call of romance in most homosexuals, it was welcomed—"

"As overwhelming as that must have been," I said, "wasn't anybody scared to death?"

Phil laughed. "Only at first. Here perhaps was the Ideal for which so many were looking—the real male who'd sweep away the yearning heart . . . the ultimate Heathcliff of *Wuthering Heights* . . ."

"Why not call him the ornery sonofabitch all too eager to fulfill the melting masochistic hungers of gropers for romance?"

"You've always had that tendency," Phil said, "ever since we've known each other."

"And what's that, pray?"

"In the past, every time I felt the least romantic—which was not too often—you've always taken a kind of perverse delight in bringing me back to earth with a thud. Like just now—with the 'melting masochistic hungers' and the 'ornery sonofabitch' . . ."

"I'm only trying to preserve nature's exquisite balance," I said, "Moderation in all things. But Wally's enthusiasm could very well counter the dullness of the first column on our scale—the ones who 'made the plank.'"

"I suppose," Phil said, "that you could say his taking charge began where that of the peachiest fuzz left off. Not only would he run through the entire bag of tricks that two men can do together, but quite obviously he'd enjoy it all . . . greedily, completely."

"The demon-lover of sex."

"Yea," Phil said. "And even with all the hazards of love-amongst-the-dunes, where grease attracts sand the way a magnet pulls iron filings to it, he always kept things moving smoothly."

"Was he expensive?"

"From what I used to hear from satisfied customers, after everything had come to its exhausting but exhilarating end, no one ever objected to giving Wally every damned cent he had on his person, and then borrowing back enough bus fare to get home. If he didn't have enough payment for Wally, he'd promise to meet him a week away. And Wally somehow knew that the new one would always show up when he said he would."

"Sounds like a real treat," I said, and then looked at my notes. "Was that the last of the columns?"

"I've lost track," Phil said. "But we haven't said anything about the 'specialists' — the ones who advertise their services in the specialized journals, like the foot fetishists' club in Cleveland, or the groups devoted to rubber, to bondage and discipline, to piercings, fistings or other dangerous pastimes. Those guys have all advanced to the top stage, even beyond that of 'anything goes' — 'anything' itself meaning much more than the ordinary gamut of what's called 'vanilla' sex."

"By which you mean sex without embellishments or elaborations?" I said, and he nodded.

"Tell you what," I said. "Let's postpone those topics until we get to a discussion of what actually goes on behind the green door. Our own little detailed Kama Sutra."

Phil sighed. "Are you planning to have me expose all my secrets?"

"Every damned one."

"Just like any writer," Phil said. "Sucking all the information out of a guy, and then taking all the credit for it."

"We call it getting the nut without cracking the shell."

"How about 'I tell it, you sell it'?" Phil said.

"That too," I said, grinning. "I am a part of all that I have met. Or else I make it all a part of me."

Chapter VII

Shoppers of the Night

1. A VERY FEW POINTS OF LIGHT

We had returned from an excellent lunch, this time at a Thai restaurant which had been receiving good reviews in the press, and which had the added charm of a menu announcing that you could order your food as "hot" as you wanted. Both of us chose the extreme limit, and ordered a strange, milky iced tea to take away part of the heat.

Back in the house, as we settled into our chairs, one of which had to be angled so as to face the other, I noticed in diagonal corners of the room two small gold-toned objects that looked like reliquaries.

"Do those belong to you?" I asked Phil.

"No way," he said. "They belong to Ward Stames."

"What are they?" I asked. "I mean—what's in them?"

Phil chuckled. "When he was young, Ward was looking for a lot of answers. He even tried the Catholic church for a while, but he had become too materialistic for it actually to 'take' for very long. Year and a half, maybe. But during that time—when he was about twenty years old—he was confirmed in the church, and his godfather gave him the reliquary in that corner—which contains a fragment of blond hair, about an eighth of an inch long, from the head of Sainte Thérèse, the Little Flower of Jesus. First-class relic, and there's a Latin document to prove it. Bad Latin, Ward says . . . but an impressive paper."

"Does it cure things?" I asked.

"I think Ward tried it on one of his dogs once," Phil said, "but only briefly, because he decided if it cured the dog, he would have to go back to the Catholic church in gratitude."

"And what happened?"

"Unfortunately, the dog died. So Ward felt freed."

"And the other reliquary?"

This time Phil laughed loud. "You'd never guess," he said. "It's a tiny bit of Rudolf Valentino's pubic hair."

"Good lord," I said. "I didn't know Ward was that old."

"In his eighties," Phil said. "He actually was with Valentino in 1926, shortly before Valentino died. You'll have to get him to tell you the story sometime."

"Where's Ward now?"

"In Europe," Phil said. "For about another year. Mostly in France."

"This sort of leads us into the area of morals and religion and —"

"Movies?" Phil asked.

"Maybe, with Valentino, who was a fairly expert hustler himself. Of course, if there were no demand for sexual hustlers, the breed would never have appeared — right?"

"I suppose so," Phil said. "But that would mean that somewhere along the line of human endeavor, there would have to have been a surgery performed on the human psyche — to remove the libido and every other kind of sexual urging."

"Impossible to achieve," I said, "except with certain medications."

"Right. If it could be managed for everybody, the race would die out in one generation. But if the urge stays as strong as it is, then the need to fulfill it remains as well. No legislation of pope or church, or city or state or national government can remove it entirely."

"Saint Augustine realized that, being a practical man as well as a reformed lecher. Remember what he wrote in his *City of God*? He admitted that brothels were as necessary in a city as cesspools — not that they were equal, but that both were required for the health of the city."

"All too many of the laws in this country," Phil said, "are tied to the religious precepts found in the Bible . . ."

"Not only in the New Testament," I interrupted, "but in the Old Testament as well, appropriated by the Christians although it was concerned only with the Jews."

". . . and you can use those precepts to prove almost any arguable point," Phil went on, "either pro or con."

"The horrible thing is," I said, "that those axioms and maxims laid down by humans hundreds of years ago, still govern and control so much of today's legal and political and social thinking. Those in power think that those moral precepts are correct and unchangeable."

"Very sad," Phil agreed. "They ought to realize that the word *mores* — from which 'morality' is derived — means simply 'customs of the community.'"

"And those customs," I said, "are continually in a state of flux and motion. If they weren't, the community would certainly die . . ."

"Just the way the Latin language died when Cicero's writings were taken as the standard from which no departures were permitted."

"Let's drop all this," I said. "I'll grant that there may be some connection between prostitution and morality, but there's no point in our arguing about it in any way."

"Especially since we're both on the same side," Phil said with a wry grin. "I think the Bible may not have much farther to go as the unbending guide of conduct and law. If there should be no animus against homosexuals — as the Bible insists there should be — then there would be few laws against the sexual urges. Hustlers and whores — like lions and lambs — could lie down together. Censors would disappear, and Shelley's vision of the lovely future — as in his *Queen Mab* — would become about as accurate as the TV commercials predicting the wonderful life of the twenty-first century — 'only a few years away.'"

"Let's really drop it," I said. "This is a horrible bore."

"Okay," Phil said. "I suggest that the next topic ought to be concerned with what sorts of persons find it absolutely — or partially — necessary to patronize hustlers. We should start off with those not only in the closet, but in the closet behind the clothes. The deep-seated distaste of the public for homosexuality is so strong and intolerant that the slightest hint of it can ruin a person's reputation in many fields and professions."

"But in some," I said, "it's shrugged off lightly as a coloring of no importance."

"Public school teachers," Phil said, "are thought to be among the most vulnerable of all — as a result of the worry of parents about their young.''

"Yes," I said, "one breath of suspicion against a teacher of the very young, and his career is finished forever."

"Did you ever see or read *The Children's Hour*, a 1936 play by Lillian Hellman?"

"Yes, of course," I said. "But as a play about lesbianism it couldn't be made into a movie without adding a male character to 'normalize' the liaison. And the title was changed to *These Three*. So it's small wonder that public school teachers, both elementary and high school, are among the most secretive patrons of hustlers.''

"In the 1930s," Phil said, "I understand that a popular news commentator shocked the American public by saying that a student never graduated from high-school without having passed under the tutelage of at least four homosexual teachers. So hustlers were the best solution for teachers as a group. They had to conceal their leanings with greater discipline than almost any others except Boy Scout troop leaders or Big Brothers.''

"But in the 1920s and 1930s," I said, "there was a wide-spreading umbrella of ignorance protecting the majority of homosexuals. Many persons could successfully hide their secrets without too much trouble. People thought that homosexuals existed only in wicked faraway places like Paris or Berlin.''

"That was all before Kinsey came along and spilled the beans about American men," Phil grinned. "Thirty-seven percent to orgasm.''

"Yeah," I said. "In the English department at Ohio State University there were two notable cases of popular professors with a seeming disregard of publicity — not flaunting their obliquity, but at least partly protected by the innate politeness of their colleagues. Or ignored.''

"I had no idea Academia could live without gossip," Phil said.

"I think everybody just took homosexuality for granted about one of them — a harmless twinkling blue-eyed gentleman who liked handsome students. The recipients of his old-fashioned 'crushes' found themselves deluged with volumes of poetry, taken to symphony concerts and on long automobile drives, dined occasionally, and even asked to stay overnight once in a while — with nothing

more than a few caresses exacted in payment for such royal treatment. He was an intense Anglophile, and often hired British hustlers when he went abroad."

"Kinda reversed the techniques of A. E. Housman, didn't he?
who left England to collapse into the brawny arms of his Italian
gondolier-hustler in Venice."

"Yes, he did," I said. "And there was another professor at Ohio
State — a Francophile and an idol of the intellectuals — who lived
quite openly with a young painter, who had early hustled his way
into the graces of his suave and sophisticated older patron. This
elegant and dazzling man, who had written several books, including
The Innocents of Paris, which furnished Maurice Chevalier with his
first American film vehicle, had arranged his life so that he might
spend six months teaching and six months in France. There, he
would sink down into the life of Paris, escaping from the watchful
eyes of his major mignon often enough to have as many hustlers as
he wanted in the City of Light, as well as in Morocco and the Forbidden Atlas."

"Sounds like a well-arranged existence," Phil said.

"Those two professors, because of their academic reputations as
well as the umbrella of ignorance, were able to live with much more
permissive freedom than teachers in the less tolerant ambience of
elementary and high schools."

"I think perhaps," Phil said, "that they may have been luckier
than most other university professors. That despicable homophobe
Robert Frost hounded Newton Arvin from his university position
because of his homosexuality."

"Yes, the two at Ohio State were very fortunate," I agreed.
"Academia with its inbred communities and politics, and all the
whisperings and back-biting and power-plays, always made life
more hazardous than it would have been even in a blue-collar job —
where intolerance is the norm, at least with regard to sexual matters."

"What's the next rung up on our caution ladder?" Phil said.

"I'd be inclined to say people with backgrounds in religion," I
said. "Priests and televangelists need hustlers badly, if they aren't
in control of their instincts. The story of Cardinal Spellman has
been told often enough — and in print, by C. A. Tripp and others, so

that we don't have to repeat it. Nor do we need to rehash the tale of Jim Bakker of the PTL ministry.''

"Why do you suppose Catholic priests have always been more suspect than Protestant preachers?" Phil said.

"Might be partly because of the mystery surrounding the Catholic religion and priestly celibacy in a mainly Protestant/Jewish/atheist/sexual nation.''

"Who's next?" Phil asked. "I guess I'd vote for the politicos."

"Good choice," I said. "In the 1920s you have the disasters that befell political figures such as David Walsh and Sumner Wells when they were 'uncovered'; and today's figures such as congressmen Gerry Studds and Barney Frank . . .''

"Frank really got into the soup, didn't he?" Phil said.

"He may have trusted his hustler too much," I said, "or else shouldn't have left him alone in his apartment . . .''

". . . to operate a call-boy service therefrom," Phil said, chuckling. "Still, the climate of opinion is changing somewhat today. Even if you're caught in fragrant delicious with a male prostitute.''

"We haven't said anything yet about athletes and jocks of all kinds. Dave Kopay's coming out some years ago delivered a body-blow to football from which it seemed it never would recover.''

"And there's always the military bigwigs who have to keep secret. They can't all be like Leonard Matlovich — so I should imagine that quite a few of them have to avail themselves of *very* discreet hustlers.''

"Just how many athletes or military people are gay will probably never be known, nor how many use hustlers.''

"Still, I should imagine it's easier for some of them to maintain their anonymity with a hustler — ''

"Just why?"

"Because young gay men active in prostitution are not too well-informed, maybe, about the personalities in games, whether football, baseball, or basketball. Now if they were ballet dancers . . .''

"Damn it, Phil," I said, slightly irritated. "I never thought you'd be guilty of such a stereotypical statement.''

"I apologize," Phil said. "I didn't mean it. Don't tell anyone. I'd lose my reputation for being tolerant. Anyway, I said 'maybe.'''

"All right," I said. I looked at my notations. "Another rung up the ladder—movie stars."

"Middle America sure as hell got one bad shock when it learned that Rock Hudson died of AIDS, that he was homosexual, that he had known lots of hustlers, and finally that his last companion walked off with several millions in palimony. And up to the moment of disclosure about Hudson, his old buddy Ronald Reagan—"

"An actor in a number of Hollywood B movies," I added.

"—had considered AIDS to be no more serious than a case of measles."

"Movie stars are a strange sort of category," I said. "A few of them always take homosexual roles in movies, and are gradually accepted as the real thing—although indeed they may not be. Others who've become known for their machismo or rough-and-tumble screen roles turn out to be great users of hustlers."

"Somebody once said that all actors are empty vessels, and that their personalities are either weak or non-existent, until someone furnishes them with words to say or persons to be. But if they're gay, they get the death-kiss in Hollywood—that is, if they're openly *known* to be gay."

"Most of the really gay actors in Hollywood keep their lids on tight," I said, "and there's also that somewhat special group we've mentioned, the ones who always take gay roles—or troubled gay roles such as transvestites or transexuals. Oddly enough, their private lives are rarely dissected in the supermarket scandal sheets."

"By now we ought to be able to make up our own axiom," Phil said. "The more deeply closeted a person is, the more likely to employ hustlers—unless he's asexual or ascetic."

"A brilliant conclusion," I said sarcastically. "Are we ready now to move on to another topic?"

"Why not?" Phil said. "We might consider the wonders of red herrings and also the value of letting the fog rise around oneself, or *making* it rise."

"There's a great number of cases in which the 'fog' as you call it has proved invaluable in goosing a person upwards."

"One of my favorite stories," Phil said, "concerns what Gertrude Stein said to movie mogul Sam Goldwyn in Hollywood in 1934."

"I'm not sure I ever heard that one," I said.

"Goldwyn asked her how she managed to get so much free publicity when a like amount would have cost him hundreds of thousands."

"And—?"

"'First,' she said, 'there are a few a very few articulate people who write and talk endlessly about me and what I am trying to do, and second and just as important I have let a lot of fog rise around me and lots of people are fascinated by enigma and fog, but otherwise it costs money to advertise and you have to pay lots if you want anybody to listen.'"

"If we're going to make this a major classification," I said, "we'll have to admit right off that all the ones in it are less deeply closeted, and so their hiring of hustlers is not so extraordinary as it would be for those deep in the closet."

"And there are many in the category—writers, musicians, composers, rock stars, comics, painters, and artists of all kinds," Phil said.

"They tend to answer questions about the vagaries of their sex lives with a kind of Mona Lisa smile, or else they won't comment in any way about their lives inside the glass bowl."

"I suppose," Phil went on, "the fact that they are surrounded by so many groupies or camp followers keeps them supplied with what Gertrude Stein called the 'few articulate people.' And it's quite possible—in fact it's happened a lot of times—that the star bestows a sexual favor on one he picks out, or gives him free tickets, or even pays him in money, thus technically and eventually turning him into a real hustler."

"The kids today certainly have more tolerance and understanding of such adventures. The '60s and '70s had so many gender confusions and revolutions that hiring a hustler really didn't mean any more to them than getting laid on Saturday evening. Fog and rumors may be valuable in many cases, but also not necessary in many others."

Phil laughed. "I knew a guy once who was teaching English in Pullman, Washington. He had written a letter to Somerset Maugham, who answered, and there was a brief correspondence. On the strength of that and a few innuendoes dropped by the teacher himself, along with hints that he had published many books under pen-names which he wouldn't reveal, quite a few gay students were attracted to his classes. He'd always reward them with a few bucks and let on that their silence would earn them much more. I suppose you could say he also created quite a few hustlers."

"I think we may be getting off the subject somewhat," I said, "or else straining too hard to make a point. How about the business of red herrings? I suppose the most common device in that case is the marriage of convenience."

"Yes," Phil said. "Many a gay male tries that. Sometimes the woman he marries knows he's gay, and thinks that the love of a good woman will cure him of his queerness. Sometimes she doesn't know he's gay, and so she is doomed to unhappiness. Or when she finds out that hubby is spurning her for the golden-haired Adonis he picked up in a hustlers' bar, she's likely to explode. The fragments will certainly appear in the *National Enquirer* if hubby's name merits the attention, and — man! — he's out of the closet with a bang."

"'Outing' seems to be gaining favor. Malcolm Forbes's body was hardly cold when the word was put out about him."

"We can hardly debate the morality or the ethics of that topic," Phil said. "It would be endless. What's next — I mean, what other categories remain?"

"There's one quite obvious one," I said. "Jean Genet called them 'les mal foutus.'"

"I suppose you'd translate that as something like 'the poorly-put-together ones,'" Phil said.

"You won't find the expression in the French dictionaries of Larousse or Cassell," I said. "But if you're diligent, you may come across it in a dictionary of argot — the French underworld language which along with English seems slowly to be taking over the pure French allowed by the Academy."

"I guess 'les mal foutus' is a large umbrella term," Phil said. "It covers a potpourri of cripples, Calibans, Quasimodos, paraplegics, armless and legless ones, and those who because of some physical defect like acne or atrophic rhinitis with its dreadful rotten odor are denied the possibility of ever finding someone to love them — or maybe even go to bed with them."

"Perhaps certain fetishists will also have to be excluded at this point," I said. "Grossly overweight persons are often pursued by what are called in the ads 'chubby chasers,' and the foot and rubber clans have their own clubs and groups, as do the enema boys and those into water sports."

"Although we seem to be discussing the patrons of hustlers at this point," Phil said, "we might mention hustlers who are themselves physically damaged in one way or another."

"Like the handsome hustler in Tennessee Williams's story called 'One-Arm.' In a rather brief space that story reaches a peak in hustling literature."

Phil agreed with a nod. "And I suppose 'les mal foutus' will also have to include the old ones," he added.

"Yes," I said. "The beginning hustlers are often extremely picky about their clients. They'll ask the client's age, and if it doesn't fall within their tolerated limits, they'll turn him down. That's finicky and fussy."

"I should imagine it would quickly cut down their numbers of clients," I said.

"No great loss to the profession," Phil said. "The middle-aged and the old ones make up one of the largest groups an experienced hustler can have . . ."

". . . and one of the most profitable, I suppose."

"Yes," he said. "That group's been through the mill — time and money wasted in bars and fruitless evenings. In a sense it's not right to put them with the 'mal foutus,' because often they're well-groomed, intelligent, not very demanding, and of course well-heeled —"

"Sometimes called 'whops,'" I said, grinning.

"Which means — ?"

"An acronym for 'well-heeled older persons.'"

"And further," said Phil, "sometimes they can add to a hustler's enjoyment by having false teeth. Many a hustler will tell you that you haven't lived until you've had fellatio from a white-haired gentleman who has slyly removed his teeth before beginning."

"We should be nearing the end of trying to find the ones who need hustlers," I said. "Is there another group?"

"Ward Stames once told me that if there was one thing Kinsey loved, it was finding a record-keeper among the thousands he interviewed for his volume on the human male."

"Did he find many of them?"

"Quite a few, according to Ward. And *his* enthusiasm for *their* lists and detailings made many of them more eager than ever to 'keep up their numbers of contacts for Doctor Kinsey.' But these came to be looked on by the Kinsey staff as artificial ones whose reported numbers of 'releases' did not readily indicate the strength of the male libido."

"But weren't there others who were genuine sexual . . . er . . . athletes?"

"Oh yes . . . the real ravenous ones, many with impressive numbers in their files, and these made frequent use of hustlers. If they were accustomed to five or six contacts a day, it was often very difficult to find a reservoir of fresh males in the smaller cities unless there were a naval or military base nearby. Hustlers became a prime necessity, the quantity depending on the size of the patron's pocketbook. I don't imagine the numbers ever reached the totals of the stockpiles of Heliogabalus or Caligula, nor the magnificence of the rewards the Roman emperors gave, but they were astounding for the mid-twentieth century."

"Finally," I said, "I suppose there are those who were *afraid* to go cruising — or couldn't go for one reason or another . . . the city in which they lived, the location of the meat-rack, the smallness of the town . . . or some such. Inborn timidity or common-sense. Maybe they preferred to use the telephone to answer an ad, thinking it safer."

"For many in whom the blood runs too hot," Phil said, "there is no such thing as common-sense, and in some the libido overrides even the all-powerful instinct of self-preservation."

I shuddered a little. "Let's move on," I said.

"There is evil everywhere," Phil said with mock seriousness.

Chapter VIII

Power

The next morning when I left the motel to walk the block and a half to Phil's house, I sensed that it was going to be a scorcher — one of the no more than five days in the year when the usually cool climate of northern California became almost unbearably hot . . . somewhere near eighty-five degrees. People in this part of the state were ill-equipped metabolically — or just ill-accustomed — to handle extremes of either heat or cold.

I was sweating when I arrived. I opened the door and walked in, calling "Phil! I'm here!" to an empty room. Then I heard the shower running in the bathroom, suddenly stopping and the curtain being pushed aside.

Phil stepped out, naked. Not that I expected him to be clothed. It was a good moment, for nothing delighted or pleased me more than the sin which the church called *delectatio morosa*, though the reason why the particular delectation of the eye should be called morose, and a sin to boot, was something which lay far beyond my mortal grasp. The sight of a handsome young man nearly always impeded the smooth functioning of my zipper.

Honestly, Phil at a distance of fifteen feet still looked no more than twenty years old. His curly black hair was now plastered flat to his head, reaching down halfway to his thick eyebrows, and the water had straightened his chest hair to lie flat and down-pointing on his strong square pectorals.

"Good morning!" he hollered, seizing a huge red turkish towel and vigorously drying himself, one leg up on the tub edge while he bent over to dry it, his genitals hanging free for a moment, and then obscured while he tended to the other leg.

"This is going to be a hot one," he said, his face hidden under

76

the towel while he dried his hair. When he had finished, he reached behind the door for his trousers, and put them on. There was always a kind of magic for me in watching a man step into — or even better, out of — his trousers, and Phil was as graceful about it as any athlete could be, or even for that matter as a premier danseur from the ballet.

He came into the living-room and sat down shirtless in the leather chair.

"You'll stick to it on a day like this," I said.

"No matter," he said. "Unless the noise of pulling away bothers you."

"It would be canceled by the pleasure of looking at you."

He grinned. "Always the flatterer." He reached down to scratch the ears of one of the long-haired dachshunds which made a small sound of pleasure.

"Mighty damned good looking dogs," I said. "Got papers, I suppose."

"Oh yeah," he said.

"Ever think of showing them at a dog show?"

He shook his head. "Nah," he said. "I don't need dogs to bolster my ego. It ain't that fragile, and I don't really think that wearing a blue ribbon is all that important to them. They seem to be happy enough just to be companions, without being champions. They're champs anyway, as far as I'm concerned. Sure, they've got papers, but that doesn't make me love them any more than I already do."

"Wouldn't their being champions increase your self-esteem in any way? Gertrude Stein used to say that it was necessary to be important to yourself inside yourself."

"Sure — but just how the hell would a dog's championship status contribute to that?"

"I dunno," I said. "You'd have to ask for explanations from the old maids of both sexes who follow the dog-shows. Seems to work for many of them. Blue ribbons give them a sense of power."

"Who needs that?" Phil said shortly. "The dogs furnish me all the real companionship and love that I need at present."

"This is just a roundabout way of getting at something that we touched on briefly a coupla days ago," I said, "but I'd like you to talk a little more about the topic of power. The balance of it between hustler and client. Or the exchange of it. Or what it depends on — and not just the money changing hands. I have seen very little about the matter — nothing, really — in the literature about hustling or hustlers. It's something that's quite noticeable in the matters between a man and a female whore where it's been widely explored and examined in both novels and dramas, but in homosexual literature not much has been said on the topic.''

"Well, first of all the power's in the wallet of the score,'' Phil said. "When I started hustling, it was quite definitely centered there.''

"But where was it centered for the score himself?''

"I suppose it was to be found in the hustler leaning against the lamp-post, thumbs hooked in his belt, 'la bourse' thrust forward, shirt open to the navel . . .''

". . . and eyes full of smoky lightnings that promise wild nights of horizontal sport on satin sheets under mirrored canopies on bouncy beds.''

Phil laughed. "Say rather faintly malodorous sheets on lumpy mattresses,'' he said. "But I'll grant you — a certain power radiates from the hustler.''

"It catches the night-shopper and draws him into the web. Maybe the pheromones are at work.''

"Something was working,'' Phil said, "before we even knew about pheromones.''

"To go on,'' I said. "One speaks to the other, predator and victim.''

"Which is which?'' Phil asked.

"Ah,'' I said. "We don't know yet. A bargain is struck. A sum of money is agreed upon . . .''

"Certain restrictions may apply,'' said Phil, "as the airlines say. Exclusions of activity.''

"Tell me if I'm wrong. With the final agreement, a subtle shift takes place. The element of power slips towards the one who will pay the fee. Right?''

"I think the exchange may still be only a partial one,'' Phil said. "I believe the hustler still retains a large portion of his power. Within himself.''

"Nobody has ever said it better than Walt Whitman," I said, looking ceilingward to see the words scrolling forward on my mind-screen:

> It is within him . . . dress does not hide him, it is curiously in the joints of his hips and wrists; it is in . . . the carriage of his neck, the flex of his waist and knees . . . his strong sweet quality strikes through the cotton and broadcloth . . . I linger to see his back, and the back of his neck, and the shoulder-side . . . the play of masculine muscle through clean-setting trousers, the strong set of thighs, well carrying the trunk above . . .

The magic of the lines made me shake my head a little, so that they would leave me.

"As a matter of fact," I said, "perhaps the hustler is still in control and has lost little or none of the Power so far."

"Maybe," Phil said, "but once the bed has been reached, the shift is bound to occur. As soon as the patron has made his wants known, the Power begins to wobble and gradually return to the john's side of the bed . . . almost entirely, unless the hustler happens to be like Wally-of-the-dunes . . . really firm and aggressive."

"Foreplay begins," I said, "progresses, advances to a high point."

I paused. "Shall we in honor of old Sigmund spell 'fore' f-o-u-r?"

"Why on earth . . .?" Phil asked.

"Because towards the end of his life, Freud said that the more he considered two persons in an act of intercourse, the more he was convinced that there were four people taking part in it."

Phil looked puzzled. "I don't exactly . . ." he began.

"He meant that each of the two was enjoying his own particular fantasy . . . which might have been that he was in bed with someone other than the person beside him."

"Or underneath or on top," Phil said, laughing. "I'm afraid that's all too true in many cases."

"And so instead of finding himself abed with a scrawny young man with pimples, the john can imagine he lies beside any current male heart-throb of the silver screen, or maybe a lost lover, whilst the hustler himself may be screwing any female rock-star or movie-queen he worships from afar.''

"But when the waltz is over . . ." Phil said.

". . . and the dime-a-dance partner is paid, then the moment of the future begins. If the dancer was awkward or inept or stumbling, the score may not want to see him ever again, and so he says farewell without any regret.''

"But if he has been carried to the heights," Phil said, "he'll ask for a repetition, at which point the dance-card will be consulted and another tango arranged.''

"Doesn't that mean," I asked, "that still another shift has taken place? The Power has been entirely in the patron's pocket after it's all over, and the money has changed hands. But at the final moment, doesn't the hustler find that he may be in charge again?''

"To a certain extent," Phil said. "But that's a really delicate minute. Up to that time the hustler has been nothing but the hired hand — and then suddenly he's favored with an unexpected bequest. You've gotta know how to handle things just then.''

"In what way?''

"You've got to be agreeable and enthusiastic, even grateful — but you mustn't overdo it. Fawning will get you nowhere.''

"How about a small pretense of being unable to find a date in the week ahead?''

"That gets the hook in okay," Phil said, grinning, "but you've gotta watch out not to overplay it. If you're just a beginner, and you leap at the invitation too quickly, you may find that the patron will soon tire of you, or think you too easily available to be really much good. If a guy is too shallow he's the one who wears out first, since he's got nothing left to be discovered, the body having already given up all its secrets. No substance left. And if his 'brains can be sucked dry in five minutes' he's in more difficulty than if his vesicles are empty.''

"I guess these power movements are really rather important considerations for the futures of both the hustler and his score, aren't they?''

"The trouble is," Phil said with a smile, "that for hustlers the future is not what it used to be.''

Chapter IX

Literary Illuminations:
Portrait of the Ideal Hustler

In the house belonging to Ward Stames, where Phil was at present living, there were many mementos of Ward's "literary" career—the persons he had known much earlier in his life, having sought them out because in his youth he had been afflicted with a desire to own something tangible that had been associated with them. A kind of early groupie, really. Thus on his bedroom wall were signed photographs of Gertrude Stein, Thomas Mann, André Gide, Jean Cocteau, Romain Rolland, Kinsey, and a few others not so well known. Elsewhere in his house were Stein's small silver rose-embossed stamp box and a tie-dyed scarf, Alice Toklas's favorite tomato-slicing knife, and innumerable books signed by Thornton Wilder, Sigrid Undset, A. E. Housman, Theodore Dreiser, Sherwood Anderson, and many others from the great period of the 1920s and 1930s.

Within the house one could almost sense the presence of these tangible witnesses to the great past, and both Phil and I were extremely conscious of it.

"To which," I said more or less jokingly, "we shall of course have to add the name of Phil Andros eventually. It will become a shrine to be visited by gays."

"Oh, of course," said Phil, with the biting sardonic inflection he often used to put himself down. "Like the testicles on Oscar Wilde's monument in the Père Lachaise cemetery in Paris."

"I guess I'm not really aware of their importance."

"The monolith by Epstein," Phil said, "the extremely modern sculpture has the penis and scrotum hanging down from the figure's midsection . . ."

". . . And where else would they be hanging from?" I murmured.

He paid no attention. "Well, before the privates were all broken away by vandals or souvenir hunters or mad old ladies with rocks, it used to be the custom for homosexual Parisian boys to visit the monument on the anniversary of their 'wedding' to touch the balls, thus insuring another year of domestic tranquillity. The stone appeared to have a high polish at one time."

I laughed. "We'll have to have a large stone bas-relief affixed to this house later on."

"No thanks," Phil said. "If anyone's going to come around stroking my balls, I want to be in them — "

He paused. "Wait a minute," he said. "I guess that doesn't sound quite right. But you can undoubtedly grab my meaning."

"We are talking in double tenders," I said, adding one more linguistic twist.

"Uh-huh." Phil picked up a small plastic dome in which was sealed a ceramic rose of a particularly obnoxious violet and rose color combination. "Ward filched this from the ledge of the Epstein monument at one time," he said. "It was one of a bunch of six someone had left there. Ward thought he was doing a favor for Oscar, who would have been utterly devastated by a tribute in such detestable taste."

"And now," he said, returning the rose to its dusty place, "what do we discuss today?"

I shook the several sheets of my notes at him. "Today we ought to talk about your literary output, and I'd like to have you remind me of a few descriptive passages of self-analysis that you composed or at least talked about to me at one time. It might turn into a sort of 'know thyself' session."

"I am embarrassed," Phil said. He looked down, pretending to flutter his eyelids.

"The hell you are," I said. I referred to my first page. "I have it down here that John Rechy's novel about hustlers, *City of Night*, appeared in 1963 — just about when you had started to send your first stories to Copenhagen to be published in *eos* and *amigo*."

"I guess that's right," Phil said.

"The book became a best-seller, but there was a heluva storm about it. The Supreme Court had not yet tried to define obscenity, not until 1966. A reviewer said that '*City of Night* was a brilliant collection of chapters that had appeared in some of the little magazines, the avant-garde ones like *Evergreen Review* and *Big Table*. The never-named hustler traveled the night cities of America, and gave the readers a fascinating account of a sub-culture which Kinsey had revealed about fifteen years before.'"

"The novel really had the seeds of belligerence in it," Phil said, "but it couldn't measure up to the — what to say? — real roar of defiance and outrage that he later produced in *The Sexual Outlaw*."

"Well . . . *City of Night* was the first, and it is always good to be the first in anything," I said. "But you were writing at the same time for the European magazines, and creating the persona of Phil Andros. Funny how few people noticed the joke in your name — 'Phil' from 'philos' . . . love, and 'andros' from the Greek word for 'man' — as in 'philanderer' or man-lover . . ."

"Or lover-man," Phil said, ironically. "'Philanthropic' might have been just as close."

"Oh sure," I said, consulting my notes. "You were also writing stories for *Der Kreis* in Zurich."

"Not under the name of Phil Andros," he said. "They hated him. Thought him too outspoken by far. You had to be very delicate with Zurich — sighs and sidelong glances, hand-holdings, discreet little embraces, a peck on the cheek for friendship, and all that kind of twaddle. Nothing more. No explicit sex."

"I guess Ward helped write the blurb about you that appeared on the hardcover edition of *$tud* in 1966."

"It tickled both of us," Phil said. "I told him it sounded as if Norman Vincent Peale had got together with Dale Carnegie to produce a being almost beyond reproach."

I handed him the flimsy yellow paper on which it had been first printed. "Just have a look at that, if you want to see how really fine you were in those days."

He read it silently, and then handed it back. "You're not going to reproduce that, are you?"

"Of course," I said. "If we're doing a complete interview with America's premier hustler, we'll have to go clear back to have a piercing look at his roots."

"Oh gawd," Phil groaned. "I suppose I'll have to agree."

"That's my boy," I said. "Be brave. Real manly. Matter of fact, I think I'll stick it in right here."

"Watch your language," he said.

"You — a censor?" I said. "If I don't include this rare piece of early information, it may be lost forever. And you know how important it is to have a full record about you."

"I give up," Phil sighed.

"The passive-aggressive tactic always works," I said smugly. "So here we go."

Phil Andros is a hustler. The word has developed many meanings, but in this case it means that he lives by renting his body to all male comers. In a savage moment of self-accusation he once explains the term to a country boy he has picked up: "I'm a male whore, a guy who sells his body to queers for money."

And *$tud* is a novel in the picaresque tradition, with the "hero" an adventuring, lusting rogue, partly uncertain whether he belongs to the homosexual world, but finding his own channel as the book moves on — meeting bank presidents and blacks, college boys and professors, weightlifters and policemen, fetishists and motorcyclists, millionaires and narcissists, factory workers and interior decorators — all of whom he beds, some free, but most of them for money.

Yet Phil wears his hustler's uniform — of tight chinos and black leather boots and black leather jacket with a difference. He has a tremendous advantage over his other 'colleagues.' He can observe and he can relate what he observes, with wryness or with venom, with unconcealed pleasure in the things that belong to passion, and with a surprising gentleness for those that are of the intelligence and the spirit . . .

These stories comprise a Dantesque journey into a dark and underground world that may shock or repel, but will surely fascinate . . .

College-trained, he has been a bellboy, pro basketball player, masseur, taxi-driver, merchant mariner, gym instructor . . .

"There's just a bit more," I said, "but that's the main thrust."

"There you go again," Phil said, "with your dirty language."

"I guess what you were really trying to do," I said, "was deliberately to make each chapter of *Stud* appeal to a different sort of homosexual — foot fetishist, motorcycle enthusiast, admirer of blacks, weightlifter nut, cop-lover, and so on. You are the anti-hero in the book, the hustler — "

"That's what I knew most about," he said, "and a hustler can easily enter into any level of society."

"I think I can perceive either a certain laziness with regard to plotting, or else just a general disinclination or lack of ability in that matter."

"You pays your money and you takes your choice."

"Your college background enables you to think about yourself and to analyze — "

"Somewhat," Phil said.

" — the changes that went on inside your personality. I seem to remember that when you began to tell your stories you were still a bit uncertain about whether or not you were totally homosexual . . ."

"Yeah, but midway through I came to the conviction that I was."

"You had to produce about eight volumes of novels and short stories to come to that final realization."

"Ah yes," he said, with the dreamy, theatrical irony that always softened the edge of his mocking. "My *oeuvre* . . ."

"The Phil Andros of the stories and novels is really constructed out of many hustlers whom you knew, wasn't it?"

"I've always said the adventures were about eighty-five percent true, and that they had either happened to me or to someone I knew."

"This reminds me of the theory that I learned in high-school biology class — that ontogeny recapitulates philogeny. My, how we used to love saying those big words!"

"You've got me by the short hairs," Phil said. "I never really understood that, but I do remember hearing it somewhere along the line."

"Simple. Just as a developing embryo repeats, in miniature, the phases of animal evolution, so does the individual contain all the traits of the group; in analyzing and dissecting yourself it may be possible to learn about the entire genre. Thomas Mann thought the same thing, but in literary terms. He thought if he understood himself and wrote about himself with sensitivity, he would be writing about all mankind, universally.''

"Sounds like a pretty good theory to me," Phil said.

"Of course, within the phylum there is an infinite number of separate entities — ''

"Yup," he interrupted. "From sullen, surly, and monosyllabic to extroverted, happy, and charismatic. But the basic traits exist in common, no matter how disguised or deeply buried."

"Except we've found out," I said, "that the 'broken-home syndrome' is *not* to be found in every one of them."

"I am Everyman," he intoned with mock solemnity. He turned his head to the left profile, and thumped his chest with his fingertips splayed apart in an early silent-movie gesture.

"Oh lord," I said in dismay. "We may have gone too far. Lillian Gish made the same hand gesture when she said 'Who, me?' in one of her movies."

We both laughed.

"Seriously, though," I said, "maybe you remember writing in one novel about spending your birthday alone in the California hills above Berkeley. You were undertaking the kind of self-examination that hits most people on New Year's day when they make their resolutions, or when a sinner makes an 'examination of conscience' prior to confession."

"That must have been in *Shuttlecock*," Phil said.

"Pages 101 and 102,' I said. "I brought it along. And I'm going to read it out loud so your memory can be refreshed."

"I never knew an ex-professor who wasn't in love with the sound of his own voice," Phil said.

"Humph," I said, and began.

Twenty-nine years old, and you began hustling at sixteen . . . thirteen years of it, thirteen years of a *completely* sexually oriented life — through high-school (the druggist, the jazz pianist, the football coach, and about forty others before you left the small Ohio town), and then four years at Ohio State, where

you earned your tuition by selling your cock and your body —
to a coupla English professors (regulars), wealthy students,
members of the "art" colony that lived on the fringe of the
campus, a librarian, a football hero (for free), a campus policeman, a black doorman at the theater, half a dozen members
of a repertory acting company, a Methodist minister, a Boy
Scout leader, a tennis champ (free), a visiting dramatist, the
"poet laureate of New Jersey" (a trip to Europe out of him)
. . . and a long side-involvement with a huge Junoesque lez,
whom everyone thought me about to marry.

And memorable nights . . . tied spread-eagled on a bunk
and screwed by a total of sixteen overheated young fraternity
brothers . . . the expanding into sexual variants, ranging from
the S/M scene to the finest and most delicado flower-fruits, the
blacks, the Asians, the Chicanos — the golden showers delivered, the tits pinched and pierced . . . the countless mouths
. . . Ah, *Shuttlecock* is my real name!

"Well," I said, closing the volume, "that's a kind of overview
of the earlier part of your life . . ."

"A little scary when it's condensed like that," Phil admitted.

"One of the things I believe you were looking for was affection," I said. "It might hurt you to admit it. But if you were, then
how many other hustlers do you think might have been looking for
the same thing?"

"It doesn't hurt me to admit it," Phil said. "In the earliest days I
certainly *was* looking for affection, and I think many hustlers also
were. But most of them would have sneered at such a statement.
They would've said 'You're outa your fuckin' gourd.'"

"The revelations about your character go on in *Shuttlecock*," I
said, opening the volume again. "Even more to the point, I think.
They reveal the bottom nature of the hustler — yourself, and I am
sure many many others — so I'm going to read some more from that
same chapter. You listen — and then you can tell me if by now
you've changed anything in your attitudes or worldviews."

"Do I really have to put up with this?" Phil said. "It's making
me a little uncomfortable, this going over my past feelings. It's the
future that's my concern now."

"I'm still interested in the past," I said. "And yes — you're gonna have to listen. I'll skip some of it, however, just to speed it up a bit.''

"That's welcome news," he growled.

"At this point in the book you feel that you must disagree with them when they reject the idea that they want affection.'' And then I began again:

> Hardly true. Most of them slipped into hustling because they obscurely felt that their clients placed some value on them. And so they offered their cocks, rampant, and took money for the use of them. But what a hustler really secretly wanted was to be admired for himself alone — and he hardly ever was. It was like an artist's coming into contact with a tasteless newly-rich wife, who bought his painting because its attractive gold frame would go well in her powder room. And since the hustler (the artist) was thus himself rejected (the painting unimportant) for the frame (his body), a sense of frustration developed in him. And how did he protect himself? By setting up his own rejection of the "goddamed queers" — by slipping the contents of fat wallets into his own pockets while his customers washed up . . .
>
> Yet it was true that the hustler who ripped off his john never really got far in the business . . . The affection of the hustler for his score was always buried or disguised, hidden from his ineffectual probing, his incompetent reasoning. To him hustling seemed only a business venture, and in the dimly conscious three pounds of meat that passed for his brain, he could not see that each encounter was really a brief love-hate relationship, sharp and intense, without which he could not maintain his ego.
>
> . . . And yet . . . he always sensed that his customer must have liked him a little or he would not have been there — that the client desired or wanted him. But after the act — the money was given, the door opened and the hustler ejected. And rejected . . .
>
> I'd gone through all those stages and they were painful. Until you could manage to think it through, you suffered. You allowed your client to come so close, you liked him a little because you thought he liked you for yourself — and then it

turned out he just wanted the temporary feeling of your cock in him, your body on top of his. Repeat it a thousand times (that sexual rental followed by discarding) — and what happened? Damage and destruction to the ego — so great that most hustlers could not stand it long. And that was why . . . so many quit hustling . . .

But if you were a sensualist, a hedonist such as I hoped I was, if you really by God *liked* the feel of a warm mouth around your prick, or the clamping anal muscles seizing you in their tight grip . . . well, you had it made. You'd just have sex and enjoy it. And get paid for it — a wholly incidental factor, but pleasant when it came to paying the rent.

"You were still pretty unsure of your bottom nature when you began hustling, weren't you?" I asked him.

"Yeah," he said. "And so were all the others, I reckon."

"An observation confirmed by Phil Sparrow in his tattoo shop," I said. "What helped you to get over the uncertainty? To consolidate you, or to make you happy with the orientation?"

He grinned. "As the dough began to pile up, and the payments increased," he said. "Plus — as you just read in the passage — the fact that, by damn, I just plain *enjoyed* sex."

"All of which turned you into a number six on Kinsey's rating scale."

"It sure helped," he said.

"But one of the strangest things about your career in hustling," I said, "was the fact that you actually developed a kind of obsession about policemen, and very few hustlers would try to do what you did with the street-person you picked up, change him into a bona-fide cop. I'd like to quote just one more small passage from *Shuttlecock* . . ."

Ah, damn — I had finally begun to see what was really in ole Maugham's mind when he used the words "of human bondage," and at last comprehended the power and danger of such enslavement . . . I had never understood why the poor club-footed hero had simply never bothered to see his pale green-skinned waitress again . . . had not simply told her to go to hell after the insults she gave him. But after knowing Larry, I understood at last.

The filaments of desire, rooted in the cock at one end and spreading into the grey valleys of the brain at the other, seem to be cut only by death or madness . . .

"That's pretty damn complex," I said, looking at Phil.

"Nobody ever said that homosex relationships weren't equally as complicated as hetero ones . . . or even more so."

"That comparison between the hustler and the painting and the picture frame was fairly esoteric," I said, "and things might seem to be well settled for you. But lo! your fantasy during an encounter does seem to take an unwanted direction."

"In what way?" Phil asked, faintly belligerent.

"Listen to this," I said, and read from *Greek Ways*. "It's on page 149, and you're sort of dozing in bed:

> . . . the face of Larry, old Supercop, who stood scowling over me . . . With his foot he flipped me over on my back, his hard cock poking and prodding but never quite getting into my cunt for some reason, and yet myself feeling as if it had, sliding down the slick walls of my vagina, rubbing the clitoris . . .
>
> Ah, goddamn! No female crap . . .! With almost a roar, I opened my eyes."

I put the volume down and smiled a bit cynically at Phil. "It does seem to me," I said, "That once in a while even those of us who try to maintain the hardest macho shell do find that a bit of female fantasy slips up from some region of the unconscious, especially when one is taking a passive role . . . to which one is presumably unaccustomed."

"Ah, shut up," Phil said, with a grin.

"By the way," I said, "didn't Christopher Isherwood express his special admiration for one of your novels a few years ago?"

"He did that," Phil said. "He liked *Shuttlecock* a great deal. Said that the most impressive thing in it was the drama of the relationship between Larry and Phil Andros. He was also of the opinion that it would make a terrific movie—*will* make one, he said, when gay films 'of that scope begin to be made.'"

"Very kind of him," I said, and turned again to the *Greek Ways* volume. "It just occurs to me that you do know yourself pretty well — because every now and then in your *oeuvre* you tuck in — or someone adds — a paragraph or two revealing what a narcissist you are. There's a dandy one here on page 19 . . ."

"There's as much diversity even among narcissists as there are persons falling into the category," Phil said. "I am at least faithful to myself without interruption. In periods when I may be somewhat dark in the head, I know that I am always there to admire myself."

"My god," I said, "I'll certainly agree to that. But here you are, proving that you certainly *are* your own 'type:'

> There was a full-length mirror on the back of the bathroom door. I closed it, threw the towel aside, and took a good hard look at myself, not too displeased at what I saw, for twenty-nine, the deep end of the twenties when the mold and rot begin. Six feet tall, black curly hair on my head, fairly short, and a big fan of hair on my chest that narrowed to a wrist-wide line as it crawled down the center of a flat belly and below the navel expanded into a thick crisp black bush. And from the middle of that hung a long prick, still swollen and heavy, turgid from the morning on the beach and the toejob . . . I flexed my leg, drawing one knee up, and saw the hard-bunched muscles jump out satisfactorily. The definition was still good — shoulders, washboard belly (from all that subconscious holding-in I'd trained my stomach muscles to do), muscular biceps, hairy forearms and enough on the legs. I was what they called a white Greek . . . even a little sun turned my skin a dark tan . . ."

I closed the book. "In order to avoid any charge of literary favoritism — or nepotism," I said, "I scanned a half-dozen popular novels about hustlers — the two separate ones both titled *The Happy Hustler*, by Forbes and Saxon, and *10 1/2!* by Marc Stevens as well as Dotson Rader's *Gov't Inspected Meat*. But there was no extended physical description to be had in any of them, aside from the perhaps exaggerated dimensions of their work-tools. Moreover, the 'purity' of these books as accounts of homosexual hustling is greatly sullied by the inclusion of many hetero episodes scattered here and there."

"What's the best one?"

"The one by Dotson Rader," I said. "Brilliantly written. 1972. Done by a real writer. All of them are entertaining to read as fictionalized history, but none makes any great contribution to the matter of male prostitution."

"I think there aren't any women in my books at all," Phil said, "except old Aunt Elena in Columbus, where I stayed once upon a long ago time."

"Ah, there's one other I remember," I said. "In 'The Tattooed Harpist' a girl comes to the door and you look at her, noting that 'she had the usual number of arms and legs and boobs, all in the right places.'"

Phil chuckled. "I had no idea I was such a misogynist."

"That's why it's all the more curious that groups like Women Against Pornography sometimes wander into the direction of male homosexual erotic writing. It has absolutely nothing to do with women or their denigration."

"Very few female zealots seem to realize that."

"It's not that you have anything like the pathological *horror feminae* that the psychiatrists talk about. It's just that the world according to Andros is entirely free of dead and withered orchids in rubyfruit jungles."

"We might as well also note here," said Phil with a wry grin, "that my fellow-collaborator and amanuensis is much given to 'the associational enrichment process with which he embellishes his writing and talking,' as one academic critic said some years ago."

Chapter X

Behind the Green Door:
What Do They Actually Do?

1. IN THE KINGDOM OF THE BLIND

"I suppose you're familiar with what William Dannemeyer has been saying about homosexuals," I said.

"Just who the hell is William Dannemeyer?" Phil said.

"He's the latest homophobe. Every once in a while one of them comes along and just happens to hit the publicity button from the right angle — and lo! a new attacker is born!"

"The last major one I remember," Phil said, "is that orange juice lady — was her name Bryan, or sumpin like that? A songbird of the South."

"Dannemeyer's from southern California," I said. "Maybe that puts him out of the sotadic zone where — according to Burton — the Vice is tolerated."

"Well, southern California — LaLa Land — breeds all kinds of right wingers," Phil said, "so we might very well expect it to spew forth one more intolerant bigot."

"He's an obscure congressman, not heard of outside his district, until he started loudly attacking homosexuals in the sacred halls of Congress. His vituperation is created in 'the name of God,' the 'good people across the nation,' and Mom and apple pie too, I suppose. He will 'affirm the heterosexual ethic' — as if ethics had anything to do with sex at all."

"He sounds like a real winner," Phil said sardonically.

"Until Kinsey came along to tell us what homosexuals actually did — the activities between two males in bed, or two females for

that matter, remained largely a matter of hearsay and street whis-
pers.''

"But what about earlier investigators like Krafft-Ebing and Stekel and Havelock Ellis?'' Phil asked.

"Well, Krafft-Ebing was about in Dannemeyer's class regarding
tolerance and scientific objectivity; and Ellis was not a creative
thinker — just a synthesizer, one who gathered everything together.
Stekel was wrong about everything nearly eighty percent of the
time. Anyway, such persons reached only the well-educated, not
the common man. The arcane knowledge of the techniques of love-
making among gays and lesbians remained hidden from all save
those who took part in it. But the brouhaha that Kinsey started made
considerable numbers of people aware of what went on, especially
after they digested the fact that thirty-seven percent of adult American males had had a homosexual experience to the point of orgasm.
And that was in 1948.''

"Hey!'' Phil said. "What do you suppose it is now? No wonder
business was booming when I stopped. The boys must have discovered that they really liked it . . . even from other boys.''

"Like any ignorant amateur, Dannemeyer made a lot of very
funny mistakes in his terminology. So he says that 'with every subtly [sic], with every bit of imagery I can conjure . . . and with the
grace of God' he will insert his attacks on gays — with much forth-
right language — into the Congressional Record.''

"Available to anyone?'' Phil said.

"Of course. Just look at the June 29, 1989 edition. It's there for
all the world to see.''

"What's so funny about the mistakes?'' Phil asked.

"First off, he speaks of oral sodomy. I suppose he means analingus, but 'oral sodomy' is enough to boggle the mind. Any definition of sodomy makes it clear that anal penetration by cock is
meant. Just how the 'oral' can enter into such a thing takes you into
a Wonderland stranger than any Alice ever knew. A place where the
monsters and gargoyles of Hieronymous Bosch roam around the
weird landscapes of Escher and Dali.''

Phil's laughter made him almost choke. "I can't picture oral sodomy,'' he finally said. "A sixty-nine by Moebius?''

"And not content with that eerie and bizarre foray into a region of mythical beasts, he goes on to speak of '*mutual* oral sodomy' and finally describes 'rimming' as 'one man using his tongue to lick the rectum' of another man. To me that suggests teeny little figures crawling up the waste-chute to get into the rectum, deep inside the body, closed off by the stern guardian sphincter muscles . . . not easily breached . . .''

". . . As many persons from the earliest times have discovered, including tyro hustlers and undoubtedly several legislators,'' Phil added.

"He says that he got his information from a book by Alan Bell and Martin Weinberg called *Homosexualities*, but their terminology was accurate. This ignorant congressman should have consulted a dictionary.''

"It sounds as if a lot of his information came from the streets, maybe even hustlers. All inaccurate. Could he be pulling a te-levangelist's trick on us? How much more delicately the French describe rimming with their euphemism of 'faire les pétales de la rose.' ''

"Making rose petals,'' I said. "Or even the Germans — with 'the dark kiss.' ''

"His failure to know the difference between 'rectum' and 'anus' reminds me of that old saying — ''

"Which is — ?''

"He don't know his ass from a hole in the ground.''

"Right on,'' I said.

"Well, I suppose there's no way to stop his sad little crusade to restore medieval darkness and general ignorance . . .'' Phil said.

I shook my head. "No, I suppose not,'' I said. "Except with laughter. They've even got a song about him down in the south-land — it's to the tune of 'Danny Boy,' but it's too dull to bother quoting.''

"Let us now move on,'' Phil said, "out of this depressing mish-mash.''

" 'At last he rose, and twitched his mantle blue — ' ''

" 'Tomorrow to fresh woods and pastures new,' '' Phil finished.

2. A HUSTLER'S KAMA SUTRA:
HOW TO PRODUCE GOLDEN EGGS

The next morning when I arrived at the Institute of Higher Hustling, Phil was fiddling with the remote control on the VCR, pushing buttons seemingly at random.

"What in the world are you doing?" I asked him, watching the flashing of various static patterns on the TV screen.

"I can't seem to get the damned thing to rewind," Phil said, irritated.

"We are at the mercy of the mechanics," I said. "Life used to be much simpler. I do hope you haven't been watching dirty films."

"Yes, I was," he said. "The star was a guy I used to know. We even occasionally went on double dates."

"Good grief," I said. "You mean with each other?"

"No," he said. "I mean—two hustlers with two johns. A four-way."

"What's he doing now?" I said.

"I dunno," Phil said. "I haven't heard from him or of him for almost a year. I hope he's all right, but there's no way of knowing."

I felt it necessary to change the subject—quickly. "The Dannemeyer Canon may well have been a model of brevity," I said, "but those brief so-called definitions certainly don't lead in any way to an understanding of the niceties of love-making between two males, even if one of them is—in effect—the hired hand. Instead of curtness, we need the kind of full treatment used in the diabolic scholarly technique called *explication de texte*. Or, for that matter, in this volume. It's one of the earliest how-to books."

I opened a French copy of the *Kama Sutra* which I had brought with me. "I suppose you remember it was written in the eighth century," I said.

"Oh sure," Phil said, rather caustically. "I'm surprised you can't date it any more exactly than that."

"To our purpose, nothing," I said. "Here's one sentence from it:

But since all the acts involved in copulation are privately performed, and the nature of man being as inconsistent as it is,
how can one ever know what a man indulges in behind the
locked doors of his chamber?''

"How indeed?" Phil murmured.

"One of the simplest ways," I said, "is to consult an expert — in
this case, *you*. The expert furnishes the data, and if he is reasonably
intelligent, he tries to arrange it in some kind of order, and not
simply ramble at random over his randy facts, no matter how ram-
bunctious or romantic they are."

"How you rant when you go on a rampage!" Phil said.

"I'll stop it if you will," I said. "But in asking you about such
matters I realize the question has to be very carefully phrased. You
remember the story about the Chicago doctor?"

"Can't say as I do," said Phil.

"He was an expert on arsenic, and had been called to testify in a
murder trial. The defense challenged him, and asked him what he
knew about arsenic. The doctor asked the judge to direct a withdrawal of the question, but the judge refused."

"So what happened?"

"The doctor sighed . . . and began. The first day he discussed the
discovery of the drug — eight hours worth. Second day — its properties, plus topics such as atomic weight, appearance, virulence, shelf
life, and so forth. Third day — both sides, and later the judge —
asked him to stop. He would not. He finally finished in five and a
half days. So . . . you represent the same hazard. I gotta phrase the
question carefully."

"Go ahead, then."

"Well, let's see . . . how about: Please discuss the ways in which
the human male body reacts to sensory stimuli, and the best spots
an experienced love-maker/hustler/partner should concentrate on.
How's that?"

"One point," Phil said. "Those spots might vary with the individual — so why not drop the word 'best'?"

"Okay," I said.

He paused a few moments. I had been kidding him when I
spoke of his rambling at random — he really *did* have a fairly orderly

mind. It might not have belonged in a think-tank somewhere, but I could almost feel him secretly composing an outline with headings and all sorts of sub-headings.

"Well," he said at last, "it seems to be taken for granted that the penis is the point of concentration of attention—that its particular size and shape are the focus of most males' interest, and that if arousal is to occur, the penis must be stimulated at once. I always found that was dead wrong—unless it happened to be a quickie in an alley doorway. Then it had to be all business—pronto."

"Clearly," I said.

"A really successful hustler ought to get his john's imagination working first," Phil said. "I discovered that a slow and sensual undressing was very effective in that regard—just like a female stripper performing in a club. A slow unbuckling of the belt, an equally slow pull on the zipper, or one button at a time, a leisurely taking off the boots and peeling off of the socks, a lifting of first one foot and then the other out of the jeans, all to be accompanied by words carefully chosen to stimulate the listener's fantasy . . . Or perhaps no words at all, but smoldering glances and half-smiles to the extent of effectiveness, but not overdone to caricature or parody. In effect, this undressing could be a substitute for foreplay, although *that* should really occur as well."

"And when it comes to the actual foreplay, what then?" I asked. "What do you do, and how much?"

"Sheez," Phil said, "you can't make any statements about that. Each case might be different. You just *know* when to stop and begin the real thing. I saw a porno flick not long ago in which the guy tongued his partner for a full twenty minutes, and by the end of that time, the poor guy was so raging hot that he came right away."

I chuckled a bit. "Phil Sparrow told me once about how the whores in a brothel used to treat the boot sailors who came in. They did a slow undress such as the one you described, and then helped the sailor take his clothes off. They might then take his cock in hand or pat it underneath a coupla times, and the poor kid would shoot. So the ladies could collect without even being screwed at all."

"Once in a while I've had guys like that," Phil said. "Repressed, but with strong imaginations. It can happen."

"To go on—how about deep kissing?"

"Some do, some don't. I always tried it as a part of foreplay unless I could sense the score's withdrawal from it. But it really got things moving unless the score was too fearful of it or tried to avoid it. It always involved tongue touchings of lips and teeth, tongue and lip sucking, gentle nippings of lips and tongue, and if it went on for a few minutes it might even turn the shyest individual into an aggressive fellator. But it usually shortened the head-bobbing time, which got to be a real pain in the neck as I got older."

"Hah!" I said. "The confessions of love! We are getting right down to facts. Move on!"

"If you are sure that the cock is the center of attention and activity," Phil said, "and that you've read your guy right, then the moment has arrived. Often a simple act of fellation was all that ever took place—with me usually on the receiving end of it. Of course, I might come out of the encounter wounded, or at least painfully scraped by an amateur. That's why all of us looked on guys with false teeth as a kind of heavenly bonus."

"What if you were the active one?"

"You had to learn the 'deep throat' business . . . taking the head through the membrane arch at the back. Simple, really . . . but you had to do it without gagging. That always tended to cancel the . . . er . . . erotic response."

"I can understand that," I said. "I think we are leading right up to the *auparishtaka*, the 'wedding with the mouth,' as it's described in the *Kama Sutra*. By Vatsyayana, chapter nine of part two," I said, thumbing through my copy. "By the way, I seem to remember that you gave a shortened and somewhat modified version of that technique in one of your novels."

"I think it was in *My Brother, My Self*," Phil said.

"Yes," I said. "Wasn't the *auparishtaka* expressly forbidden in Hindu holy writings?"

Phil nodded. "But it was practiced by two classes of persons—eunuchs dressed as women, and those dressed as men. The male type was usually employed as a masseur to conceal the real practices. As masseurs, they used a subtle technique of thigh caressing, and if they found an erection, they made their intentions clear. If the client was silent, this was taken as permission, and the ritual began.

But if the client got aroused and ordered the masseur to continue, he would refuse — only continuing after begging and bribing.''

''Such coy subterfuge has been largely abandoned today,'' I said ironically. ''How does it happen you know so all-fired much about the *auparishtaka*?''

''Once upon a time,'' Phil said, with the same irony, ''while I could still read and didn't have to listen to the announcer read the writing on the TV screen, I also read the *Kama Sutra*.''

''It is amazing how long certain skills stay with one,'' I said, ''like swimming, or bicycle riding . . .''

''. . . or fucking,'' he said matter-of-factly. ''Well, there were eight stages to the *auparishtaka*, as you know all too well, and after each step the eunuch would stop and refuse to continue, but the interruptions only excited the client more, who begged him to continue, and paid him extra each time for his troubles.''

''Troubles?'' I said, doubtfully.

''Depends on your point of view,'' Phil said. ''Are you going to include them in your magnum opus?''

''Indeed I am,'' I said, ''so here they are:

Stage 1. The Ordinary or Nominal Union. The eunuch takes his client's lingam in his hand and caresses the tip lightly with his lips.

Stage 2. Then he takes the head of the lingam in his hand, closes the fingers tightly as if on the bud of a flower, and roughly kisses and bites the stem of the organ.

Stage 3. If the client begs him to continue, the eunuch seizes the lingam and thrusts it into his mouth, closing his lips tightly and then pulling with his lips as if he wished to separate the organ from the body. This is called the Exterior Pressure.

Stage 4. If the client's response is favorable, the lingam is inserted more deeply into the mouth, pressing it firmly with the tongue and then with air forcing it out of the mouth; this is called the Interior Pressure.

Stage 5. The eunuch holds the lingam in his hand and gently bites the sides; this is called the Kiss.

Stage 6. He caresses the lingam with his tongue, especially the end; this is known as the Polishing.

Stage 7. The eunuch takes half the organ into his mouth, caresses it with his tongue whilst sucking it with great force; this is called Eating the Mango.

Stage 8. The climax comes when the eunuch pushes the entire organ into his mouth and presses on it with great force clear to the root, as if he wished to swallow the lingam whole. This is known as the Absorption.

"So," I said.

Phil adjusted his position, arranging his heavy purse a little. "Such simplicity, such directness. Even after all these years, it still gets to me."

"Amazing," I said. "You have never been entirely able to maintain your psychic distance. That's probably why you were such a success in your chosen field."

"Just call me empath," he said.

"But now, having disposed of what is generally considered to be the main focus of any 'romantic encounter' among us he-men," I said, "we can have a look at what goes on elsewhere during foreplay. Or what might go on. I suppose you're fixing to say that the sense of touch is more important than any single one of the other senses, and that the leading spot most responsive to touch is still the penis. Am I right?"

"Yup," Phil said. "And on the dingdong the two most sensitive places are the corona of the glans, and the underside of the glans beneath the cleft. The nerve endings there, if you touch or rub them lightly, seem to increase the blood flow into the shaft, as do purely mechanical pressing and squeezing movements on the shaft if they are directed from the root towards the head."

"My boy," I said, "you are talking to an ole farmhand who used to milk the cows."

"So that's where you learned such a technique," Phil said with a grin.

"I am a part of all that I have met," I said sententiously.

"It may sound heretical to many people," Phil said, "but after years of experience I almost conclude that the penis seems more important than it really is. Sure, it's the focus of attention, and its changing size when stimulated is remarkable and quite evident — but often it gets a kind of consideration that is almost obsessive, a genuine primary concern. The ones who are really trapped by it may insert things into the urethral canal, or have penile piercings and wear rings or jewelry near the frenum or on the glans. And do you know what?''

"No — what?'' I said.

"A lot of hustlers, even experienced ones, are sorta scared about such things. They seem dangerous to them, and quite often they might even refuse a client on such grounds. I think the truth is that they believe their john might ask to insert things in themselves, and unless they are really experienced along those lines, they feel quite nervous. Even frightened.''

"How about the scrotum and the regions surrounding it?''

"For some persons, the scrotum is very important, and fondling it or taking the testicles into the mouth or otherwise manipulating them is very exciting. I knew a hustler in Chicago who said that mouth-testicular contact excited him almost to the 'point of madness.' The small spots on the inside of the thighs near the neck of the scrotum are particularly sensitive to any kind of tactile stimulus, especially with the tongue.''

"How about the perineum?'' I asked.

"Ah, that,'' Phil said, grinning. "What the French call the 'little bridge, *le petit pont*,' the space between the scrotum and the anus . . .''

"And also, we might mention,'' I said, "the name of the 'Press' which published most of your books.''

"Yes,'' Phil said, "a small 'in'-joke. Did you ever have *your* perineum pressed?''

"Once in a while,'' I said. "Are you aware that Kinsey found that strong pressure on the mid-point of the perineum was one of the surest ways to bring a person to erection?''

Phil looked at me as if he thought I were half-witted. "Lord,'' he said, "that's one of the first things any hustler learns if he's worth his price. Most of the time it works when everything else fails, so it's used when there's not much time to be leisurely.''

"And the anus?"

"It's a dandy erogenous zone — although occasionally you find someone who reacts unhappily — either he's too goosey or he finds it painful. But when it's erotically sensitive, it causes things to happen even a long distance away. A stimulation of the sphincter with a finger will make the nostrils flare or cause deep breathing. One of my physician clients once told me that if there were difficulty in bringing a person out of anesthesia, a finger inserted into the anus often caused a deep gasp and a start of deep breathing."

"How do you feel about analingus?"

Phil shook his head. "Not for me," he said, "nor for any hustler who knows enough to tie his shoelaces. That's one of the surest ways to catch hepatitis that there is. I wouldn't even let anyone do it on me — not only because of the danger of by chance infecting the one doing it, but also because I don't want *any* saliva inside me. There are too many bugs in it."

"But isn't saliva one of the old traditional lubricants — for masturbation, for instance."

"Oh sure, your own saliva on yourself for something like that. But no saliva from anyone else on anything to be inserted. Once I heard that there are around three thousand different bacteria and such like in the saliva. Most dentists nowadays when they clean teeth on a person insist on his taking antibiotics before disturbing the plaque or tartar — the bugs travel to the heart and there's danger of endocarditis."

"How has anyone in these days managed to live beyond the age of five?"

"A mystery," Phil said. "Our parents and grandparents must have been extraordinarily immune to thousands of modern dangers."

"Female breasts are the focus of desire in the American male, somehow," I said. "I don't know whether that's because he wants to continue breast-feeding beyond the weaning time, or just *how* to account for his obsession with the hooters. But how about male breasts and nipples?"

"I think that the hetero male's attention to female breasts tends to obscure the fact that the male breasts are almost equally susceptible to stimulation. Not many hetero males are even aware that their own nipples are one of their most sensitive zones, usually because their female partners ignore the male nipples completely, most of the time. The males are too busy getting at the female nipples, and that puts the male nipples too far away. Besides, many males feel that attention to their nipples indicates some sort of female structure in themselves, and they won't permit it.''

"In the homosexual world, didn't it use to be that gays also mostly ignored the male nipples? But with the popularity of sado-masochistic games, wasn't all that changed?''

"Sure," Phil said. "It's now recognized as being capable of adding much to erotic arousal.''

"Don't some followers of the s/m cowpath concentrate their pain/pleasure techniques on the male nipple almost entirely?''

"Yeah . . . with all the varieties of clothespins, pincers, and clips—and fingers and lips and teeth. Or winding dental floss tightly around the nipple to make it grow larger.''

"One of your stories called 'The Broken Vessel' is about a paraplegic who could be brought to orgasm by the manipulation of his nipples alone.''

"It can happen. Sometimes a real breast enthusiast, whose nipples have been excessively fondled and played with, finds their size greatly increased under sexual arousal, and often the mouth on one particular nipple rather than the other will trigger the orgasm. You can always tell when you find the trigger-nipple. There's an involuntary gasp, so then you know where to concentrate.''

"How about ears?''

"Unpredictable," Phil said. "Some like caresses with the tongue on the lobe and inner tunnel and shell, but others hate it. I've noticed that the ear lobes become engorged with blood when a guy's aroused, but I think in all my experience I can't remember more than one person who popped just by having his ears worked on.''

"'Yet all experience is an arch wherethrough . . .''' I began.

"Spare me," Phil groaned. "No more Tennyson, for heaven's sake.''

"Okay then," I said. "Let's move on to the buttocks.''

"Everyone knows that they're sensitive," Phil said. "And I'm not talkin' just about goosin'. A hand sliding over the great gluteus gets immediate attention.''

"Sometimes such tactile stimulation is met with a response of great energy," I said, humming a bit.

"And in the act of screwing," Phil went on, "the muscular contractions take on a rhythmic pattern that certainly helps to build up the erotic pyramid."

"A moment ago you mentioned the spots on the inside of the thighs up near the scrotum, saying they were extremely sensitive. But aren't the insides of the thighs all along their length extremely sensitive also?"

"Sure are," Phil said. "On those areas, if you unexpectedly — and swiftly — trail the backs of your fingernails from the kneecap towards the crotch, you'll get an astonished gasp from your john — without fail. That surprise touching will also sometimes make the legs roll together or else suddenly spring apart. That's just another step in building the tensions which lead to the erotic release when they accumulate enough."

I sighed. "I guess when you get right down to it," I said, "there's hardly a square inch of skin anywhere on the body that doesn't respond to tactile stimulation with an erotic end-result . . . if properly attacked, and if one knows that the body is looking forward to an orgasm and not just a massage. There's the throat and nape of the neck, the navel area, the lower end of the back, the entire abdominal and pubic areas and the groin . . ."

". . . and don't forget the armpits," Phil said, "which to masochists in the s/m merrymaking seem particularly attractive on a macho hustler, especially if slightly unwashed or sweaty."

"Havelock Ellis in his pioneer work on sex tells about the success of a British guy in making out with his female dance partners. The fellow kept a handkerchief tucked into the armpit of his shirt while dancing, and then would give it to his female partner to wipe the sweat off her face when they paused. Remarkable success in bed for him."

"It'll do wonders sometimes," Phil said, "and the dance partner doesn't have to be female."

"And then down at the bottom of everything are the feet."

"Ah . . . yes," Phil said, and there was a long pause. I remembered that he had been involved for several months with a foot fetishist in what he called "pedalian delights" and had told about it years ago in his story called "The Green Monkey." He had been aware of the symbolism of the foot, shoe, and boot in his early days, but had not realized the vast potentialities for erotic arousal to be found in that area. Later he learned of the existence of three or four clubs such as the Foot Fraternity with several thousand members devoted to the adoration of the foot—some as a symbol of domination and masculinity, others as the source of extreme erotic response when oral attention was paid to the toes and planar surfaces. Such attention usually made for almost immediate erections and long-lasting and intense erotic arousal.

"Yes . . . the feet," I repeated, for Phil seemed lost somewhere in a forest. "There seems to be a deep American prejudice against oral manipulation of the foot and toes. I think such a bias does not exist in Europe."

"No, it doesn't," Phil said. "The foot is rather highly regarded there as an erotic object. Sophisticated masseurs in Turkish baths who want to entice their customers into some sort of sex always concentrate on the toes and feet—and as a result the customer often asks for 'special' treatment in the form of fellatio or masturbation with oil."

"Don't the Japanese know about its possibilities, too?" I asked. "I've heard that they often manipulate the foot as a prelude to orgasm and ejaculation."

"The techniques of oral 'figure-eighting' around each toe are easily learned," Phil said, "and the results are gratifying even to the most experienced hustler. Talk about driving one to the point of madness! When it's done to me I really go to pieces."

"I'll note that in my daybook," I said. "Or as I asked you once before—shall I alert the media?"

"The daybook will do," Phil said. "But even the novice hustler, if he's smart enough to realize the potentialities of foot caressing, will find that many clients will call him back again and again for vespers and evensong."

"I do believe," I said, "that we're coming to the end of our short treatise on what goes on behind the green door."

"Except for one more major activity that we've barely mentioned so far," Phil said.

"Yes," I said. "Sodomy . . . and not the Dannemeyer kind of 'oral' sodomy."

"No," said Phil. "The real thing. Remember the old joke about the good lawyer who got a charge of sodomy against his client reduced to tail gating?"

"Never heard it until now," I said. "But anal penetration is something that many beginning hustlers won't allow, right? If they maintain they're in it just for the money, and that they're straight, they create such a major taboo against it in their own minds that they can't permit it at all and still hold on to the straight image. When you mentioned 'prior restrictions,' didn't you include that angle?"

"Yes," said Phil. "But they soon find out that if they don't allow it, they are losing customers, or else that they can't increase their fees or even receive their expected fees as long as they refuse. And so gradually they overcome their 'macho' prejudices and suc-cumb, only to find in it, sometimes, an entirely unexpected plea-sure. To paraphrase Tennyson — 'the sliding past the prostate helps the hurt that honor feels' as likewise does the 'jingling of the guin-eas.'"

"You wouldn't let *me* quote Tennyson," I grumbled, "and then you go and pull something outrageous like that. So much for sod-omizing the beginning hustler. What about the old pro, such as yourself?"

"If I'm asked to screw someone — and within the last two or three years of my being active, I was certainly wanted for that more than anything else. I always went in slowly unless asked to do otherwise, using many small forcings instead of a great lunge, so that the sphincter had a chance to relax. And there was one way of doing it that really turned everyone on, without exception . . ."

"And that was . . .?"

"If I could position myself on the balls of my feet with bent knees, so that I could manage a kind of circular movement of the pelvis using the asshole as a fulcrum, I could bring any guy really close to ecstasy."

"But suppose you were . . . the . . . er . . . receptor?"

"You must mean the fuckee," he said with a grin. "If that's going to be happening to you a lot, you have to learn how to control the sphincter muscles, a tightening and relaxing pattern of rhythms to imitate the real orgasmic contractions.''

"How did you ever learn to control those muscles?"

"Coughing, sneezing . . . you can do it, but it takes practice, I'll admit."

I was silent a moment, trying . . . "It's the same muscles with which you make your penis jump upwards," I said. "Or force the last drops out of the urethra."

"Bright boy," Phil said ironically. "Don't tell me you're just learning about them."

"No—of course I've known about them since high-school," I said indignantly. "But I never knew their names. And I still don't."

"Neither do I," said Phil. "A rose by any other . . .''

"Oh, hell," I said.

"I think there may be another pleasure in addition to the prostatic one," Phil said after a moment. "A kind of psychic pleasure, maybe . . . the satisfaction of knowing a deep engagement has been achieved . . .''

"Yeah," I said. "The feel of the body on top. I was once told by a young kilted Scot in Paris: 'Ay, an' if ye are lying with your face in the sweet heather, and ye feels yer man atop ye and in ye under the night sky, and him a-breathing in yer ear, then ye knows ye are in heaven or close.' ''

"Right," Phil said. "That can be of great importance. Just like the tactile pressure of the naked body against the buttocks of the client. Perhaps the weight and the full body contact pinning the john down may be of psychic or physical importance at that moment."

"All of these things together," I said reflectively, "would certainly make for a successful entrepreneur. You've had a damned good career . . .''

"Both profitable and enjoyable," Phil said, stretching his long legs out.

"Both rewarding and fruitful, you might say. But alas—even as you master the last of the tricks that have placed you at the top of your profession, there's one barrier against which you can't prevail . . .''

"Sure," he said. "Growing old. Every year diminishes you, as

John Donne might have said. He might have added — makes you so jaded that you can no longer fantasize."

"You could shift your goals a little," I said, "and go on to be a 'daddy' for several more years."

"But even that would fade," Phil said. "A good man knows when to call it quits. If your fantasy mechanism breaks, you're done for, and all the repetitions have bent mine badly. Then you will find — as the comic says — that you can't shoot pool with a rope, and that the younger and stronger have captured the world."

Chapter XI

Sailing on Perilous Seas: Hustling in the Dark Age

1. HELP FROM MR. BELL AND AN ANCIENT INVENTION

We had been at our discussion for a very long time, or so it seemed. But I realized as I arrived at Phil's house on a rather over-cast and somewhat muggy day, that it was really only the sixth morning—not yet time for our seventh day of rest. Even so, there hung in air, along with the humidity, Huxley's definition of Ameri-can life as routine interrupted by the orgy of the weekend.

When I entered the house, Phil was sitting on the oversized sofa reading from a large binder.

"What's up?" I asked.

He closed the pages and said, "Here's a . . . publication, I sup-pose you'd call it, describing a sort of exposition about AIDS that was held recently at Ohio State University, me old almy mayter. I'm not sure that anything like this could have taken place while I was going there."

"The country has been very slow in waking up to the danger," I said. "Lots of deep prejudice."

"There's some really vivid material here," he said. "Look at this, for instance."

It was the reproduction of a poster—the flat black silhouette of a male figure, cut off about mid-face and mid-thigh, with legs apart and arms akimbo. At the crotch in the genital position, pointing straight at the observer, was a handgun. The stark flatness of the man's figure and the detailed representation of the revolver said it all.

"Very effective," I said.

He folded the paper and put it aside. "I was watching the telly for a while last night," he said, "and there was an Australian television commercial that carried a great wallop. It opened with the close-up of a young couple naked in bed — man and woman — discreetly covered up to their chests with a sheet. They were embracing each other tenderly. Meanwhile, the announcer's voice-over was saying that each of them might have been to bed with other persons, and those other persons might have been to bed with still others. He said this while the camera continued to withdraw, to take in more and more of the scene — a huge room, big as a football field — dozens of identical beds, each containing one couple, until the whole screen was covered with beds, seemingly hundreds of them — and at the final moment the announcer cautioned that condoms should always be worn."

"Wow." I pronounced the word flatly with no emphasis.

"Those are only two out of hundreds of warnings and admonitions," Phil said. "We are really being bombarded with advice about this mysterious HIV virus . . ."

"Or whatever it may be called in its final naming."

Phil was thoughtful for a moment. Then he said. "I never would have believed that a few years ago I would be making such a statement as . . ."

"As what?"

He took a deep breath. "That the single most dangerous person to go to bed with in the last twenty years of the twentieth century is a male hustler."

"Jaysus," I said. "Such a statement might be made by a falwell or an advertiser trading on fear, but to hear it coming from a wise ole codger like you really is stunning."

"Maybe the wise old codger has been around and knows the ropes," he said soberly.

"There's a lot of people who would reject such a warning, saying — what of junkies? of female whores? of hemophiliacs? of victims of bad transfusions?"

"Sure, all of those, too," Phil said. "But my statement refers to male hustling as the single most dangerous *profession*."

"And is there a second?"

"Sure," Phil said. "Tattoo artists and their dealings in blood.

I'm afraid that many of their shops are inexpertly 'sterilized.' Third—nurses and all health technicians. The 'life-giving blood' has now become death-dealing.''

"The poison can be everywhere, I'm told," I said. "It can hide in even a single drop of pre-coital mucus . . .''

"Or perhaps anywhere else, for all we know," Phil said. "In the beads of salty sweat on the hustler's handsome chest, or in the tears of joy over the perfect orgasm, or in the saliva of the sweetest mouth . . .''

"To say nothing of the copious gouts of semen spilled on the buttocks of the handsome porn star. I can just imagine how Sir Thomas Browne might have phrased it—'Who would clasp the rotting corpse in the crypt, or make love amidst the worms?'"

"Or," said Phil, falling in with the macabre mimicry, "There is no longer gold in the showers that fall on Danäe, nor do diamonds lurk in the hidden crevices of the colon.''

"Let's drop it," I said. "There's nothing even vaguely amusing about this disease.''

"You're right about that," he agreed. "Before 1970 the venereal dangers for hustlers—or for anyone engaging in promiscuous sex for that matter—were common enough, and after antibiotics were discovered most of them were easily treatable.''

"Maybe too easily," I said dourly.

"Yep, they weren't scary any longer. Of course, there were stubborn things still around—like genital herpes and venereal warts and hepatitis.''

"Books like Edmund White's and Charles Silverstein's *The Joy of Gay Sex* are certainly an ironic remnant of the past," I said, "and deadly if they should fall into the hands of young and unaware kids. They emphasized the 'joy' of the new freedoms and liberation. But when the Plague arrived with all the bureaucratic fumbling and prejudice . . .''

"'No worse than a case of measles,' as our beloved leader said, until his old buddy Rock Hudson died of it . . .''

"To say that the case was dramatically altered," I went on, "is perhaps the mildest statement that could be made.''

"So you see," Phil said, "that perhaps there might have been another reason than age for my retirement.''

"Indeed," I said.

"I was being very careful," Phil said, "and following all the precautions. But I realized slowly that in the heat of arousal and passion —"

"No matter how phony," I said, smiling to take the edge off the comment.

"Sure — in the excitement, who may not occasionally forget? A quick deep kiss, an engulfing mouth, an unprotected insertion — to be followed by the dread realization and remembering . . . which is then rationalized into 'Oh well, I've been lucky so far — why not this time?' . . ."

"Sounds to me as if you might have slipped up once or twice," I said.

"I guess I have," Phil said. "So now for the next eleven years — is it? — I'll be living under the sword."

"Like so many," I said. "Hardly anyone nowadays can be sure of his own immunity . . . by saying 'It happens to others, but not to me.' Trouble is — they're dead wrong. And . . . dead."

"I hope I'm not that young or inexperienced," Phil said. "But if one day a dark patch appears on a thigh, and I find myself wondering how I got that bruise . . ."

"Let's move on," I said, "to one stop-gap pastime for hustlers that resulted from the implications and horrors of the fatal syndrome."

"Which is what specifically?"

"The one made possible by the advent and popularity of credit cards, the three-minute egg-timer, and Mr. Bell's handy little invention."

"Ah yes," Phil said. "Obscene phone calls have been around for a very long time. But there's not really too much new about telephone sex. It's always been useful for those whose Mister Wiggly has been on a diet of bread and water."

"The merchandising of it in all the gay publications is new," I said.

"Back in the beginning when I was doing some advertising myself," Phil said, "I used to kinda *like* getting an occasional obscene phone call. I liked the heavy breathing and the rhythmic quality that the hand movements gave to the caller's voice."

"The Plague turned the obscene calls into a profitable business for those early, far-sighted entrepreneurs," I observed. "You paid a certain amount for the first minute, and then lesser amounts for the following minutes, and you got a choice of a fireman, a cowboy, a cop, a trucker, a construction worker, a lumberjack, a mountie, a football or basketball player, a jock, a college student, or any other type calculated to churn the adrenalin and stir up the bloodstream . . ."

". . . directing it towards the penile girders," Phil said. "And then the entrepreneurs hired hack porno writers to create one-page monologues of sex talk — all kinds of instructions about what to take hold of and what to do with it, all sorts of threats, promises, pleadings, beggings . . ."

". . . directions, orders, injunctions, assurances, intimidations, menacings, ordeals, appeals, entreaties, implorings and such like," I finished for him. "The new businessmen didn't have to make much of a capital outlay to get started. The cost of a phone and line, a dollar a page for the speeches so they'd have continuing streams of dirtytalk. Then they'd hire college students for a few bucks an hour to read off the erotica and make sextalk with the customers."

"Certainly it was the safest sex possible," Phil said.

"It created a whole new sub-group of hustlers and pimps overnight. The gay periodicals from about 1987 on were filled with ads of naked young men in tantalizing positions with telephone held near the crotch, or otherwise posed invitingly to handle the horny calls — paid for by credit card."

"Never thought I'd see the day when the phone replaced the masseur's table or the model's posing."

I shook my head. "But dammit, there was no physical contact! What's sex without that?"

"Something won-der-ful," Phil said breathily.

"You sound like Howard Carter peeking into King Tut's tomb," I said.

"*You* ought to realize just *how* wonderful," Phil said. "The imagination is mighty powerful. And effective. Formerly, if someone answered a hustler's printed ad in which he described himself as a hunky black-haired Mediterranean-type weightlifter — and a scrawny kid with zits and pipestem arms showed up at the door, there was often a complete breakdown of simpatico and communication. To say nothing of rapid detumescence.''

''Yeah, you're right,'' I admitted. ''Phone sex has the same advantages the old radio dramas had over television: the power and effectiveness depended on the listener's imagination. The drama's hero could be as handsome and compelling a hunk as your imagination could produce.''

''In some ways,'' Phil said thoughtfully, ''the telephone could give you more satisfaction than even a hustler could furnish.''

''Oh, perhaps,'' I said grudgingly. ''But listen, kid—the touch of a warm body and what it could do gave the hustler a mighty powerful advantage.''

''Jean Genet said that he was in favor of starting a cult of masturbation because only that way could a 'perfect gratification' be obtained.''

''Good grief,'' I said. ''What did he mean? *Start* a jack-off cult? It probably had its beginning among the cave-dwellers.''

''Well,'' Phil said. ''In view of today's paranoia and real fear of hustlers, what are we gonna do? I retired.''

''We are now,'' I said, aping a scholar's nasal twang, ''brought to a consideration of the condom.''

''Ugh,'' said Phil. ''Ward Stames once told me that back in the 1920s it was called a 'cuntrum.'''

''The great unwashed,'' I said, ''could no more than approximate the unusual words they had perhaps heard only once. 'Hermaphrodite' used to be 'mor-free-dite.' It was only logical that hoi polloi would say 'cuntrum' because it was associated with the vulgar word for a woman's rubyfruit jungle—as lesbians are sometimes wont to say.''

''Some say that the condom was invented by a British doctor named Condon—seventeenth century. Or a British colonel.''

''It is probably a heluva lot older than that,'' I said. ''The idea was of great antiquity, really. In China and Japan, rounds of oiled silk paper were used by prostitutes to cover the mouth of the vagina, to prevent conception. In Europe they are first heard of in mid-sixteenth century Italy—linen sheaths in the shape of a penis. Later they used the caecum of a lamb—and afterwards, even isinglass.''

Phil shuddered. ''Cracklin' good,'' he said.

"Then they used goldbeater's skin," I went on. "Madame de Sévigné mentions them. She didn't like 'em. Called 'em 'armour plate against voluptuousness, and spider webs against disease.'"

"When Ward was young," Phil said, "little high-school boys used to feel very worldly and wicked when they carried a 'rubber' around with them, purchased from the town's 'agent,' usually a barber or else the town drunk. They used them just to masturbate in — and frequently washed them out and dried them to use again, because they were sort of expensive back then. But Ward said that if the boys were wealthy enough they purchased the small aluminum box containing three rolled 'Merry Widows — Agnes, Mabel, and Beckie.' Three dollars. Prohibitive price in those days."

"What about the controversy over condoms today? The Catholic Church is in a dilemma. How can it keep its young men free of the Plague and still not recommend that hated birth-control device called a condom?"

"They'll probably find a way around it," Phil said, "as brilliant as the rhythm method of planned parenthood which they devised."

"For today's hustlers and their clients, and also for all the porn movie producers and stars, the condom is perhaps just as difficult an issue as for the church," I observed.

"To use or not to use?"

"A ticklish matter," I nodded. "Long years of avoiding it entirely in gay encounters have made everyone scornful of its use. Some reject it without any discussion at all."

"I've known several hustlers — and clients, too," Phil said, "who've said that either to use them or not use them has been so violently discussed that the encounter has been ruined, even called off. If the hustler is to give a blowjob and demands that the client wear one, maybe the client is offended. On the other hand, not all hustlers are careful enough, some feeling that rubbers are for old fuddy-duddies. They may believe that their own immortality is assured for their three-score-and-ten into the next century."

I shook my head. "The wise hustler certainly ought to insist on their use. He can't rely on his customer's promise not to come in his mouth. Such a statement is about as trustworthy as 'the check is in the mail.'"

"Man," Phil said, crossing the elegantly *fines attaches* (as the

French say—the fine attachments) of his ankles out in front of himself, "in the last months before I quit I heard nothing but complaints against condoms from the beginning unsophisticated hustlers, as well as clients in a hurry or those used to the freedoms of the 1960s and earlier. And lord—the kinds of complaints you wouldn't believe."

"Such as—?"

Phil took a deep breath and began. " 'They cut down on the sensation. I can hardly feel anything with one of the damned things on. They're no protection anyway—I've heard the viruses can go right through them. I can't stand that gassy smell. The powder—or something—inside 'em makes my cock swell up. I always get them on inside out and they don't roll on right. They slip off. They bust. If you use any grease on 'em they either won't slide, or else they break right away. All the statistics say they aren't really safe, or don't really protect you. They have tiny holes in them. I never go to bed anyway with anyone who's tested positive—I always ask them about things like diseases. And rubbers make my cock itch. They ain't never big enough—I always feel strangled. Jeez, I forgot to bring any with me. Don't you trust me, man? I can't come with one of the damned things on.' "

Phil stopped for breath. "And on and on," he said. "Lots of excuses and rationalizations. That's just a sample."

"Even with a condom," I said, "there's no universal protection against syphilis, herpes, genital warts—and really against AIDS, except for two small areas—the orifice and the entering organ. Tears, saliva, and sweat carry the spirochetes of syphilis, and although they say that there have been no proven cases of AIDS developing from tears, sweat, or saliva—that's not the same thing as saying it isn't possible. No one yet actually knows, I guess. The authorities also say that anal intercourse is the most dangerous because of the virus that may enter and hide deep in the crypts of Morgangi in the rectum."

"I just happened to remember that as early as 1964 you wrote a piece called 'The Narrowing Circle' for one of the Copenhagen magazines, didn't you?" Phil asked.

"Yes, I did," I said. "It ended with a view of love-making in the future—and I settled on the year 1975 to describe that future."

"I read it once," Phil said. "Didn't you point out other dangers connected with gay sex?"

"Lots," I said. "Mononucleosis, if you preferred your lovers to be on the side of eighteen or nineteen. Syphilis, with the bugs in blood, sweat, and tears. Gonorrhea—both buccal and rectal. Tetanus—or worse—from boot-licking. Histoplasmosis—if you made love in a hay-mow or near a chicken-coop. Hepatitis—if you went for analingus. Trichomoniasis—if you picked the unlucky husband of a still more unlucky wife. But the AIDS virus had not yet appeared on the scene in 1964. Or if it was hanging around, it hadn't yet been identified, finger-printed, or mug-shot."

"Ward Stames has some bound volumes of *amigo* in the bedroom," Phil said. "It was 1964, you said?"

"Yes."

"I've sort of forgotten the part about the future," he said. "I'll go get it."

"I think it was in the June issue," I called after him.

He returned in a moment with the green-bound volume, flipping through the pages. "Here it is," he said. "I'll read it out loud." He sat down and began.

> ". . . and the vision of the future is discouraging . . .
>
> Here, for example, are two handsome young men in bed in 1975, let us say. The camera zooms down to find them, lying on spotless hospital-clean sheets, tightly drawn and unrumpled. The bodies of both are naked, save for the faces and midsections. On the face of one is a mask of surgical gauze; on the other's a kind of cylindrical metal purifier containing the latest chemical air-filters. The hands of each person are encased in elbow-length surgical rubber gloves. And each wears a pair of tight-fitting rubber drawers covering the entire midsection of his body from navel to mid-thigh, with only one thing protruding from a circular opening in the rubber.
>
> These young men are homosexuals. They are about to have sex. Let us watch them. Slowly the right hand of one young male reaches across the body of his buddy to press a button on a container of sterile lubricant; with some of this on his glove, he returns his hand to manipulate his friend's rosebud. And

then his lover-boy does the same. Thus flat on their backs, breathing the sterile air, our friendly homosexuals of the future make love . . .''

Phil closed the volume. "Jaysus," he said. "That's scary. If you'd made it 1981 instead of 1975, you'd have been right on the button."

With affected modesty, I buffed my fingernails on the lapel of my sweater. "Even for Nostradamus," I said, "the vision of the future was not always unclouded. We do the best we can."

"Oh my," Phil said.

2. EITHER BRAVE, FOOLISH, STUPID, GULLIBLE, OR YOUNG

Phil was in the yard in front of his house, playing with his long-haired dachshunds when I arrived the next Monday morning. He had put on a tight bright red teeshirt and a pair of well-worn and skin-tight chinos which showed off his buttocks and his bourse to great advantage. As I opened the gate he was engaged in gently prying open the mouth of the younger dog, and extracting a piece of orange plastic from between tightly clenched teeth.

"There are three girls in the yard next door," he said. "*Little* girls, about two or three years old."

"Sounds as if the hubby had more than his share of X chromosomes," I said. "Maybe a trisomic."

"Whatever," Phil half-growled. "They are at the savage monster stage of development — not old enough yet to have any sense or responsibility or to pay attention to prohibitions of any sort. They persist in poking sticks through the fence at my small beasties, and feeding them an assortment of pebbles, stones, sticks, and bunches of green fox-tails. I guess the only solution is to get the dogs inside the house when I hear the girls out in their backyard . . .''

"Kids are sometimes a great problem," I said.

". . . or else kill them — the girls, I mean. Not the dogs."

"Sh-h-h," I said. "In today's society you mustn't even say things like that in joke. Aren't you afraid that poppa or momma may hear you and accuse you of raping the children? That is, if they have heard of your reputation.''

"I think they haven't," Phil said. "And the last thing I would ever be likely to be accused of is being a child molester. The people I prefer to molest are men at the period when they're just beginning to rot—about thirty," he said grinning.

"You probably then don't approve of the boy-love group of homosexuals, I take it."

"No way," he said. "First off, as I told that Matthias Brown character in Milwaukee years ago—''

"Ah yes," I said. "You told his story in 'H²' in *$tud*. You accused him of being unable to face another adult on the battlefield of the bed—not able to control anything but a youngster.''

"Good memory," Phil said. "And while we're discussing my prejudices and intolerances, can you think of anything else to hit me with?"

"Sure," I said, slightly amused. "Why is it in talking about hustlers, you have never said a damned word about the very large group of them—?''

"What group have we left out?"

"The cross-dressing drag queens in skirts who go out at night, all bound tight around their dingdongs, everything flat up in place, looking for straight men only, wanting to give them a blowjob or to be screwed.''

Phil's faint scowl disappeared, and he laughed a little. "I haven't anything to say about them," he said, "because I haven't got the foggiest about what makes them tick.''

"Ah, c'mon," I said. "You must've known plenty of gay boys who wanted to bring pleasure only to straight men, and who wouldn't even go to bed with another gay.''

"Sure I have," said Phil, "but that doesn't mean I understand them, and I particularly don't understand the drag-queen hustlers. I could barely read through that book called *Mr. Madam* some years ago. If you want to write about hustlers, their kind, you've certainly crawled into bed beside the wrong breed of person . . . me.''

"Don't blow a basket," I said. "Er . . . *that's* a Freudian slip! I meant gasket. No—someone else will do the definitive book on them. Not I. It should be a person of infinite wisdom and tolerant understanding—a Freud or Jung or Kinsey.''

"Well, now that we've excluded the man-boy group and the drag-queen hustlers, what do you wanta talk about today?''

"Well," I said, "something else quite unpleasant. Last year or so—I haven't been able to find out exactly when it happened—there was a memorial service in Los Angeles for twenty young porno stars, all of whom died of AIDS. The event wasn't given much publicity, and anyway, among the legions already dead, twenty more did not mean much to the keepers of statistics at the Center for Disease Control.''

"I heard a little something about that," Phil said.

"More to our point," I said. "Eighteen of the twenty were also hustlers on the side. Both professions—quite hazardous. Nobody knows how many more have died since that memorial service but I wouldn't be surprised if another memorial service were due.''

"The transition from porno star to hustler is an easy thing," Phil said. "I've known a lot who started out in films—or maybe reversed the order and ended up in films. The tapes present the talents and endowments of the newcomers to the world, and so it follows as the night the day . . .''

" . . . thou canst not then be kept from any man," I said, misquoting Donne.

" . . . the advertising churns the adrenalin and the libido into a frenzy that's strong enough," he went on, ignoring my brilliant interruption, "to compel the film watcher to seek out the handsome new man, he of the unbelievable dimensions and the perfect musculature that's moved a thousand hips.''

"I saw a few examples of screen tests given to those young men," I said. "None of that particular batch seemed to have elevators that went clear to the top floor.''

"I've seen some of those filmed screen tests too," Phil said. "The guys I knew who were porno stars had been brainwashed by some of the most skilled operators in existence.''

"The articulate persuasion they practiced seemed to me the equal of that of any lawyer or Jesuit. They conned the young man into posing, into having his perineum and anal areas shaved, and into believing that his whole future life lay under the benevolent guidance of the film's director or producer. The new guy is then lulled into a sense of security about the things he is required to do—no danger at all, he is told. We have been very careful in screening your partners, they are all negative, no one likes to see condoms in these fantasies and encounters, and besides they bunch up and slide off most unattractively, and all of our attempts to create a sexy fantasy are destroyed when the condoms can be seen . . . and so on."

"You're really steamed about all this, aren't you?" Phil said.

"Any man's death diminishes me . . ."

"Therefore do not send to ask for whom the bell tolls . . . " he finished. "And you're really hung up on Donne today, aren't you?"

"Sorry," I said. "I'm about to do something rash. Something you don't particularly approve of. But I can't help myself."

Phil looked vaguely alarmed.

"What's Donne today doesn't have to be Donne tomorrow," I said.

He looked heavenward and bit his lip—but gave no protest but a sigh. "There are no statistics available on the deaths of the porno stars," I said.

"I don't imagine their occupations are recorded on death certificates."

"One of the more realistic producers—who wouldn't be identified—said that he estimated the average life expectancy of a porno star to be two years after the start of a guy's film career."

"And still, new faces and fresh bodies appear."

"One reviewer of porn films said he sits through about forty films a month, and that condoms are seen on the screen less than ten percent of the time—and even in those cases, their use is erratic and sporadic. Used in one or two scenes, and then absent in four or five. And never appearing in fellatio segments. It seems to be an old wives' belief that stomach secretions kill the virus. That's never been proved."

"If anything, the tragic evidence is to the contrary," I said. "I guess, then, there's no questioning the fact that hustling is one of the most dangerous occupations in the world, as you said earlier . . .

maybe the most unspectacularly fatal, too. No flaming death-crashes on a race-track with souped-up cars."

"Yeah — very quiet," Phil agreed. "Once the organism is invaded, it begins its gradual decay. A slow progression towards the tomb . . ."

I shivered a little.

"Even the most optimistic scientists on the cutting edge of research believe that an infected person will have to spend the rest of his life on medication just to slow the progress of the virus. And as of today, there seems to be nothing to stop it, unless the blood-boiling, the simple artificial fever treatment, turns out to be the ultimate — but expensive — cure."

"Well, on your retiring you've at least got your pharmacist's license to fall back upon," I recalled.

"It's other hustlers I'm pessimistic about," Phil said, gloomy. "So few of them have anything to look forward to. They're not prepared."

"There are always careers in dishwashing, ditch digging, politics, televangelism, janitorial work — provided any of them live long enough."

"That's a mighty bitter statement," Phil said after a moment. "But one almost has to agree. Their chances are not the best."

There was a long, uneasy silence. On the backdrop of my imagination was projected the vision of a bleak and devastated future, unrelieved by any glow of hope, darkening slowly to a somber twilight.

Chapter XII

The Mystery of the Hidden Linkage

The next day was even hotter, and the announced morning temperature was already eighty degrees. I approached Phil's house, feeling that the interview was winding down, or else that I was beginning to lose control of it. And when that happens, even the most carefully planned schemes begin to fall apart, to degenerate — even though quite pleasantly — into aimless gossip accomplishing nothing except occasional insights of no great importance. But the truth was that I still had a few more points I wanted to discuss with Phil.

He was again in the backyard with the dogs. He had discarded the revealing chinos in favor of an even more eye-opening costume — a pair of skimpy, ragged-edged denim cutoffs that revealed his 'bourse' more tantalizingly still. His legs had always induced in me a kind of trembling admiration — they seemed to my eye perfectly formed — classically proportioned with the thigh curling into the ideal calf, and tapering to the elegant ankles, all given a kind of grave and dusky luminance when the sun fell at a certain angle on the dark hair that covered them.

A fugitive memory from my own university days came to me — an observation from a prose essay by Alice Meynell, written sometime in the 1880s. Alice was a devout Catholic lady-poet, but now and then she seemed to slip a bit in her rigorous moral discipline, and the one I recalled hinted at that most subtle and esoteric of all the Church sins, mentioned previously — *delectatio morosa*, the 'morose' enjoyment of the 'sins of the eye,' committed by those who looked upon another human being with lust in the heart . . . or at least somewhere in the body.

She had been commenting on the clothes that men wore in the

nineteenth century, and what she said was something like this: "It is a shame that the handsome configuration of male limbs should be encased in those long straight tubular coverings, with straps under the instep, that men are compelled to wear because fashion so decrees."

Bully for Alice, I thought as I closed the gate and said hello to Phil.

"It's going to be a real stinker today," he said. He had been placing a few bricks at the bottom of the fencing between his yard and the neighbor's, so that the dogs would be discouraged from digging underneath. "Every animal, human or not, has a desire to roam," he said, "or wants to be free."

"Questionable," I said, "but not really a good topic for debate. You remember that the other day we were talking about power and the elements it depended on—the hustler's attractiveness and youth, the patron's pocketbook, and what a volatile situation was caused by the back-and-forth flow of power."

"For heaven's sake," Phil said. "We don't need to say any more about that, do we?"

"No way," I said. "Be comforted. But it occurred to me as I lay abed this morning—"

"A dangerous time for you," Phil said with a grin. "You seem to plot all sorts of mischief when you can't sleep in the mornings."

"Some of my very best scheming and manipulations," I said. "But what I thought of this morning is even more subtle, I think, than the power bit. And just as deeply buried. It seems to be a kind of magnetic pull which a hustler can exert on a client. I got a letter from an old friend not long ago—just listen to this paragraph from what he says:

> I hardly know how to explain Tim's hold on me. At first he seemed to be just another hustler—a cut above the ordinary street hustler, yes, but no great shakes. As time went on, however, and I saw him on several more occasions and listened to some of the tales of experiences he had had [all told without mentioning identities, of course], I began in a sense to *see through him*, not that he was trying to hoodwink me in any way, but that I was seeing through him and looking at the long

line of persons he had been to bed with, and after that he took on an odd kind of magic for me that was even stronger than the attraction of his good face and trim young body. . . .''

"He seems to be groping around a lot," Phil said, "but not quite sure what he's reaching for."

"Do you understand what he's trying to say?" I asked.

"Sure," Phil said. "I've heard it before, or at least listened to people trying to express the deep unconscious urging which hustlers seem to create in many who use our . . . services."

"How does this mechanism work, exactly?" I asked.

"I dunno," Phil said. "Beats me."

"I had one idea but I'm sort of afraid to tell you about it. Sounds a little far-fetched."

"Give out," Phil said. "I promise not to laugh . . . very much."

"In the reign of Elizabeth I," I said, "there was a certain Dr. John Dee who was doing topographical and mathematical studies under her sponsorship. But he also dabbled in occult and alchemical matters, not exactly a legitimate complement to the other stuff. At any rate, he developed what he called a 'gazing-stone,' a shiny black flat ovoid stone you held comfortably in the palm of your hand, which was used to 'free the mind,' or at least help it to become blank so that a person could all the more easily receive the impressions and associations which flowed up from the unconscious."

"Just like crystal-gazing," Phil said.

"I suppose so. But it seemed to me that Tim the hustler became a kind of Dr. Dee gazing-stone for my friend Jack, because through him he could see the long and winding line of former clients extending as far back into infinity as Jack's imagination could carry him."

"Yup, that's the way it works," Phil said, "at least as far as I could judge from what I heard a few of them say."

"Could it be that somewhere in that long line, then, the client might feel that there had been an encounter with the ideal man of his dreams?"

"Possible," Phil said. "One of the main reasons for the promiscuity of many male homosexuals is that endless search they feel compelled to make for the ideal dream-figure."

"The one who most perfectly answers all of the impossible ideal-izations demanded by the fantasy of the searcher. Did you ever have any clients who questioned you about your former customers?"

"Sure thing. Some even were really obsessive about it," Phil said.

"Any success for them?"

"Fruitless," he said, with a grin. "But the search doesn't end with that."

"Hardly," I agreed. "Everyone is subject to the same kind of haunting that memory compels. Proust used the taste of a madeleine to begin his outpouring of hundreds of thousands of words in his *Remembrance of Things Past*. We have all experienced how a scent — maybe a hint of honeysuckle on an evening breeze — can recall a memory, perhaps an entire country childhood, or an idyllic summer visit to a long forgotten spot. Then suppose you add to the search some small characteristic of a forgotten love — the profile of a favorite uncle, the large hands of your first lover, the copper-red hair of a swimmer buddy at a summer camp . . ."

"Hey!" Phil said. "Gad, you're lyrical today!"

". . . or any of a thousand details useful in your continuing erotic search, and then imagine also that suddenly the same gesture, the same coloring, is seen in the hustler . . ."

"Yeah, it's happened many times to my johns," Phil said, "but if you're wise you avoid getting tangled up with anything that's not erotic, unless you're hired especially as a companion. Or escort. Things like that lead nowhere. Oh sure — to a pleasant hour. I don't like to sound materialistic, but they were all without profit. And furthermore, they weaken your hard shell."

"You've got a hard shell?" I said in astonishment. "Over your soft center?"

"You've gotta protect your ego," Phil said. "Your importance to yourself inside yourself, remember?"

"Yes," I said. "Mustn't be naked to the ravages and buffetings lying in wait for your self-esteem."

"There's always a kind of romantic aura to hustlers," Phil said. "I suppose I don't need to do more than mention it. But I've heard you yourself speak of the kind of fascination which the virgin Desdemona felt when she learned of the romantic and dark past of the Moor Othello.''

''She was conquered long before they met. The stories of his exploits did it before he began his entreaties. She was a victim of her own fantasies. The modern patron of the hustler is the captive of his own imaginings.''

''Or of his filled-up-to-overflowing vesicles,'' Phil said.

''Guess we can't ever prove all these fancies about a hustler's aura,'' I said. ''Your clients can stammer about it, but they're just as awkward as I am when it comes to analysis.''

''We see through a glass darkly,'' Phil said in mock piety. ''But actually I know that many johns felt these things deeply, even though they're only romantic dreams.''

''Perhaps to be sighed over,'' I said, ''but not acted on.''

''That's my friendly old realist,'' Phil said, slapping me on the shoulder. ''Want a glass of bittermilk?''

''You must mean buttermilk,'' I said.

''No,'' Phil said. ''Or I would have said so.''

''Thanks,'' I said, ''but it's too early in my day to start drinking.''

Chapter XIII

In Faerie Lands Forlorn:
Is It Then at an End?

"That was a very short session we had yesterday," I said.

"Too damned hot," Phil said. "Takes all the starch out of your cerebellum."

"What a novel idea," I said.

He had searched through the house until he found Ward's hassock fan, which distributed a violent current of air in a full circle throughout the room. He still wore his cutoffs, and I did my best to conceal the glances that I sneaked at his legs. He had, however, removed his shoes and socks, and from time to time dug his toes into the deep pile of the dark maroon living-room rug. I noted that the second toe was of classical length, slightly longer than the big toe, in accord with the best designs of the Greek and Roman sculptors as well as God's own template. I said nothing about the distraction of his costume, or lack thereof, thinking that with his considerate nature, he might just go and put on his trousers if he thought I found his nakedness disturbing. And that was a conclusion I devoutly wished him not to reach at all.

"This is just a minor matter, I suppose," I said, pretending to shuffle papers to create a business-like air, "but do you have any anecdotes about the sorts of accidents that may befall hustlers? Aside, of course, from the chances of contracting one of the many ailments which are the scourge of your profession. I mean an event that might only temporarily interrupt a career, *or* perhaps end it permanently. I mean, apart from the possibility of the hustling life so palling on, or disgusting or discouraging or boring the hustler that he willingly gives it up. Perhaps he might even join the ranks of the Born Agains . . ."

"That would be the unlikeliest adventure of all." Phil crossed one ankle over his knee, drumming his fingers on the chair arm. "But I do think of one — a serio-comic event. To the one involved, however, not funny at all."

"Wanna tell me?"

"Poor Duncan!" Phil said, a hint of humor in his voice. "He was a very elegant and young curly-blond hustler, quite well endowed, who had already made several film appearances in pornos. He had been called from Louisville to a rather small town in Kentucky where there lived an extremely wealthy patron who had seen him on the screen, and also heard of his services. After a satisfactory encounter, Duncan left the isolated estate to find his way back to civilization through several small Kentucky towns."

"You make it sound like a setting in darkest Appalachia."

"Yeah — well, almost, except for the estate. The score raised horses and had quite a spread of land, as they say."

"Sorry for the interruption."

"Duncan had to stay overnight in one of those small towns, and the only toilet facility available was a tiny outside wooden two-holer with an old Sears Roebuck catalog hanging nearby on a nail. And hanging also close at hand was a branch with leaves on it, the purpose of which escaped him. He let down his pants and was seated, and within two minutes was bitten on his dangler by a violin spider resenting the intrusion into his kingdom."

"Good heavens!" I said. "How would you ever get a tourniquet on that!"

"Just the point," Phil said. "He later learned the branch was to swish around the underside of the hole to dislodge any varmints who might attack at one's most defenseless moment."

"What happened?" I asked.

"Duncan lived . . . but barely. By the time he got out of the hospital, the lesion with its blackened eschar left by the kiss of the violin spider had been replaced by a skin graft from his formerly impeccable butt, and the systemic symptoms treated with the appropriate chemicals and an O^2 facemask improvised to apply oxygen to the ulcer formed when the bleb ruptured. Duncan's hustling career never quite recovered from the trauma inflicted on his machinery."

"Quite a story," I said. "Luckily not too many hustlers have to go to two-holers."

"Sometimes," Phil said, "the damaged hustler finds that the loss he's had really increases his attractiveness. I knew a hustler in Chicago who had lost a leg—and clients seemed to enjoy him. One of them said that certain positions were made easier since nothing got in the way."

"Loss and gain," I said. "I once knew a guy who'd been born missing one hand. He found that for certain purposes his forearm was more than adequate."

"Didn't you mention that you liked Tennessee Williams's short story, 'One Arm,' the one about the hustler with the torso of the young faun of Praxiteles—the one who murdered a guy one drunken night, was caught and electrocuted?"

"A brilliant and haunting story," I said. "Unforgettable. I really don't comprehend the quirks of such attractions, but broken vessels do seem to be mighty successful sometimes."

"Or just odd vessels," Phil said with a grin. "In Gould and Pyle's book on the anomalies and curiosities of medicine, they tell of a man 'whose testicles were elevated each time the east wind blew, which caused him a sense of languor and relaxation.'"

I exploded with a laugh. "Sometimes it's difficult to keep enough balance," I said, "to be able to say that nothing which is human is strange to me."

"Aside from the ordinary hazards of the profession," Phil said, "there's a double condition which defies everything, the two things from which no one has ever been able to free himself."

"One thing obviously is time, I suppose. The passing of it. Growing old."

"Yeah," Phil said. "And the other part of it?"

"Give up," I said after a moment.

"Gravity," Phil said. "The two things can end the most brilliant career. I think gravity is even more wicked than time."

"Dread mistress of the universe," I murmured. "Einstein's nemesis . . ."

"Turns the most impressive pectorals of weightlifters into the shrunken dugs of old women. Makes the stomach sag."

"Draws the jowls downward. Makes the nose bulbous."

"Flattens the firm ass, makes the belly hang over the belt."

"Kings and athletes shrink and diminish," I said, "and handsome lads turn into wizened pot-bellied monsters with spindly legs."

"And then a hustler's career is really finished," Phil said.

"You could have coasted along for quite a while on your reputation," I said. "Wigs, cosmetics, transplants."

He shook his head. "You can't really do much about the ravages of time and gravity," he said. "The telephone rings fewer times, and finally stops. While all my non-hustling contemporaries were busy climbing the ladders to become head ribbon-clerks at Macy's—"

"I know," I said, "you were spending on silken sheets in silken or leather boudoirs, and like the happy grasshopper bouncing from one bed to another, wasting your substance."

"Well, not entirely . . ." Phil said, grinning. "More likely not always the cleanest sheets in sometimes dingy bedrooms."

"Do you have any recommendations to make for people who will have to do without hustlers?" I said, almost giggling. "Substitutes for your abilities?"

"Dozens," Phil said. "There's the hand—old Mrs. Palm and her five daughters. The merkin—tied to the back of a straight chair, latex with a hole in it, formerly a pig bladder. Sun-warmed melons for delight. Dream control. Vibrators, and the best of all—the Accu-jac. And to keep excited: butt plugs, shaving with its later prickling, cock rings, holes in pants pockets, accupressure points, yohimbine, and desyrel if you want to develop a real case of priapism. Or just thinking and imagining."

"Then we don't really have to go flaccid into that good night," I said.

"Hell no," Phil said, chuckling.

"There's one final point," I said. "Would you like to make a personal statement about yourself? Or about your life in general? Maybe some nugget of wisdom that might help future . . ."

"Hustlers?"

"Not necessarily," I said. "Just people."

"I'm no good at things like that," Phil said.

"Aw, g'wan," I said.

"Well . . ." A long pause. "There was a period in my life when I somewhat cynically said that the ideal epitaph for me would be 'Every body is of *some* use,' but I sort of got over that."

"You were never that selfish," I said.

"I guess I might say that I've never deliberately hurt anyone . . ." I scribbled it down.

" . . . and that I have probably brought a good deal of pleasure to a lot of people. And finally, I've never been afraid of love."

"That's good enough," I said. "I hope someone can say something like that of me when I die. I think I'd be satisfied."

I closed my notebook. "I'm only sorry," I said, "that you decided to retire before I had one last encounter with you."

Phil stood up, and cupped his hand over his heavy bourse, slowly moving his fingers.

"I haven't stopped having sex, silly," he said. "It's just that I don't charge for it any more. Uncle Wiggly would never submit to being kept on a diet of bread and water. And there's no greater troublemaker than a rebellious Uncle Wiggly."

"True," I said.

He pointed. "The workbench is through that little corridor and to your right," he said.

The door to the bedroom was a solid wooden one with four panels. I noticed that at one time they had been painted green by a former hippie tenant of the "Invisible House," and traces of the color still lingered faintly on the surface of the wood.

He followed me. The bed had no top covers on it, just a sheet which was stretched to military tautness. You could have bounced a quarter on it.

Phil knelt and pulled a shoe-box from under the bed. He stood up and placed the box on the sheet, and removed the lid. An invisible and potent odor of latex gas arose, the sort that comes from condoms. And indeed, the box was full of them — all kinds, rolled and unrolled, wrapped and naked, blue, green, red, striped, gold and black and wine-dark, with heads of roosters, lions, and griffins, studded with projections, ribbed, glow-in-the-dark ones.

"Good grief," I said.

"One should be prepared at all times for anything," Phil murmured, grinning. "Even safe sex."

He dipped into them, picking up a handful and letting them slide from his fingers. The odor — a very potent sexual stimulant to me — was strong in the room. It took me back to simpler younger days, to car rides on summer nights, and handsome jocks in the back seat.

I was quivering a little. "E*specially* . . . s-s-safe sex," I said, gulping some air.

He bent again, picking up a plastic container from the floor. "And a bottle of lubricant," he said. "The very best Nonoxynol-9, with aloe. Guaranteed to kill all nasty little visitors. If any." He shook it gently, and looked at me, his dark eyes hot and intense. He put the bottle on the bed beside the shoe-box, and then reached out and took the top button of my shirt between his fingers.

"I think you'd be cooler without your clothes," he said.

A Modest Bibliography

Andros, Phil. (pseud.) *Greek Ways*. San Francisco, 1984.
_____. *Shuttlecock*. San Francisco, 1984.
_____. *$tud*. Washington, DC, 1966.
Augustine, Saint. *Civitas Dei*. [City of God]. London, 1931.
Austen, Roger. *Playing the Game*. Indianapolis/New York, 1977.
Bishop, Donald. (pseud.) *Der Kreis/Le Cercle*. Zurich, 1963. Vol. XXXI. July, pp. 35-40.
Burton, Sir Richard. *Terminal Essay: The Sotadic Zone*. New York, 1930.
Ellis, Havelock. *Studies in the Psychology of Sex*. New York, 1936.
Fitts, Dudley. *Sixty Poems of Martial*. New York, 1967.
Forbes, Jason. *The Happy Hustler*. Chatsworth, CA, 1974.
Gould, G.M. and Pyle, W.L. *Anomalies and Curiosities of Medicine*. New York, 1956.
Grant, Michael. *Eros in Pompeii*. New York, 1975.
Gregory, Horace. *The Poems of Catullus*. New York, 1956.
Henry, G.W. *Sex Variants: A Study of Homosexual Patterns*. New York, 1941.
_____. *All the Sexes: A Study of Masculinity and Femininity*. New York, 1955.
Humphreys, Laud. *Tearoom Trade*. Chicago, 1970.
Kinsey, Alfred C. et al. *Sexual Behavior in the Human Male*. Philadelphia & London, 1953.
_____. *Sexual Behavior in the Human Female*. Philadelphia & London, 1948.
Lloyd, Robin. *For Money or Love*. New York, 1976.
Magie, David. transl. *Historiae Scriptores Augustae*. London, 1921.
Myers, H. and Ormsby, R.J. *Catullus*. New York, 1970.
Rader, Dotson. *Gov't Inspected Meat*. New York, 1972.
Rechy, John. *City of Night*. New York, 1963.
_____. *The Sexual Outlaw*. New York, 1977.
Reiss, A.J. *Social Problems*, Vol. 9, pp. 9-13. 1961.
Saul, Jack. *The Sins of the Cities of the Plain*. London, 1881.
Saxon, Grant Tracy. (pseud.) *The Happy Hustler*. New York, 1975.

Stevens, Marc. *10 1/2!*. New York, 1975.
Steward, Samuel M. *Bad Boys and Tough Tattoos*. Binghamton, 1990.
Suetonius. *The Lives of the Twelve Caesars*. New York, 1931.
Talsman, William. *The Gaudy Image*. New York, 1958.
Tripp, C.A. *The Homosexual Matrix*. New York, 1987 [1975].
Vatsyayana. *Kama Sutra*. New York, 1963.
White, E.B. & Silverstein, C. *The Joy of Gay Sex*. New York, 1977.
Williams, Tennessee. *One Arm*. New York, 1948.

Consultants

The following list contains the names or initials of a great many of the young men — and some not so young — whose input or output or interfacing has been of value in preparing this study. It is not possible to identify them additionally, for in many instances their current lives might be adversely affected. They have been interviewed or questioned during the past twenty-three years, and their identities discreetly retained, despite the fact that some of them are certainly aliases or "business" pseudonyms. The author's tendency to be a record-keeper — a factor which delighted Dr. Kinsey — accounts for their preservation and inclusion here.

Chuck Ad, Tom Ad, Albert Af, Joe Al, Robert Al, Frank Am, Marc Am, Mark An, Norm An, Bill An, Anon (16), Joe Ar, Art Ar, Jim Ar, Bob Ar, Dave Ar, Jon As, Jim Au, Dick Av, Pat Ba, Everett Ba, Bill Ba, Elbert Ba, John Ba, John Ba, Junior Ba, Harold Ba, Bob Ba, Leslie Ba, Steve Ba, Emile Ba, Hubert Ba, Bert Ba, Larry Be, Glen Be, Bachir Be, Jack Be, Arthur Be, Bob Be, Glenn Be, Myron Be, Carver Be, Frank Be, James Bi, Audrien Bi, Eddie Bl, Lemuel Bl, Joe Bl, Tab Bo, Tom Bo, Dave Bo, John Bo, Earl Bo, Paul Bo, Michel Bo, Jim Bo, Carl Bo, Don Bo, Victor Bo, Bruce Br, Jim Br, Buddy Br, Paul Br, Kirk Br, Al Br, Bill Br, Gene Br, Glenn Br, John Br, Don Br, Vic Br, Hank Br, David Br, Jerry Br, Joe Bu, Bill Bu, Jim Bu, Noel Bu, Harvey Bu, Bob Bu, Bill Bu, Lenny Bu, Mike Ca, Dan Ca, Mike Ca, Michael Ca, Bob Ca, Tony Ca, William Ca, Othello Ca, Harry Ca, Tony Ca, Jim Ca, Winston Ca, Steve Ca, Wally Ca, Clarence Ch, Judd Ch, Perry Ch, Art Ch, Frits Ch, Bob Ch, Art Ch, Glenn Ch, Bob Ch, Bob Cl, Johnny Cl, Willis Cl, John Cl, Lou Cl, Bill Co, Ray Co, Glenn Co, Jerry Co, Marco Co, Don Co, Pete Co, Burton Co, Frank Co, Douglas Cr, Roy Cr, Guy Cr, Bill Cr, Ted Cr, Phil Cu, Norbert Cz, Bob Da, Joe Da, John Da, Jim Da, Terry Da, Merle De, Charles Da, Ray Da, Jack De, Larry De, Frank De, Art De, Jerry De, Russ

De, Frank Di, Bill di, Jerry di, Sid Di, Salvator di, Jack Do, Matthew Do, Alfred Do, John Du, Michael Du, Jack Dy, Ken Dy, Ralph Ea, Buck Ed, Tommy Ed, John Eh, Ray Ei, Harry El, Wayne El, John El, Allan El, John En, Bob En, Roy Er, Jack Fa, Joe Fa, Hugh Fe, Ken Fe, Hays Fe, Jimmy Fe, Jim Fe, Cal Fe, Joe Fi, Jim Fi, Roy Fi, Lee Fl, Walt Fl, Benny Fl, Juan Fl, Wesley Fl, Joe Fo, John Fo, Ed Fr, Claude Fr, Paul Fr, Leroy Fr, Joseph Fu, Buzz Ga, Wally Ga, Jimmy Ga, Jonathan Ga, Raymond Ga, Lee Ge, Leroy Ge, Ted Ge, Clifford Gi, Ray Gi, Jon Gi, Gus Gi, Barry Go, Mel Go, Joe Go, Gene Go, Jimmy Go, Peter Go, Dick Go, Jack Go, Bill Gr, Guy Gr, Bill Gr, John Gr, Georges Gr, Rudi Gr, Herbert Gr, Harold Gr, Jacques Gu, Rudolfo Gu, Earl Gu, Roland Gu, Joseph Ha, Jack Ha, Ron Ha, Robert Ha, Bill Ha, John Ha, John Ha, Leland Ha, Bob Ha, Mel Ha, Fleming Ha, Sam Ha, Monroe He, Morry He, Paul He, Ed He, Stan He, Clark He, Bill He, Wally He, Jack Hi, Ken Hi, Red Ho, Fred Ho, Ben Ho, Triville Ho, Daniel Ho, Harry Ho, Adam Ho, Jimmy Hr, Art Hu, Bob Hu, Jeff Hu, Richard Hu, Herb Hu, Dave Hy, Cliff In, Don Ir, Dick Ir, Al Iv, Evert Ja, Red Ja, Roger Ja, Bud Ja, Jack Ja, Hill Ja, Howard Je, Philippe Jo, John Mc, Dick Jo, Bob Jo, Laurence Jo, Salvador Ju, Jacob Ka, Art Ka, Jim Ka, Paul Ka, Bernie Ka, Wally Ka, John Ka, Neil Ka, Bob Ke, Jim Ki, Don Ki, Larry Ki, Dick Ki, Kenny Ki, Ralph Ki, Neil Kl, Robert Kl, Dick Kn, Allan Kn, Bob Ko, Foy Ko, John Ko, Ken Ko, Adam Kr, Frederick Kr, Theodore Kr, Ejnar Kr, Bob Kr, Carl Ku, Ted Ku, Gilbert La, Marcel La, Jimmy La, John La, Ralph La, Casimir La, Pete La, Bob Le, John Le, Daniel Le, Serge Le, Bob Le, Charles Le, Eugene Le, Quigley Le, Paul Li, Tony Li, Chester Li, Art Li, Jim Li, Julius Lo, Russ Lo, Ted Lo, Gene Lo, Ervin Lu, Ed Lu, Jack McC, John McC, Max McC, Richard McC, Hal McC, Ken McC, Bill McD, Bob McD, Bill McG, Charles McG, Brian McG, Bob McG, Bob McH, Joe McI, Doug McN, Martin McN, Gene Ma, Phil Ma, Thomas Ma, Heinz Ma, Dean Ma, Jimmy Ma, Don Ma, Carlo Ma, Bob Ma, Jack Ma, Harold Ma, Wally Ma, Sylvester Ma, Syl Me, Reinhardt Ma, Frank Ma, Mike Ma, Johnny Me, Miguel Me, Guy deM, Bill Me, Phil Me, Jerry Mi, Johnny Mi, Mike Mi, Bob Mi, Allan Mi, Frank Mi, Mel Mi, Dick Mi, Daniel Mo, Eddie Mo, Bill Mo, Lloyd Mo, Warren Mo, Bill Mo, Charles Mo, Henri Mo, Dick Mu, Jim Mu, Jack Mu, Pete Mu, Benjamin Mu, Vincent Na, Fernand Na, Bill

Na, Lou Ne, Bryan No, Ray No, John No, Horace Nu, Charles Ny, Louis Oc, Joe Od, Doc Ok, Dan O'L, Pete Ol, James O'N, Tim Or, Noel Or, Patrick Os, Al Os, Russ Ot, Wesley Ow, Jimmy Pa, Donald Pa, George Pa, Pasquale Ro, Jim Pa, Bill Pa, Earl Pa, Karl Pa, Johnny Pa, Marty Pa, Browne Pa, Al Pe, Joe Pe, Lyndon Pe, Edgar Pe, William Pe, Pete Pe, Rogert Pe, Karl Pf, Bob Ph, Wally Ph, Herb Pi, Daniel Pi, Innocencio Pi, Argel Pi, Gordon Pi, Art Po, Robert Po, Kirby Po, Bob Pr, George Pr, Bob Pr, Leo Pr, James Pu, Philip Qu, Juan Ra, Jean Ra, Luis Ra, Jimmy Ra, Georges Ra, Clyde Ra, Charles Re, Bob Re, Don Re, Frank Re, Jean Re, Steve Re, Charles Re, Eugene Re, Olin Re, Tony Ri, Pablo Ri, Vic Ri, Robert von Ri, Hal Ri, Bob Ri, Larry Ro, Pat Ro, Phil Ro, Roy Ro, Bill Ro, Francisco Ro, Joe Ro, Charlie Ro, Larry Ro, Bob Ro, Rocky Ro, Don Ro, Don Roz, Walter Ro, Arthur Ro, Gene Ru, Lupe Ru, Dean Ru, Charlie Ru, Clifford Ru, Willard Ru, Bob Ry, Bernard Sa, Tommy Sa, Enrique Sa, Don Sa, Jose Sa, Bob Sa, Roberto Sc, Bill Sc, Bob Sc, Harry Sc, Willard Sc, Ken Sc, Billy Se, John Se, Charles Se, Fred Se, Jim Se, Ron Se, Dave Se, Clarence Se, Everett Se, Jack Se, Bill Sh, Bud Sh, Hank Sh, Charles Sh, Jack Sh, Joe Sh, Danny Sh, Denny Sh, Bill Si, Gene Si, Art Si, Leo Si, Erik Sk, Eddie Sl, Ed Sm, Alexander Sm, Leon Sm, Vern Sm, Len Sm, Gerhardt Sn, David Sn, Carlo So, Marc So, Eddie Sp, Chuck St, Clarence St, Bob St, John St, Steve St, Bob St, Hal St, Joe St, Sam St, Harry St, Thomas St, Eugene St, Bob St, Jim St, George St, Tom Su, Gene Su, Ron Sum, Heinrich Su, George Sw, Ike Sy, Cranford Sy, Ed Sy, Arthur Ta, Ed Ta, Jim Ta, Al Ta, David Ta, James Ta, Carl Te, Ruffian Te, Thad Te, John Th, Tommy Th, Paul Th, Edward Th, Lou To, John To, Al To, Don To, Bill Tr, Phil Tr, Louis Tr, Jean Ts, Frank Tu, John Tu, Jerry Tw, Hans Ul, Nick Um, Bart Up, Steve Va, Frank Va, Mark Va, Gene Va, John Va, Eric Vi, Pietr Vo, Bill Vo, Henry Wa, William Wa, George Wa, Jack Wa, Dave Wa, Danny Wa, Harlan Wa, Charles Wa, Paul Wa, Sherman Wa, Buzz Wa, Marvin We, Robert We, Bill Wh, Douglas Wh, Paul Wh, Thornton Wi, George Wi, Alex Wi, Marshall Wi, Robert Wi, Roy Wi, George Wi, Bill Wi, Bob Wi, Clark Wi, Dwight Wi, Howard Wi, Alex Wo, Ernest Wo, Dick Wy, John Wy, Ernest Ya, Jim Yo, Lucien Yu, Teddy Ze, Mohammed Ze, Alvin Zo, Tony Zo, Jimmy Zu.

Index

RECLAIMING
LITERATURE

RECLAIMING LITERATURE

A Teacher's Dilemma

WILLIAM A. GLASSER

Westport, Connecticut
London

Library of Congress Cataloging-in-Publication Data

Glasser, William.
Reclaiming literature : a teacher's dilemma / William A. Glasser.
p.   cm.
Includes bibliographical references and index.
ISBN 0–275–94959–1 (alk. paper)
1. Literature—Study and teaching (Higher)—United States.
2. Criticism. I. Title.
PN70.G53 1994
807′ .1′ 173—dc20   94–17005

British Library Cataloguing in Publication Data is available.

Library of Congress Catalog Card Number: 94–17005
ISBN: 0–275–94959–1

First published in 1994

Praeger Publishers, 88 Post Road West, Westport, CT 06881
An imprint of Greenwood Publishing Group, Inc.

Printed in the United States of America

∞™

The paper used in this book complies with the
Permanent Paper Standard issued by the National
Information Standards Organization (Z39.48–1984).

10 9 8 7 6 5 4 3 2 1

Copyright Acknowledgments

The author and publisher gratefully acknowledge permission to use the following materials that were previously published by the author.

"Moby Dick." First published in the *Sewanee Review*, vol. 77, no. 3, Summer 1969. Reprinted with permission of the editor.

"A Farewell to Arms." First published in the *Sewanee Review*, vol. 74, no. 2, Spring 1966. Reprinted with permission of the editor. Also published in *Explicator*, vol. XX, no. 2, p. 18, October 1961. Reprinted with permission of the Helen Dwight Reid Educational Foundation. Published by Heidref Publications, 1319 18th Street, N.W., Washington, D.C. 20036-1802. Copyright 1961.

"The Catcher in the Rye." First published in *Michigan Quarterly Review*, Fall 1976.

The author also wishes to thank Susan Lamontagne for her indefatigable help in preparing the manuscript.

To Laura

Contents

Introduction

Teachers of literature face an intensifying need that arises every time they stand before a class, trying to explain away what appears to be a major flaw or confusion in a classic literary work. When we turn for help to hosts of literary critics who have written about the work, we too often discover a wilderness of incongruous and conflicting readings. Attempting to find our way through the wilderness, we are confronted by entrenched camps of literary theorists defending increasingly abstruse positions, including the ultimate claim that there is no valid reading for any literary work.

Teachers are now challenged to reclaim each literary work from the current profusion, and accompanying confusion, of the critical camps surrounding it. The central issue becomes one of focusing again on the author's primary accomplishment, and not the critics' secondary concerns. Each major literary work offers a specifically crafted experience of great value, one that we can clarify and share with our students to extend and enrich their lives. Therein lie the excitement and rewards of teaching.

RECLAIMING
LITERATURE

---——— 1 ——————

The Author's Viewpoint

How do we, as teachers, know when we have grasped a novel
adequately enough to teach it? Consider these classic American
novels: *Moby-Dick*, *The Portrait of a Lady*, *Adventures of Huckleberry
Finn*, *The Turn of the Screw*, *The Red Badge of Courage*, *A Farewell to
Arms*, and *The Catcher in the Rye*. Each of these novels, from the time
of its publication, has brought forth from its many readers a multitude of disparate and contradictory responses, not simply to
different aspects of the novel, but to the most basic experience it
conveys. Critical attempts to clarify each work, to define its central
accomplishment, have resulted in an overwhelming accumulation
of disagreements. And within that flood of published commentar-
ies, there flows a strong undercurrent, not against the contradic-
tions of the critics, but against each of the novels as a defective work
to be held responsible for eliciting such confusion.

   The confusion is reflected, indeed compounded, by the hosts of
critical camps that have arisen around literary works. We have
reached a point in literary criticism where the text of a novel can no
longer be viewed as autonomous. Each novel is now placed within
such critical frameworks as historicism, structuralism, Marxism,
feminism, psychoanalysis, semiotics, deconstruction, and a variety
of other seriously delineated perspectives, including the "neo"s and
"post"s added to many of the above labels. Considering these

multitudes and their prolific outpourings, growing numbers of teachers have been tempted to share the conclusion reached by one of the leaders of deconstruction, Paul de Man: "There are no such things as valid texts. There should be no fundamentalists in criticism. . . . Neither is there a valid reading. There is no final authority."[1]

The most recent of our seven classic works appeared in 1951, the oldest in 1851. What is there about the nature of each that has evoked such critical discord over so many years? And how do we, as teachers, cut through this discord to reclaim the literary work, to grasp each of these elusive novels firmly and confidently enough to teach it to others?

Certainly, when we come to any of them, we anticipate finding that foundation upon which E. M. Forster, in *Aspects of the Novel*, regrets all novels are built: a story.[2] One thing happens, and then another, and then another. And if anyone were to ask us what the novel was about, we would most probably tell him, in a matter of minutes, the story line, that sequence of events running through the novel that keeps us reading in search of some satisfying answer to "And what happened next?"

But in simply recalling the story, we would obviously not yet have grasped the novel. If we were asked, while relating the story, why something took place, then we would move into the realm of those causal relations Mr. Forster labels "plot" and illustrates with "The king died, and then the queen died of grief."[3] So we might listen closely to Ishmael's or Lieutenant Henry's narration of not only what took place within the world inhabited by each character, but also why it took place. With this approach we might arrive at a consistent perspective toward the causes behind everything occurring in the novel, a much richer response than simply following the story line. And still we would not have grasped the novel. For if we allow our view to be delineated by any character within the work, even the main character, then the novel will ultimately elude us. We will not have gained the most comprehensive viewpoint it offers us, that which encompasses and controls every other perspective established within the novel: the author's viewpoint. I would like to define this term by quoting from M. H. Abrams's Forward to *Literature and Belief*, where he refers to "a neglected topic in recent criticism": "the sense we get, even in the work of writers pursuing a strict policy of authorial noninterference, of a

pervasive ethos, of an intelligence and moral sensibility (Henry James's "quality of mind") which expresses itself less in manifest doctrine than in the silent understructure of suppositions, norms, and beliefs which have controlled the choice, conception, and management of the literary subject."[4]

Perhaps one qualification should be added. When I speak of the "author," I have in mind the individual revealed to us through his novel. If the Hemingway we discover in *A Farewell to Arms* is not in accord with the Hemingway known personally by others, we must not be too troubled. As Wayne Booth so aptly stresses in *The Rhetoric of Fiction*, "A great work establishes the sincerity of its implied author, regardless of how grossly the man who created that author may belie in his *other* forms of conduct the values embodied in his work. For all we know, the only sincere moments of his life may have been lived as he wrote his novel."[5]

Although point of view has long been a subject of central concern in modern criticism, greater emphasis needs to be placed on distinguishing the author's viewpoint as established through his craft. If we wish to perceive the nature of a fictional world, we must not simply listen to the voices of its inhabitants. We must give our closest attention to its creator, whose vision is always transcendent. The vast front of the house of fiction, as Henry James tells us, is pierced with as many individually shaped windows as there are authors looking out through them upon the human scene. We may enter the house, but we can never, as readers, look directly out for ourselves. We may sit in the room and listen to the figure at the window telling us what he sees. If we listen closely, and if his account is vivid enough, we may even end our stay with the sense of having crossed the room to stand beside him and share his vision. But at that moment, we will have lost sight of reality. And the author, who has paradoxically striven to achieve that very end, will have lost his control over us as readers.

The more successful the novelist is as craftsman in creating his illusion that we are looking directly at the world of the novel, the more assuredly does he lose control over our responses, encouraging us to believe that he has positioned us to look for ourselves and so to shape our perceptions according to our own natures and sensibilities.

However, the viewpoint we gain is, after all, second-hand. Everything comes to us through another pair of eyes. And so we must heed James's cautioning words that our visit will lead to nothing if we do not direct our attention to our host: "The spreading-field, the human scene, is the 'choice of subject'; the pierced aperture, either broad or balconied or slitlike and low-browed, is the 'literary form'; but they are, singly or together, as nothing without the posted presence of the watcher—without, in other words, the consciousness of the artist."[6] To get hold of a novel adequately, then, we must grasp it as the author has done, no more and no less.

But is that possible? Allan Tate, in "Techniques of Fiction," dooms us to failure: "The novelist keeps before him constantly the structure and substance of his fiction as a whole, to a degree to which the critic can never apprehend it."[7] Indeed, if we turn to the beginning of Percy Lubbock's famous study in *The Craft of Fiction*, we find our doom being tolled in deeper tones: "To grasp the shadowy and phantasmal form of a book, to hold it fast, to turn it over and survey it at leisure—that is the effort of a critic of books, and it is perpetually defeated. Nothing, no power, will keep a book steady and motionless before us, so that we may have time to examine its shape and design."[8]

Faced with this perplexity, advocates of the New Criticism nevertheless remained deeply committed to establishing the literary work as having an existence and an authority separate from the reader. The New Critical approach was firmly based on the belief that, however wide or variable the range of enriching responses elicited by each work, a central, definable experience had been created by the author within the work, an experience that could essentially be recreated within the mind of any adequately educated, responsive reader.

But such proved not to be the case in practice, for generations of critical readers have persisted in offering us their disparate responses to many of our best literary works. All too often critics have arrived at completely contradictory readings based on supposedly irrefutable evidence cited from the very same text.

Literary theorists, confronted with such glaring inconsistencies, have responded by shifting attention away from the text and focusing instead on readers and the act of reading. Jonathan Culler

examines this shift in his work *On Deconstruction: Theory and Criticism After Structuralism*: "One reason for interest in readers and reading is the orientation encouraged by structuralism and semiotics. The attempt to describe structures and codes responsible for the production of meaning focuses attention on the reading process and its conditions of possibility."[9] Culler explores Roland Barthes's belief "that the text is not a line of words releasing a single 'theological' meaning (the 'message' of an Author-God) but a multi-dimensional space in which a variety of writings, none of them original, blend and clash." But all meaning is not lost in the process, for, as Barthes adds, "there is one place where this multiplicity is focused and that place is the reader, not, as was hitherto said, the author. . . . A text's unity lies not in its origin but in its destination."[10] Barthes's objective is "to make the reader no longer the consumer but the producer of the text."[11] By doing so, Barthes views disparate critical readings of the same text not as a problem, but as a normal and acceptable outcome of the reading process. Culler adds a perceptive thought:

This has implications even for critics who reject notions of readers constructing texts, for emphasis on the variability of reading and its dependence on conventional procedures makes it easier to raise political and ideological issues. If the reader always rewrites the text and if the attempt to reconstruct an author's intentions is only a particular, highly restricted case of rewriting, then a Marxist reading, for example, is not an illegitimate distortion, but one species of production.[12]

However, as multiple readers of the same text continued to elicit varying degrees of critical discord, further attempts were made to impose some workable consistency on the unfettered responses of readers. Structuralist critics, seeking some authoritative mode of control, undertook a pervasive attempt to define and employ those underlying "structures" by means of which we elicit meaning from language. But critical readers, taking this approach, discovered that they held, not a clarifying lens, but a kaleidoscope. As Christopher Norris comments in *Deconstruction: Theory and Practice*, "Far from providing a 'window' on reality or (to vary the metaphor) a faithfully reflecting mirror, language brings along with it a whole intricate network of established significations."[13] Thus, Norris states, since "*all* forms of writing run up against perplexities of meaning

and intent. . . . the deconstructive reading of 'literary' texts" is based on the premise that "There is no longer the sense of a primal authority attaching to the literary work."[14]

The ultimate doomsayers are thus the more recent critical camp of deconstructionists. Paul de Man has asserted unequivocally that "commentary in all its forms," including literary criticism, "is illusory at all time" and that "patterns of totalization," which we must assume would include any clarification of the author's crafted accomplishment, are always open to "demolition."[15] Or as another critic has described Jacques Derrida's deconstructed philosophy: "Derrida seems to believe that . . . all that remains is the ultimately meaningless play of words which refer not in any way to 'reality' but only to more and more other words, in an endless drift, deferral, or dissemination of undecidable meaning (*différance*), words without end, an abyssmal labyrinth in which we are forever condemned to wander aimlessly about."[16]

However, the variability of language is not the central issue in responding to a literary text, as anyone who has ever worked a crossword puzzle knows. The word *sound* could mean "an auditory effect" or "free from injury" or "a narrow passage of water." The words *carry on* could mean "to conduct" or "to persevere" or "to behave in an agitated manner." Faced with these variable definitions, would the deconstructionist conclude that the "pattern of totalization," the crossword puzzle, was open to "demolition," that there is "no final authority"? Deconstructionists would have us shift the focus of our reading of a literary text to the multiple significations of words that can be elicited by any educated reader, losing sight of the author's crafting of his materials to control that multiplicity through the selection and arrangement, not simply of definitions or significations, but of shaped experiences of a fictional world and its inhabitants conveyed to, and recreated within, the reader's imagination. Writers have always faced the challenge of controlling their readers' responses, and they succeed or fail by how effectively they control the crafting of their materials. It is my sincere hope that all readers will basically apprehend my present book— and do so more readily than I did. I believe that every novelist shares this hope about his own work, and that if we visited him during the throes of his creation, we would find him undergoing his own struggle to grasp his materials and shape them into a basic, present-

able form. In "The Philosophy of Composition," Edgar Allan Poe, a meticulous craftsman, stresses this point dramatically:

Most writers . . . would positively shudder at letting the public take a peep behind the scenes, at the elaborate and vacillating crudities of thought—at the true purposes seized only at the last moment—at the innumerable glimpses of idea that arrived not at the maturity of full view—at the fully matured fancies discarded in despair as unmanagable—at the cautious selections and rejections—at the painful erasures and interpolations—in a word, at the wheels and pinions—the tackle for scene-shifting—the step-ladders and demon-traps—the cock's feathers, the red paint and the black patches, which, in ninety-nine cases out of the hundred, constitute the properties of the literary *histrio*.[17]

We need only read about the working habits of writers as different as Henry James and Mark Twain to recognize the common goal that novelists strive for: a form for their materials that is *not* phantasmal and shadowy, a form that establishes as the "final authority" each author and his crafted viewpoint. And we may be pleased to discover that their extensive labors, certainly as revealed in our seven novels, are directed by each author toward making "the substance and structure of his fiction as a whole" more readily accessible to us than it was to him. Having confronted the infinite possibilities of a blank page, each novelist offers us his final choices, and we are guided every step of our way by selections and arrangements already made.

Neither authors nor readers are able to hold every word of a novel in mind. Nor do authors expect to control completely every localized response each reader might make as he proceeds through the author's work. But no one ever seriously intended novels to be conceived in this manner. Each of the novelists included here does not give us his work as an object to be held up statically to view, or as a text that by its very nature will elicit contradictory responses that demolish any possibility of a basic reading. He offers us, instead, the opportunity to undergo an imaginative experience, to recreate a set of happenings that he has selected and arranged according to some particular significance they embody for him. The happenings may be extensive, but he recognizes them as forming the basic experience of his novel, and expects his readers to do so, too. If he succeeds in conveying them to us and leaves us

at the end with a reasonably clear awareness of the significance they held for him, he has fulfilled his role as craftsman. And we, in turn, may feel secure in asserting that we have grasped the novel.

But such does not appear to be the case with our seven novels, where we are left with a mass of divergent and often contradictory readings. Certainly, as noted earlier, the text of a novel may be viewed from many enriching perspectives that can expand our experience of the novel significantly. But every additional perspective built upon a novel must be firmly grounded in a basic reading of the work, as defined by the author's craft, or the additional perspective will be false. This last particular point, which accounts for such an overwhelming amount of wasted labor, will be illustrated later.

Perhaps at this moment, then, we should shrug our shoulders and dismiss the confusion as a technical problem of literary criticism. But what if I come to respect and wish to emulate Ahab or Lieutenant Henry or Isabel Archer, and you turn in disdain from the approaches to life they exemplify? Obviously, the influence a novelist has upon our lives cannot be considered solely in terms of literary technique. As Wayne Booth states in *The Rhetoric of Fiction*, the artist has "a moral obligation, contained as an essential part of his aesthetic obligation to 'write well,' to do all that is possible in any given instance to realize his world as he intends it."[18] The authors of our seven novels certainly attempted to fulfill their obligations to their readers. But the question nevertheless remains, Did they do so successfully?

To arrive at an answer, we must explore the differing perspectives established within each novel. We will discover as we enter these works that each author is primarily concerned with characters who view their world inadequately. They do not, in other words, see the world as the author does. With this thought kept in mind, we must focus in particular on a basic disparity to be found within each of the novels: between the views that the major characters have of the world, which are never completely accurate, and the viewpoint that the author holds, through which we should receive his sense of "things as they really are."

Each author, however, strives to keep his artistic manipulations, and himself as practicing craftsman, hidden from the reader's immediate awareness. He purposefully dims our sight of reality as

he works to enlighten his fictional world. He creates an illusion that we have somehow been positioned as another presence within that world, seeing and listening to the characters of that world for ourselves. And so he inadvertently encourages us to experience his world, and to define its significance, within the limitations of our own sensibilities—and the author's more encompassing awareness is lost beyond the boundaries of our own perceptions.

How can we, as teachers, resolve this dilemma as we stand before our classes? To extend the boundaries of our students' perceptions through classic works of literature we must awaken our students to the author's craft, to the means by which authors shape their materials into significant experiences. If we succeed in doing so, not only will we open to them the exceptional worlds of these particular novels, but we can send them on by themselves with increased capacities to engage other works. The happenings of each novel we are about to examine are radiant with an imbued significance. We must be able to illustrate to our students that, although a multitude of educated readers have responded to each novel with an uncontrolled diversity of readings, there are guideposts pointing the way through that critical confusion, along a pathway cleared by our most accomplished authors practicing the fiction writer's craft.

Author as Narrator

THE PORTRAIT OF A LADY

How can we, as teachers, grasp a novel in which the author, as craftsman, works to keep his artistic manipulations hidden from our eyes? Recognizing that each of our authors has attempted to do so in a different way, we begin with the novel in which the author allows us most clearly to delineate his controlling viewpoint. In *The Portrait of a Lady* Henry James speaks to us and supplies us generally with clarifying comments about the attitudes he holds toward the material he is presenting. There is less chance for us to go astray—so long as we stay in the company of the author, and so long as he continues to assert for our benefit the viewpoint he has taken.

James introduces us to Isabel Archer, an attractive young woman of limited means and background, who is taken to Europe by her aunt, Mrs. Touchett, so that Isabel might experience more of the world. Shortly after her arrival in England, James has Isabel avoid a pursuing American suitor, Caspar Goodwood, and decline a proposal of marriage from Lord Warburton, a friend of the Touchetts, for James is intent upon characterizing Isabel as a young woman who wishes to be free to choose her own direction in life. When Isabel's cousin Ralph secretly convinces his father, the dying Mr. Touchett, to leave half of his fortune to Isabel, she is given the means to maintain her own freedom as she sets out on her explo-

ration of life. Madame Merle, a widowed friend of Mrs. Touchett, connives to bring Isabel together with Gilbert Osmond, a restrictive American dilettante living in Italy. Isabel, ironically, chooses to marry Gilbert Osmond, believing that her freedom will not be impaired. James designs the remainder of the novel to dramatize the problems arising from the marriage and to test whether Isabel, caught up in the increasing complexities of her existence, has the capacity and the resolve to succeed ultimately in controlling her own destiny.

The most controversial point in the novel for critical readers has been the ending: Isabel's final rejection of her ardent suitor, Caspar Goodwood, and her return to her husband in Rome. The significance of these actions has been hotly disputed—primarily because readers are left with the sense that it is up to them to supply that significance. A sampling will illustrate the variety of their critical responses:

Arnold Kettle: It seems to me inescapable that what Isabel finally chooses is something represented by a high cold word like duty or resignation, the duty of an empty vow, the resignation of the defeated. . . .[1]

Marjorie Perloff: Her decision to return to Rome at the end of the novel can only be regarded as an unselfish, generous, and admirable act. . . .[2]

Carl Van Doren: The conclusion, on various grounds, does not satisfy. . . .[3]

Lyall H. Powers: The form of the novel *is* complete and, once identified, familiar and indeed satisfactory.[4]

William Bysshe Stein: From the beginning to the end of the story Isabel does not change. Only her situations change. In this process we are confronted with James' treatment of the stagnant emotions of the Victorian female.[5]

Rebecca West: The conduct invented for Isabel is so inconsistent and so suggestive of the nincompoop, and so clearly proceeding from a brain whose ethical world was but a chaos, that it is a mistake to subject the book to the white light of a second reading.[6]

Throughout his narration, James often intrudes to clarify any comment or event that he feels "demands an explanation." Although he speaks to the reader a good deal just before the final scene, he is much less noticeable in the closing pages. Obviously,

he wishes to avoid ending his novel with an explanation. He chooses, instead, to close with a scene of dramatic intensity, creating the sense that Isabel and Caspar are there immediately before us, that we are viewing their actions for ourselves, a direct impression of life in the world of the novel. But he does so at an expense. The success of his dramatic method depends on our losing sight of *our* reality. We must forget that we are still seated inside the house of fiction. We must lose sight of James at the window. And so, at the very last moment, as we try to draw our own conclusions from our seemingly direct observations, the novel slips from our grasp.

The only way we can possibly "see" the ending is by means of the author's craft. We must pay more attention to how James gathers together specific materials from throughout the work, and how he deftly and dramatically manipulates them in the closing moments of the novel. Only then will we be prepared to receive the final gift he offers us: *his* conception of the ending.

An axiom of literary criticism is that the author of a fictional work is never to be identified with the narrator. However, as noted earlier, since we consider the author to be the individual who is revealed to us through his work, we can make the identification in this case—in spite of the fact that James, as narrator, assumes a pose, a bit of a mask. For James does not assume the mask to conceal his identity. The voice speaking to us from behind the mask belongs to the author, as do the thoughts and feelings expressed by that voice throughout the entire work.

Then why the mask? We must turn to James's persona for the answer. James does not appear in his work as an author of fiction writing a novel about Isabel Archer. He speaks to us, instead, as "Our heroine's biographer," as though Isabel Archer had actually existed. James, as "her historian," offers us, not a product of his own imagination, but a history of her life substantiated by evidence seemingly uncovered in the real world. His evidence ranges from individually reproduced documents, such as Isabel's letter to Lord Warburton, declining his offer of marriage—"the letter belongs to our history," James asserts, and then cites it—to some larger, vaguer source of information: he states, for instance, after a particularly hurtful remark made by Isabel to Caspar Goodwood, that "it is not on record that her motive for discharging such a shaft had been the

clearest," as though her motives generally are "on record" somewhere and apparently at his disposal.

As a "historian," James employs an audacious and effective technique to give himself authority: he implicitly asks us to consider, throughout his narration, the accuracy of his interpretive comments in relation to the "factual" material he is presenting. For example, after reporting verbatim certain remarks that Gilbert Osmond makes to Caspar Goodwood, James states, "I have said that Osmond was in good humour, and these remarks will give ample evidence of the fact." By establishing this distinction between "things as he says they are" and "things as they really are," James brings off a masterful stroke: all of the material comprising the "history," exclusive of his interpretive remarks, takes on the objective appearance of reality; and since his remarks are constantly in accord with this reality, his own narration takes on the semblance of truth.

This presence of a reality existing within the novel apart from the narrator is fashioned by James most often out of seemingly direct impressions of life. In this sense, James is not a historian, for his concern is not with the past. Although he may shift time and place, being as selective as he wishes, he generally insists that when he does stop to look, what he finds before him is an event occurring in the immediate present, an event that he and the reader may directly view, but only as bystanders who have paused for a moment, unseen, at a niche in time along the span of Isabel Archer's life. For example, when Caspar Goodwood visits Isabel for the first time after her engagement, James says, after Caspar enters the room, "Whether his sense of maturity had kept pace with Isabel's we shall perhaps presently ascertain," for he would have us believe that we are going to witness for ourselves a scene that is about to begin. Having listened earlier to a conversation between Isabel and Gilbert Osmond, we find James remarking, "While this sufficiently intimate colloquy (prolonged for some time after we cease to follow it) went forward . . . ," for all such scenes, we are meant to assume, are composed of people living out their own lives, totally regardless of the narrator, who stops at points to comment on them to the reader he is leading along.

A more accurate label for the persona James takes on in this novel would be *cicerone*, for his role seems to be that of guiding us

to interesting places along the span of Isabel's existence. Not only does he supply us with enlightening information before we arrive at each place, as a competent cicerone might, but he also leads us to a vantage point from which we may gain a clear view, and then proceeds to point out things of particular significance, lest we overlook them. As a result, we find our cicerone to be a knowledgeable and perceptive man whose word we can trust, a man who offers us more exact perceptions than are attained by the inhabitants of the world in the novel, including the central inhabitant, Isabel Archer. James notes for us time and again the limitations of Isabel's awareness, and always proceeds to take us beyond them: "the reader," he asserts, "has a right to a nearer and a clearer view." For example, when we learn that Isabel, in her thoughts of poor, sick Ralph, "had been constantly wondering what fine principle was keeping him alive," James turns directly to us with the answer: "The reader already knows more about him than Isabel was ever to know, and the reader may therefore be given the key to the mystery."

Thus, we discover that James assumes a mask, not, as mentioned earlier, to hide his own thoughts and feelings, but to create an impression of authority for himself and of dramatic immediacy for his presentation. We listen to James as someone wishing to insure our understanding of the people and events, the "real" world, that he makes us feel we are viewing directly for ourselves. James, the master technician, knew that the strength of his work was not, as he might put it, in what he would tell his readers, but in what he would show them.

Near the opening of the novel, after Isabel arrives in England, James sums up for us the characteristics of her nature. Beginning with her more youthful traits, "her meagre knowledge, her inflated ideals," James carefully continues on to additional qualities, the variety of which suggests that her nature has a wide range of possible directions in which to develop: "her confidence at once innocent and dogmatic, her temper at once exacting and indulgent, her mixture of curiosity and fastidiousness, of vivacity and indifference." He concludes his summary by calling attention to a "combination" of incongruous states of being within her nature, either of which could become predominant, depending on the ultimate course she takes in developing her life: "her combination

of the delicate, desultory, flame-like spirit and the eager and personal creature of conditions." James persistently establishes throughout the novel that the strongest motivating force within Isabel's nature is her desire to keep her "flame-like spirit" predominant, to avoid becoming a "creature of conditions." The importance of this distinction has been overlooked within the abundance of critical writings questioning the unity of the novel; since this distinction is essential to our comprehension of the viewpoint James takes toward Isabel, it must be further clarified.

After Isabel rejects Lord Warburton's proposal of marriage, James poses the following question: "What view of life, what design upon fate, what conception of happiness, had she that pretended to be larger than these large, these fabulous occasions?" The answer that he fashions for Isabel leads to the central conflict of her life. Isabel's "view of life," according to James, is precisely that she believes herself capable of having a "design upon fate." James also has Ralph stress this point early in the novel: "Most women did with themselves nothing at all; they waited, in attitudes more or less gracefully passive, for a man to come that way and furnish them with a destiny. Isabel's originality was that she gave one an impression of having intentions of her own." The central conflict of the novel, which occurs within Isabel's maturing nature, is one of her determining whether or not she is indeed capable of furnishing herself with a destiny. She declares her particular "design upon fate" when, with an ingenuous faith in her untested capabilities, she states, "I wish to choose my fate. . . ." If, by the end of the novel, she does succeed in freely choosing the course of her life, then her bright and expansive "flame-like spirit" will have prevailed; if, however, her course is imposed upon her by external circumstances, then her existence must finally be viewed as predominantly that of a limited "creature of conditions."

Isabel begins the fulfillment of her intentions by setting out on a "free exploration of life," an exploration that is developed by James into the extended metaphor of a sea voyage, where the sea typifies the "conditions" that one encounters in the world, "the usual chances and dangers." If Isabel, as a "vessel" upon this sea, allows herself to "drift," or to "float with the current," or to "sink," or finally to "drown," then the circumstantial forces of the world will have determined the course of her life, and she will have

become a "creature of conditions." Contrarily, if she keeps "her hand . . . on the tiller," or continues "going before the breeze," or does not "glide into port," or into a "quiet harbor," then she can still be considered as a free spirit maintaining her own direction.

James fashions a second metaphor, that of brightness and darkness, to work in conjunction with the metaphor of the sea voyage. Isabel starts out "sailing in the bright light" with the youthful faith that she will discover only "enlightening" conditions that will not impose any limitations on her. She enters the world of the novel with the firm belief that she will find it a suitable place for her "flame-like spirit": as James remarks, "She had a fixed determination to regard the world as a place of brightness, of free expansion, of irresistible action." And she is desirous of remaining free to journey extensively, for she wishes in her explorations to gain "a large acquaintance with human life" and not to feel any sense of "exclusion." Whatever darkness she encounters, on the other hand, will be suggestive of restrictive conditions, which, at the beginning of her voyage, she too confidently believes she is more than capable of avoiding: "The only thing," she thinks, "is to see our steps as we take them—to understand them as we go. That, no doubt, I shall always do."

At the opening of the work, Isabel's most restrictive condition is a lack of substantial wealth, a strong circumstantial force that is offset by Ralph. His motive for wanting to free Isabel from this restriction by making her rich is reasonably clear. Although he is referred to as "an apostle of freedom," his own existence must nevertheless finally, and sadly, be viewed as that of a "creature of conditions"; as James characterizes him, "He was a bright, free, generous spirit, he had all the illumination of wisdom and none of its pedantry, and yet he was distressfully dying." Ralph's poor health has deprived him of the chance of exploring life, of learning the extent to which an unhindered human spirit can freely move among the conditions of this world. He arranges for Isabel's inheritance to give her the opportunity that has been denied him, for he believes that she lacks only wealth to fulfill her capabilities for determining the course of her own life. In return, he wishes only for the pleasure of watching her exist as freely as he himself would do, if his life were not so distressfully circumscribed by his physical condition. Continuing the metaphor of the sea voyage, James has

Ralph look upon the wealth that he wants his father to leave Isabel as a means of giving her the individual force that she, as a "vessel," will need to move herself through a sea of circumstantial forces. As Ralph tells his father, "I should like to put a little wind in her sails."

Isabel's subsequent decision to steer her course, with her new wealth, into a marriage with Gilbert Osmond can be better understood if we first realize why she earlier steered clear of the two other men who offered proposals of marriage to her. Isabel admits to herself that "her eager acceptance of her aunt's invitation" to accompany her to Europe "had come to her at an hour when she expected from day to day to see Mr. Goodwood and when she was glad to have an answer ready for something she was sure he would say to her." Isabel looks upon Caspar Goodwood as a stubborn threat to her intention of maintaining her personal independence, for "it was part of the influence he had upon her that he seemed to deprive her of the sense of freedom." He is capable of thus influencing her because of the forcefulness of his own nature: "Caspar Goodwood expressed for her an energy—and she had already felt it as a power—that was of his very nature." The peculiar aspect of his "energy" that most threatens Isabel's free spirit, and so causes her to evade him as she begins her voyage out into life, is, as James states, that "he could make people work his will." (James also adds a bit of spice to the metaphor of the sea voyage by mentioning of Caspar that "at Harvard College . . . he had gained renown as . . . an oarsman"; and one might be further enticed to see in his name a subtly amusing suggestion that with a "spar" of "good wood," he would indeed make a capable sailing ship.) Their final meeting before her marriage illustrates the forceful energy of his personality: he metaphorically collides with her, as James informs us, in an attempt to turn her from her chosen direction: "He had left her that morning with a sense of the most superfluous of shocks: it was like a collision between vessels in broad daylight. There had been no mist, no hidden current to excuse it, and she herself had only wished to steer wide. He had bumped against her prow, however, while her hand was on the tiller, and . . . had given the lighter vessel a strain which still occasionally betrayed itself in a faint creaking."

The second man, Lord Warburton, represents a more insidious form of suppression, which Isabel sees manifested in the life of Lord Warburton's sister, Miss Molyneux: "Isabel looked into her

quiet eyes a moment, and for that moment seemed to see in their grey depths the reflexion of everything she had rejected in rejecting Lord Warburton—the peace, the kindness, the honour, the possessions, a deep security and a great exclusion." Ralph also sees the shortcomings of a domestic life with Lord Warburton, as he candidly reveals to Isabel in his estimate of the marriage: "relatively speaking it would be a little prosaic. It would be definitely marked out in advance; it would be wanting in the unexpected." Isabel's view is clearly the same. Her sense of "a great exclusion" overbalances all of the positive qualities that Lord Warburton offers in marriage specifically because, as she sets out on her "free exploration of life," she wishes to avoid having her voyage circumscribed by any man. And so she chooses to continue on her own way, steadily strengthening her feeling of personal freedom, until, by the middle of the novel, "She had never had a keener sense of freedom, of the absolute boldness and wantonness of liberty. . . . The world lay before her—she could do whatever she chose." With penetrating irony, however, James then has Isabel proceed, at the point when her sense of freedom is strongest, into a marriage with the most restrictive man who appears in the world of the novel.

Isabel marries Gilbert Osmond for various reasons; she admits to liking him "too much," for example, and finds him attractive in appearance. However, her choice of this man after two earlier rejections can be accounted for only by noting how Isabel convinces herself that Gilbert Osmond's peculiar position is one that will accommodate her own design. As the Italianate "mond" in his name suggests, Gilbert Osmond is a man of the world. When Isabel perceives that he is not, however, financially able to live like one, her romantic imagination is aroused. She views him as "a quiet, clever, sensitive, distinguished man" being undeservedly confined to "a lonely, studious life" in Florence because of a lack of wealth. That such an exceptional man should be constrained by this unfortunate "condition," from which she had only recently been freed herself, elicits from her a feeling that neither Caspar Goodwood nor Lord Warburton could ever have called forth. Isabel believes that, with her more than adequate wealth, she is in possession of the force needed to give Gilbert Osmond that which, on the contrary, most women passively receive from a man: a course in life. Thus, she is able to feel that, while remaining in control of her own

destiny, she will, in addition, be furnishing Gilbert Osmond with one. Later in the novel, during her long nighttime meditation before the fireplace, she recalls her reason for taking this momentous step. After reflecting on Gilbert Osmond's apparent qualities—"There had been an indefinable beauty about him—in his situation, in his mind, in his face"—she continues, "She had felt at the same time that he was helpless and ineffectual. . . . He was like a skeptical voyager strolling on the beach while he waited for the tide, looking seaward yet not putting to sea. It was in all this she had found her occasion. She would launch his boat for him; she would be his providence; it would be a good thing to love him." Paradoxically, that very force with which Ralph had covertly supplied her in hopes of giving her greater freedom proves to be the key to her decision to marry Gilbert Osmond. As Isabel realizes immediately after her above thoughts, "But for her money, as she saw today, she would never have done it."

Having made her choice with little awareness of Gilbert Osmond's deficiencies, Isabel subsequently discovers that she has walked into the most restrictive circumstances of her life: "She had taken all the first steps in the purest confidence, and then she had suddenly found the infinite vista of a multiplied life to be a dark, narrow alley with a dead wall at the end." And the cause of her life's being so straightened becomes increasingly and distressfully apparent to her: "It was her deep distrust of her husband—this was what darkened the world. . . . It had come gradually—it was not till the first year of their life together, so admirably intimate at first, had closed that she had taken the alarm. Then the shadows had begun to gather; it was as if Osmond deliberately, almost malignantly, had put the lights out one by one." Instead of having chosen a man who would respect her personal independence, especially after she had supplied him with a fortune more than adequate to widen extensively the possibilities of his own life, Isabel recognizes that she has married someone who "wished her to have no freedom of mind," someone who has developed a hatred for her specifically because her nature remains so free in their relationship: "The real offense, as she ultimately perceived, was her having a mind of her own at all. Her mind was to be his—attached to his own like a small garden-plot to a deer-park." Gilbert Osmond malignantly attempts to subordinate Isabel because her very presence is an irritating

contrast to his own existence, which is, as Isabel learns with grow-ing alarm, essentially that of a "creature of conditions." Life for Gilbert Osmond, Isabel realizes, "was altogether a thing of forms"; the course he steers is determined completely by the "considera-tion" for himself that he, with feigned indifference, studiously attempts to gain from the world. As Ralph also perceptively notes: "under the guise of caring only for intrinsic values Osmond lived exclusively for the world. Far from being its master as he pretended to be, he was its very humble servant, and the degree of its attention was his only measure of success."

Faced with this deep disappointment, Isabel finds herself re-ex-amining the choice she has made. She wonders if she alone were responsible for her decision and recalls "Mrs. Touchett's theory that Madame Merle had made Gilbert Osmond's marriage"; she then berates herself for even considering the possibility of such a "petty revenge" as that of associating Madame Merle with her disappoint-ment: "It was impossible to pretend that she had not acted with her eyes open; if ever a girl was a free agent she had been. A girl in love was doubtless not a free agent; but the sole source of her mistake had been within herself. There had been no plot, no snare; she had looked and considered and chosen. When a woman had made such a mistake, there was only one way to repair it—just immensely (oh, with the highest grandeur!) to accept it."

Henrietta Stackpole had earlier criticized Isabel for having "too many graceful illusions"; "You're not enough in contact with real-ity . . . you think you can lead a romantic life. . . . You think we can escape disagreeable duties by taking romantic views—that's your great illusion, my dear." Isabel's romantic imagination plays a rather obvious role in her assumption of the above attitude: she will accept her mistake "(oh, with the highest grandeur!)." The remain-der of the book is designed by James to bring Isabel "in contact with reality," to undercut completely her romantic illusions, and then to face her with the same decision: whether or not to continue her life with Gilbert Osmond. For the novel to convey a sense of being complete, Isabel cannot assume another romantic attitude that leaves illusions yet to be uncovered. Her decision must establish that she can, and will hereafter, make realistic choices that remain in accordance with the prevailing traits of her own character.

James's challenge, as a craftsman, was to convey the concluding scene of the novel to his readers with dramatic force, as though they were directly perceiving the scene for themselves, without any distracting authorial explanations. It is a gamble that each of our authors takes as craftsman practicing the art of fiction. A dramatic presentation, uncontrolled by explanation, achieves its immediate and forceful impact on the reader at the possible cost of its significance being misunderstood or completely missed.

Briefly, then, we must note the series of revelations that James fashions to dispel Isabel's illusions. She first walks in unexpectedly on Gilbert Osmond and Madame Merle: "Just beyond the threshold of the drawing-room she stopped short, the reason for her doing so being that she had received an impression. . . . What struck Isabel first was that he was sitting while Madame Merle stood....Their relative positions, their absorbed mutual gaze, struck her as something detected." But her impression of there existing between the two a greater familiarity than that of which she was aware lasts "only a moment, like a sudden flicker of light," and so darkness, for the time, remains upon her perception of their relationship.

Isabel attains a deeper awareness of Madame Merle's deceitful role when Madame Merle visits her to ask why Lord Warburton did not follow through with his thoughts of marrying Gilbert Osmond's daughter, Pansy. Isabel is shaken during their conversation when Madame Merle reveals herself as having been insidiously involved in Gilbert Osmond's life. Implying that Isabel was responsible for Lord Warburton's sudden decision to turn away from Pansy, Madame Merle says to her, "If he gave her up to please you . . . you'd perhaps resign yourself to not being pleased—to simply seeing your stepdaughter married. Let him off—let us have him!" Isabel, sensing a "worse horror" than the insolence of these remarks, asks her, "What have you to do with my husband?" Madame Merle avoids answering, but in response to Isabel's next question, she does not refrain from openly claiming credit for having succeeded in being a strong influence on Isabel's life: " 'What have you to do with me?' Isabel went on. Madame Merle slowly got up, stroking her muff, but not removing her eyes from Isabel's face. 'Everything!' she answered."

At this point James further extends the metaphor of the sea voyage. Isabel is now almost overwhelmed as a "vessel" exploring

life by the realization that, in choosing Gilbert Osmond as a husband, she had not been completely free of external forces. She had been, on the contrary, deceitfully manipulated by this woman: " 'Oh, misery!' she murmured at last; and she fell back covering her face with her hands. It had come over her like a high-surging wave that Mrs. Touchett was right. Madame Merle had married her."

When Isabel learns from the Countess Gemini why Madame Merle has betrayed Isabel's friendship, her disillusionment is complete: Madame Merle had earlier been Gilbert Osmond's lover and had borne his child, Isabel's stepdaughter, Pansy. Madame Merle, Isabel realizes, has attempted to use her as a means of satisfying her maternal interest in her illegitimate daughter, and of furthering the life of Gilbert Osmond, although her persisting feelings for him are no longer requited. Thus, the romantic attitude previously held by Isabel toward her husband is shattered, and she is forced to face again, realistically, the decision of whether or not to continue her life with him.

To understand why Isabel finally returns to Gilbert Osmond, we must first differentiate her ultimate course from the variety of courses that others in the novel have chosen. These alternative pathways are illustrated by the lives of the women "reflector" characters that James places around Isabel.

Most obviously in contrast with Isabel's free spirit is Pansy's restricted nature, for Pansy is presented as "an easy victim of fate. She would have no will, no power to resist." Having been raised in circumstances always carefully chosen for her by others, "she was a passive spectator of the operation of her fate." Henrietta Stackpole, on the other hand, appears to Isabel as a woman of strong and free will. While living in Albany, "Isabel always thought of her as a model." But within the European setting Isabel quickly discerns the narrow simplicity of Henrietta's strictly American way of life. Limited by such an exclusively national viewpoint, Henrietta remains incapable of attaining a fuller consciousness of the world.

More pertinent to Isabel's concluding dilemma are the lives of the married women in the novel, who illustrate other pathways taken because of disappointing marriages. Mrs. Touchett stands out as representative of another narrowed existence. Although she does remain faithful to her husband, she nevertheless separates her existence, not only from him, but, as much as she finds possible,

from everyone. "She had her own way of doing all that she did," a way of life that she is able to maintain only by keeping it "unmistakably distinguished from the ways of others." The flaw in this apparent freedom is disclosed, however, when Isabel comes to realize that Mrs. Touchett's life has left her with a sadly limited nature "missing those enrichments of consciousness" experienced only by means of human interaction: "Isabel came at last to have a kind of undemonstrable pity for her; there seemed something so dreary in the condition of a person whose nature had, as it were, so little surface—offered so limited a face to the accretions of human contact." Immediately after Ralph's death, Isabel wonders sadly if Mrs. Touchett were not, finally, in her advanced age, "reaching out for some aftertaste of life, dregs of the banquet; the testimony of pain or the cold recreation of remorse."

The Countess Gemini, on the other hand, instead of remaining faithful to her unsatisfactory husband, consoles herself with a series of lovers. Attempting to lose her disappointment within "the labyrinth of her adventures," the Countess Gemini illustrates a woman who has indeed become a "creature of conditions." In the metaphorical terms established by James within the novel, her reputation is viewed as having been shipwrecked by a sea of circumstantial forces through which she had ineptly moved: James characterizes her as "a lady who had so mismanaged her improprieties that they had ceased to hang together at all . . . and had become the mere floating fragments of a wrecked renown."

Madame Merle's nature closely, and rather surprisingly, resembles Isabel's. Like Isabel, "She had her own ideas" and the individual force to put them into action, for, as James reveals, "her will was mistress of her life." As a "vessel," she has capably managed to keep herself out upon the sea, steering her particular path among the conditions of the world—until the deception that she practices on Isabel proves to be her undoing. Having succeeded thus far in furthering her own designs because of her deceit, Madame Merle is unable to continue on the sea from the moment she realizes that Isabel knows she is the mother of Pansy. Their relationship concludes, and Madame Merle leaves the novel, with her assertion that she will go to America. Her loss of further freedom of movement is described by James in terms of an ocean voyage being rather ignominiously ended: "This discovery (that Isabel knew her secret)

was tremendous. . . . Her only safety was in her not betraying herself. She resisted this, but the startled quality of her voice refused to improve—she couldn't help it—while she heard herself say she hardly knew what. The tide of her confidence ebbed, and she was able only just to glide into port, faintly grazing the bottom."

Each of these women has narrowed her existence because of her incapability, or her willful refusal, to attain the proper balance between her individual life and the lives of other people. Pansy is too self-effacing; Henrietta is too narrowly self-assertive; Mrs. Touchett is too detached; the Countess Gemini is too irresponsible and unconcerned about her reputation; and Madame Merle is too insidiously willful. By placing these "reflector" characters around Isabel, James highlights the originality of her nature. Isabel is apparently the only woman in the novel who learns to view herself as an individual existing within the larger perspective of "the human lot." To illustrate Isabel's view of her place within human-ity, James uses her response to "old Rome":

[I]n a world of ruins the ruin of her happiness seemed a less unnatural catastrophe. She rested her weariness upon things that had crumbled for centuries and yet still were upright; she dropped her secret sadness into the silence of lonely places, where its very modern quality detached itself and grew objective, so that . . . she could almost smile at it and think of its smallness. Small it was, in the large Roman record, and her haunting sense of the continuity of the human lot easily carried her from the less to the greater.

Considering her unhappy marriage from this larger perspec-tive, Isabel frankly admits to herself that the disappointing circum-stances in her relationship with Gilbert Osmond are by no means unusual in human affairs. Persevering in her desire to live up to her own ideals, she further distinguishes herself by recognizing a moral commitment to her husband well above the ordinary level of marital responsibility. Instead of adopting a conventional atti-tude toward her husband's shortcomings, she views his hatred for her as insufficient grounds for "repudiating the most sacred act— the single sacred act—of her life": "She knew of no wrong he had done her; he was not violent, he was not cruel: she simply believed he hated her. That was all she accused him of, and the miserable part of it was precisely that it was not a crime, for against a crime she might have found redress."

Isabel also sees that Osmond's hatred for her can be partially justified; she, too, had played a deceptive role at the beginning of their acquaintance. "Yes, she *had* been hypocritical," she later realizes; "if she had not deceived him in intention she understood how completely she must have done so in fact. She had effaced herself when he first knew her; she had made herself small, pretending there was less of her than there really was." Furthermore, Isabel admits to herself that Gilbert Osmond has not forcefully insisted upon placing limitations on the freedom of her movements: "She could come and go; she had her liberty; her husband was perfectly polite." However, in conflict with this rationally selfless view of their relationship is Isabel's unquenchable desire not to renounce her sense of her own individuality; Isabel remains unable to escape the feeling that "she had thrown away her life" by marrying such a man.

Isabel's trip to England against her husband's wishes offers her the opportunity of not returning to him, a temptation she desperately tries to avoid by keeping herself in a numbing state of indecision. After Ralph's death removes her reason for staying on at Gardencourt, "She lived from day to day, postponing, closing her eyes, trying not to think. She knew she must decide, but she decided nothing." During one of her strolls, "she found herself near a rustic bench, which, a moment after she had looked at it, struck her as an object recognized," an object that recalls for her Lord Warburton's proposal of marriage at the same spot. At that early time in the novel, Isabel, with her romantic illusions, was filled with her sense of personal freedom and her eager determination to sail forth upon a "free exploration of life"; now, however, this same setting heightens the ominous alteration in Isabel's present state of mind: "at this moment, she was the image of a victim of idleness. Her attitude had a singular absence of purpose; her hands, hanging at her sides, lost themselves in the folds of her black dress; her eyes gazed vaguely before her."

James has carefully prepared for the suspense of this moment which occurs just before the conclusion of the novel, by making Isabel more susceptible than ever before to the danger of becoming a "creature of conditions." His metaphor of the sea voyage aids in clarifying her dilemma. As a vessel moving freely among the conditions of this world, Isabel chose Gilbert Osmond as a husband

while he and Madame Merle were deceitfully influencing her toward doing so; before becoming fully aware of their deception, she discovered that she had sailed into the darkness of an unhappy marriage. Therefore, if Isabel now renounces her responsibility for her choice and blames her present position primarily on the machinations of Madame Merle and Gilbert Osmond, she will be admitting that her attempt to furnish herself with a destiny has failed. Furthermore, if Isabel alters, or allows anyone else to alter, her direction at this time, and she veers away from Gilbert Osmond to avoid the dark circumstances she has met subsequent to their marriage, she will additionally have succumbed to being a "creature of conditions" by allowing those circumstances to predominate.

As Isabel sits on the "rustic bench" in a weakened state of mind, she is confronted by Caspar Goodwood, whose imposition at this moment presents the strongest threat to her nature that she has yet encountered. This dramatic confrontation will establish conclusively whether Isabel has the capacity to endure as a free spirit within a world of subordinating conditions. To describe her reaction to Caspar Goodwood, James continues the metaphor of the sea voyage. Isabel is again presented as a vessel free to move in whatever direction she chooses: "The world, in truth, had never seemed so large; it seemed to open out, all round her, to take the form of a mighty sea, where she floated in fathomless waters." However, rather than moving under her own power, Isabel, for the moment, "floated," a vulnerable state to remain in, as she learns when she almost sinks completely under the torrential force of Caspar Goodwood's presence: "She had wanted help, and here was help; it had come in a rushing torrent. . . . she believed just then that to let him take her in his arms would be the next best thing to her dying. This belief, for a moment, was a kind of rapture, in which she felt herself sink and sink." Nevertheless, she does manage to save herself by performing a willful act of resistance to this force as she is sinking into it: "In the movement she seemed to beat with her feet, in order to catch herself, to feel something to rest on." Sensing her resistance, Caspar Goodwood desperately strengthens the force of his influence on her until he evokes "the deepest thing" in Isabel's soul. James established early in the novel, while examining Isabel's nature, that "Deep in her soul—it was the deepest thing there—lay a belief that if a certain light should dawn she

could give herself completely" to the man who could elicit that light. At the very end of the novel, when Caspar Goodwood kisses her, the light appears, with an intensity that again allows him almost to succeed in possessing her: "His kiss was like white lightning, a flash that spread, and spread again, and stayed; and it was extraordinarily as if, while she took it, she felt each thing in his hard manhood that had least pleased her, each aggressive fact of his face, his figure, his presence, justified of its intense identity and made one with this act of possession."

Caspar Goodwood, with "his hard manhood," has attempted throughout the novel to impose upon Isabel a fate that James considered natural to womanhood: every woman is destined, by nature, to "give herself" in love to a man. The intensified force of Caspar Goodwood's passion comes upon Isabel now like "the hot wind of the desert. . . . It wrapped her about; it lifted her off her feet, while the very taste of it, as of something potent, acrid and strange, forced open her set teeth." Only now does Isabel realize "that she had never been loved before," that Caspar Goodwood, who can touch the very depth of her soul, is a man to whom "she could give herself completely"—if only that decision did not signify her being defeated by her present circumstances.

Sensing the extreme danger of allowing herself to succumb to his passion, Isabel compares her plight with that of a shipwrecked person about to drown: "So had she heard of those wrecked and under water following a train of images before they sink." At this precarious moment, however, James presents Isabel as having the capacity to continue resisting until the "white lightning" elicited by Caspar Goodwood has passed: with a remarkable simplicity, James asserts, "But when darkness returned she was free." Contrary to the earlier associations of Isabel's freedom with light, James has fashioned here a dramatically ironic reversal: Isabel can now maintain her freedom only by avoiding the light and remaining in the darkness. Since "the deepest thing" in her soul has been tested by Caspar Goodwood, and since she still does not allow him to impose a new direction upon her life, to supply her, in other words, with another fate, Isabel now demonstrates that she possesses the strength necessary to keep her life free, not only from Caspar Goodwood, but from any external force that would act upon her against her will. Thus, James concludes his novel in part with the

revelation that Isabel will never allow herself to become a "creature of conditions."

The novel becomes complete when Isabel decides, voluntarily, to return to Gilbert Osmond. After having earlier discovered her husband's grave deficiencies, she is able to console herself with the attitude that the error made in choosing him had been entirely hers: "If ever a girl was a free agent she had been. . . . the sole source of her mistake had been within herself." Shortly before she learned of the insidious plotting of Madame Merle and her husband, Isabel reasserted to Henrietta: "I married him before all the world; I was perfectly free; it was impossible to do anything more deliberate." But after Isabel's illusions are dispelled, and she realizes that instead of being "perfectly free," she had reached her decision while being deceitfully influenced, Isabel faces the possibility of moving to another extreme attitude: that of renouncing entirely her responsibility for the part she played in her choice of a husband. If Isabel considers her present position in life as having been imposed upon her by Madame Merle and Gilbert Osmond, then they must certainly be credited with having subordinated her nature. The disclosure of their machinations temporarily suspends Isabel's volition. She remains in a dangerously lethargic state of mind until Caspar Goodwood reawakens her determination. After she has successfully resisted Caspar Goodwood's appeal, her final decision to return to Rome stresses her refusal to deny her responsibility to her husband. By no means, however, does she go back to him to perform an onerous duty to a conventional form. Her return must be viewed as an intentional act of self-consideration. She had earlier told Henrietta that she could not leave her husband because, as she said, "I can't change that way." Neither, she insisted, could she openly announce her dissatisfaction with him: "Henrietta gave a laugh. 'Don't you think you're rather too considerate?' 'It's not of him that I'm considerate—it's of myself!' Isabel answered." Isabel makes her final decision, not with a sense of suppressing her individuality, but in accordance with the dictates of her own nature, which she admirably persists in following even after they have led her into adversity. Her return is motivated by the strongest desire of her nature: that of not allowing her spirit to be subordinated by the conditions she encounters in this world. Isabel realizes that by freely choosing to go back to her husband, she will be

reestablishing the predominance of her own will over those dark circumstances that have developed in her life with him.

"She had not known where to turn; but she knew now. There was a very straight path." Rather than entering a "labyrinth of . . . adventures," or of turning to someone else like Caspar Goodwood, or of veering away from her husband to live by herself, Isabel goes directly back to Rome. She views the path she takes as "very straight" because it does not alter its direction, but continues on through the unfortunate circumstances of her married life. This particular pathway is the only one that offers Isabel the opportunity to resolve the central conflict of her life. By not repudiating her responsibility for having chosen her husband, and by willfully continuing to accept the consequences of her choice, even after it has taken her into disillusionment and darkness, Isabel perseveres in fulfilling the intention she expressed early in the novel: "I wish to choose my fate."

James thus concludes his novel by completing Isabel's portrait. He establishes that she possesses the will and the wisdom necessary to remain in control of her destiny. Isabel's return to Rome, however, should not be considered an end to her "free exploration of life." Not only does James stress that Isabel is returning to a continuance of her voyage, but he also points to the goal toward which she is heading by allowing Isabel to share with those who remain curious about her future her deep assurance of what lies ahead: "Deep in her soul—deeper than any appetite for renunciation—was the sense that life would be her business for a long time to come. And at moments there was something inspiring, almost enlivening, in the conviction. It was a proof of strength—it was a proof she should some day be happy again."

If this reading of the novel is at all accurate, it presents us, as teachers of literature, with a central dilemma regarding the fiction writer's craft. Attempting to shape our response to the concluding events, James presents them within a metaphorical framework he has constructed with consummate skill. His metaphors of the sea voyage and of light and darkness, extended throughout the novel, are brought together at the end by James to delineate for us the significance that he attributes to Isabel's final actions. The conception we should finally attain of these happenings is therefore not our own. It must be given to us by James, wrought within our

imaginations by the craft of the author. But what if he has so impressed us with his dramatic method that we tend to lose awareness of his perspective, and to be caught up, instead, in the illusion he has created of a world immediately before us? What if we assume that we may look directly at the events taking place and draw our own conclusions? Every author loses control over his readers to the degree that he allows them to make their own perceptions. Judging from the diverse and contradictory responses to this ending found within James's learned audience, should we not conclude that his readers have generally been influenced more by his skillfully wrought illusion than by his own crafted view-point? James's novel offers us the opportunity to begin resolving our critical dilemma by illustrating for our students how to distin-guish between literary illusion and authorial craft.

Narrator as Author: The Surrogate "I"

MOBY-DICK

Isabel Archer's awareness of her world and its inhabitants grew throughout *The Portrait of a Lady*, like a circle expanding within the larger circle of James's awareness. Although Isabel understood considerably more about her world and her self by the end of the novel, James never blurred the distinction he drew between himself and his main character. We turn now to a novel in which the author does not clearly maintain this distinction and creates, as a result, one of the more striking failures in communication to be found in American literature.

Critics marking their own pathways through Herman Melville's *Moby-Dick* have blazed trails in all directions. Note, for example, how they have viewed the white whale:

Richard Chase: God incarnate in the whale.[1]

J.W.N. Sullivan: the evil principle of the universe.[2]

Lewis Mumford: the sheer brute energy of the universe.[3]

Harry Slochower: the disguised form of the hermaphroditical mystery.[4]

Edmund Bergler: the infant's fantasy of the cruel, pre-Oedipal mother.[5]

D. H. Lawrence: the last phallic being of the white man.[6]

Melville, however, was after something much more complex than these individualized views of the whale. If we are to grasp his novel, we must find a way to follow him, as controlling craftsman, beyond the boundaries of this critical confusion. The novel, without doubt, is a difficult, complicated, cumbersome one to teach. But it is also a remarkable literary accomplishment, for Melville succeeded in illustrating dramatically his answer to the central question of the novel, one of mankind's eternal questions: Who or what is the cause of everything that occurs on earth? Is it God, man's free will, or chance?

Accompanying what appears to be a dazzling and often distracting wealth of materials that he brought into his work, Melville created an elaborate organizing symbol extended sporadically throughout the novel until the final three chapters, where Melville transformed the symbol into a dramatic experience of profound significance. Within those concluding chapters, where Ahab and Moby Dick engage in their final mortal conflict, Melville symbolically wove together all actors, actions, and natural forces—the winds, the waves, the whale, the whalers, the Pequod, the whaleboats—into a meticulously designed pattern conforming with, and controlled by, Ishmael's description of "the Loom of Time," thereby dramatizing Melville's answer to the novel's central question.

However, if we assume that Melville allowed us to view the closing events directly for ourselves, and if we get caught up in the compelling story line as Ahab and Moby Dick fight to the death, then we will miss the significance that arises out of the author's symbolic ordering of those events. We are confronted once again, therefore, with the dilemma we face as teachers of literature: that of encouraging our students to respond, for themselves, to the exciting events in the final three chapters of the novel, without having them lose sight of the author at work shaping their responses into a carefully crafted experience of profound import.

"Call me Ishmael." Unlike James's "historian," the persona Melville assumes to narrate *Moby-Dick* is that of a character recounting an adventure he has personally lived through within the world of the novel. As "an American whale man," he tells us, "I have had to do with whales with these visible hands." Ishmael's authority thus resides mainly in his claim of having directly experienced his tale.

To support this position, Melville has Ishmael supplement his narrative, in fact almost overwhelm it at times, with a variety of materials that actually existed in our world. Ishmael's references include, among others, "numerous fish-documents," "historical whale research," accounts of earlier explorers, first-hand talks with actual whale men, and the profusion of details derived from Melville's own experiences covering every aspect of life aboard an American whaling ship in the mid-1800s.

Melville asks us implicitly throughout the novel to test every aspect of Ishmael's tale against this wealth of factual material. He wishes to make us knowledgeable observers of the fishery so that we can judge the accuracy of what Ishmael, or anyone else in his world, tells us. For example, not only does Ishmael tell us that the heads of the sperm whale and the right whale are different; he also shows them to us as they hang on each side of the Pequod. Ishmael takes us across the deck from one to the other, and then asserts, "Ere this, you must have plainly seen the truth of what I started with—that the Sperm Whale and the Right Whale have almost entirely different heads."

But have we, indeed, "plainly seen" anything? If we listen closely to Ishmael as we sit in the house of fiction, we find him speaking of himself as a "writer" talking to his "reader." How, then, does he manage to give us the impression, not only that his account is vivid enough to be seen, but that we have actually joined him aboard the Pequod?

Ishmael accomplishes this feat by repeatedly making direct appeals to our imagination. For example: "Had you stepped on board the Pequod at a certain juncture of this post-mortemizing of the whale; and had you strolled forward nigh the windlass, pretty sure am I that you would have scanned with no small curiosity . . ." He strengthens this illusion by simply speaking to us at times as though we were there with him in the past, reliving his adventure: "Here, now, are two great whales, laying their heads together; let us join them, and lay together our own." And so past becomes present, and illusion, reality.

But Ishmael requests even more of our imagination. He asks us also to relive moments that lie outside his own experience. We cannot help noticing that once we are aboard the Pequod, we are soon confronted with peculiar disruptions in Ishmael's viewpoint.

Moby-Dick begins with Ishmael as narrator recalling his personal memories of a past adventure, but before long we look around for him at times in vain. Ishmael disappears at different moments, and we find ourselves watching other characters whose thoughts and actions were clearly outside the scope of Ishmael's awareness. For example, Chapter 37 begins: "*The cabin; by the stern windows; Ahab sitting alone, and gazing out.*"—and there is Ahab before us, alone in his cabin, and we listen to his soliloquy. There is no intermediary, no sign of Ishmael telling us what Ahab said. What we come to realize is that another presence, a larger awareness, is aboard the Pequod. Someone else has set this scene and opened the curtain for our viewing. He entered as Ishmael, for Ishmael was to be his surrogate, a naive and rather comical young man in the beginning, who would then develop into an increasingly knowledgeable individual with a profound awareness of his world and those around him. But the intensity of Melville's own nature, the uncontainable vitality of his own thoughts and emotions, steadily erodes the mask he has assumed until we are able to catch glimpse after glimpse of him throughout his dramatic presentation. Ishmael, for example, includes himself in a reference to "we harpooners." Ishmael obviously was not a harpooner. Melville was.

In *The Portrait of a Lady* Henry James gave his narrator an air of veracity by having the narrator's remarks accord with certain "factual" materials that were, after all, fictional creations: a letter from Warburton, a conversation between characters, a record of Isabel's motives. Melville, however, attempted something exceedingly more difficult. At some point during the crafting of his novel, Melville decided to transcend the boundaries of the imaginative world within which his narrator existed. Unlike James, Melville became primarily concerned with clarifying the actual world in which he lived. As a writer of fiction, he would allow his readers to experience an eternal truth. He would dramatize his answer to a question that has troubled mankind from the dawning of consciousness: Who or what is the ultimate cause of everything that takes place in this world?

Near the end of the novel, Ishmael as a character has all but disappeared, and we are left with a disembodied voice narrating the final events. Melville, as craftsman, decided that he would end his novel by positioning his readers as seemingly direct observers.

He would have us experience the full impact of his dramatic conclusion, free of distracting authorial intrusions, free of Ishmael's intermediary presence. Melville would deftly catch us up within the ultimate illusion of the fiction writer's craft: a view of events occurring directly and immediately before us.

Moving inexorably to the closing three chapters, Melville offered us an elaborately patterned but seemingly direct impression of the concluding events in his fictional world, his dramatized answer to the central question of the novel. This culminating experience was designed to illuminate the intricate workings of reality and to remain indelibly impressed upon us as we lifted our eyes to our actual world. But at this final, crucial moment, something went wrong. Melville's elaborate patterning of events, so masterfully crafted to convey his ultimate understanding, appears before us as a compelling, but somewhat confusing, series of actions. The dazzling clarity of his controlling vision succeeded only in dazzling. A sampling of critical responses will illustrate this point:

Walter E. Bezanson: Ishmael's narrative is always in process and in all but the most literal sense remains unfinished.[7]

Richard Brodhead: [The book] is magnificently resolved at the level of action, magnificently unresolved at the level of meaning.[8]

Gordon H. Mills: Moby-Dick is not a neat book. . . . Melville had no neatly worked-out scheme to which Ahab's character was to be subordinate.[9]

Bernard DeVoto: "Moby-Dick" has, as fiction, no structure whatever.[10]

If we are going to experience the ending as Melville crafted it, we must return to the house of fiction with a greater determination to focus our attention on Melville's elusive presence at the window. The viewpoints of the characters in the novel are revealed through their words and deeds; the controlling viewpoint of the author is revealed through his craft. We begin our search, therefore, by noting how the author uses his surrogate narrator to establish (1) the distinguishing features of the world within the novel, (2) Ahab's motivation for reacting so peculiarly to this world, and (3) the natures of the "reflector" characters positioned around Ahab to represent alternative ways to respond. We must watch Ishmael's circle of awareness expanding as it delineates and then transcends the limited perspectives of the other characters until it leads us,

finally, to the ultimate experience of sharing the author's encompassing vision.

The ocean, "which is the dark side of this earth, and which is two thirds of this earth," appears to Ishmael, from one viewpoint, to typify the seemingly indifferent, uncontrolled forces pervading this world, for "the sea dashes even the mightiest whales against the rocks, and leaves them there side by side with the split wrecks of ships. No mercy, no power but its own controls it. Panting and snorting like a mad battle steed that has lost its rider, the masterless ocean overruns the globe." From this singular viewpoint, the ocean may be contrasted with the land, which at times is a haven from the forces of the ocean: "The port would fain give succor; the port is pitiful; in the port is safety, comfort, hearthstone, supper, warm blankets, friends, all that's kind to our mortalities."

Ishmael also places emphasis on the contrast within this world between warmth and coldness. Discussing Euroclydon, a frigid northeasterly wind, Ishmael quotes an "old writer" who says, "It maketh a marvellous difference, whether thou lookest out at it from a glass window where the frost is all on the outside, or whether thou observest it from that sashless window where the frost is on both sides, and of which the wight Death is the only glazier." Ishmael continues, "Yes, these eyes are windows, and this body of mine is the house. What a pity they didn't stop up the chinks and the crannies though, and thrust in a little lint here and there. But it's too late to make any improvements now. The universe is finished; the copestone is on, and the chips were carted off a million years ago." In a world where "Death is the only glazier" unless "the frost is all on the outside," any warmth that man encounters, conducive to his maintaining the warmth of his own body, is generally suggestive of life; any coldness, of death. The contrast is a pervasive one. On one side, for example, are found the warm seasons of the year, the equatorial regions of the earth, southerly winds, the sun, and fire; on the other side is winter, the arctic regions, northerly winds, ice, snow, and frost. As man travels through this variable world, attempting to keep the warmth of life within him, his most unfortunate discovery is that his body, as part of the "finished" universe, has been created imperfect, with chinks and crannies that let in the cold, and that "it's too late to make any improvements now."

Ahab is conscious of being in the same mortal plight that Ishmael recognizes above, for, as he says, "I'm all aleak myself. Aye! leaks in leaks! not only full of leaky casks, but those leaky casks are in a leaky ship. . . . Yet I don't stop to plug my leak; for who can find it in the deep-loaded hull; or how hope to plug it, even if found, in this life's howling gale?" Although he experiences this general mortal plight, Ahab, at first glance, can be distinguished from other men, for his already burdened body has received an additional handicap, the loss of his leg as a result of his first encounter with Moby Dick: "Is it not hard, that with this weary load I bear, one poor leg should have been snatched from under me?" Unable to comprehend why he must experience this added loss since he is already existing in such a flawed condition, he is led once more toward a conclusion he has approached again and again during his many years of life on the ocean: that an apparent injustice pervades his world. Ahab ponders this idea as he speaks to the severed head of a recently slain whale hanging beside his ship:

"Thou saw'st the murdered mate when tossed by pirates from the midnight deck; for hours he fell into the deeper midnight of the insatiate maw; and his murderers still sailed on unharmed—while swift lightnings shivered the neighboring ship that would have bourne a righteous husband to outstretched, longing arms. O head! thou hast seen enough to split the planets and make an infidel of Abraham, and not one syllable is thine!"

Therefore, whenever Ahab finds the forces of his world acting adversely upon him, we can expect him to resist accordingly: "I'd strike the sun if it insulted me." This statement to Starbuck, which, by itself, appears to be simply a reflection in Ahab of an overwhelming egotism, is carefully qualified, however, by Ahab's next words: "For could the sun do that, then could I do the other." Ahab is asserting that if he is living in a physical universe that has the power to insult the dignity of his own being, then he must surely have the right to strike back at that world. But *how* to strike back has been a problem that Ahab was never able to solve before his encounter with Moby Dick, for the life of suffering experienced by Ahab has been inflicted upon him by larger *unassailable* forces, as is suggested in Ishmael's first description of Ahab as a man who appears to have been struck and "branded" by "lightning." We can understand, therefore, why Ahab's first encounter with Moby Dick,

resulting in the loss of his leg, compels Ahab to seek vengeance so pointedly against Moby Dick: first, the whale has inflicted upon him an injury that he, with his particular attitude toward the physical world, can experience only as a malicious insult to himself; second, Ahab is finally able to confront what he believes to be a larger, but *assailable*, force.

However, considering that "when he received the stroke that tore him, he probably but felt the agonizing bodily laceration, but nothing more," and that it was only later "on the homeward voyage, after the encounter, that the final monomania seized him," Ishmael makes us realize that it is not simply the painful infliction of a wound against which Ahab is reacting. His deepest reaction is brought about by the *thoughts* that he associates with Moby Dick while he lies wounded. To understand more fully his reaction, therefore, we must discover how the author establishes what those thoughts were.

In their first encounter, Moby Dick, by maiming Ahab, was literally the source of Ahab's physical suffering. Within Ahab's mind this particular thought, his suffering being associated with Moby Dick, is the impetus for further associated thoughts, especially as Ahab recollects Moby Dick's "prominent features," described by Ishmael as follows: "For, it was not so much his uncommon bulk that so much distinguished him from other Sperm Whales, but, as was elsewhere thrown out—a peculiar snow-white wrinkled forehead, and a high, pyramidical white hump. These were his prominent features; the tokens whereby, even in the limitless, uncharted seas, he revealed his identity, at a long distance, to those who knew him."

We find that Ahab is described as having a "ribbed and dented brow," a "wrinkled brow," an image which may well convey both the sense of deep thinking—Ishmael mentions again and again Ahab's "pondering," his "intense thinking"—and the idea of suffering or grief, which also normally wrinkles the brow. If so, then Moby Dick's wrinkled forehead may be a reminder to Ahab of his own wrinkled brow, his outward expression of all the grief and the tormenting thoughts within himself, which Ahab can now see visibly associated with Moby Dick: "in his frantic morbidness he at last came to identify with him, not only all his bodily woes, but all his intellectual and spiritual exasperations."

So, too, may Moby Dick's hump be suggestively associated in Ahab's mind with his thought of being himself humped. He asks for "a pair of steel shoulder-blades," for, as he says, "there's a pedlar aboard with a crushing pack." This statement recalls Ishmael's earlier remark about man's carrying "the burden of life in a world full of grave peddlers, all bowed to the ground with their packs." Ahab apparently feels humped with "the burden of life," the general mortal plight of man, part of which, enforced by the pun on "grave," is one's awareness of eventual death: "But do I look very old, so very, very old, Starbuck? I feel deadly faint, bowed, and humped, as though I were Adam, staggering beneath the piled centuries since Paradise. God! God! God!—crack my heart!—stave my brain!—mockery! mockery! bitter, biting mockery of grey hairs, have I lived enough joy to wear ye; and seem and feel thus intolerably old?"

Ahab is fifty-eight years old and approaching death, without having "lived enough joy." He realizes that Moby Dick, in their second encounter, could well destroy him. This literal association of Moby Dick with the thought of death is strengthened by Ahab's further association of the whale's hump with that coldness that is generally suggestive of death: Ahab exclaims that Moby Dick has "a hump like a snow-hill." Apparently seeing in the hump a suggestion of the coldness that he is attempting to keep out of his flawed, aging body, the coldness that is part of the burden of life, Ahab irrationally concludes that he is feeling humped because of the humped whale: "He tasks he; he heaps me."

Ahab speaks of the world's being like "a magician's glass," which "to each and every man in turn but mirrors back his own mysterious self." To sum up those thoughts that Ahab associates with this one peculiar part of his world, the white whale, we might say that Ahab hates Moby Dick so intensely because he sees reflected in the whale what he believes are particular physical characteristics of his own, those with which he associates the hateful, perplexing parts of his own mortal nature: his suffering and grief, his frustrating thoughts, his eventual death.

But Ahab's thoughts do not stop at this level, for by placing himself in the position of being comparable to Adam, Ahab apparently is conscious of that kind of life that man once possessed in Paradise. On the fatal third day of the hunt for Moby Dick, Ahab

sees the day dawn as though his ship had actually reached another Paradise: "What a lovely day again! were it a new-made world, and made for a summer-house to the angels, and this morning the first of its throwing open to them, a fairer day could not dawn upon that world"—a description suggesting a time when Ahab might well have "lived enough joy." But within this fair world there is still Moby Dick, the embodiment of a malicious, afflicting force, whose existence prevents Ahab from fully enjoying the day. In his desire to destroy Moby Dick, therefore, he is not simply seeking the death of a single whale. Old Ahab raises his attempt to avenge himself to a universal level: man's attempt to do battle against all those forces existing in his world that have afflicted him since the time of Adam. "He piled upon the whale's white hump the sum of all the general rage and hate felt by his whole race from Adam down." Ahab's ultimate response, therefore, is to see Moby Dick as the visible, and so now assailable, personification of "all evil," that which causes the physical and mental suffering and the death existing in man's world "since Paradise." The whale's destruction would return man to an existence in which he would no longer feel humped with the burden of mortal life. Ahab, in other words, at the deepest level of his thoughts, is attempting to grasp again what God has kept from mortal man since the time of Adam, an immortal life free from suffering: "the ungraspable phantom of life; and this is the key to it all." One discovers, therefore, that Ahab is in conflict, not primarily with Moby Dick, but with God, for Ahab comes to believe that God, by allowing man to exist in a flawed condition among such malicious, afflicting forces, reveals Himself as being unfeeling toward man. Ahab cries out, "Lo you! see the omniscient gods oblivious of suffering man."

We must, however, keep in mind a suggestion conveyed by Ahab's reference to "omniscient gods." Rather than holding a solely Christian concept of God, Ahab, apparently as a result of his many voyages around the world, has been influenced by other concepts as well—Norse, Classical, and Oriental—a sampling perhaps suggestive of all the major concepts of God held by man. Ahab's isolated life of ocean experiences, which has led him "to think untraditionally and independently," has resulted in the "unoutgrown peculiarities" of his Quaker upbringing being blended with "a thousand bold dashes of character, not unworthy

a Scandinavian sea-king, or a poetical Pagan Roman," or, one might add, a fire-worshipping Persian.

Ahab's concept of God, that which he worshipped as the source of his human life, is defined by Ahab's reference to the "clear spirit of clear fire," which he confronts in the corposants, an electrical storm that lights up his ship's masts as he sails through a typhoon. Ahab says, "Oh, thou clear spirit, of thy fire thou madest me." We discover, when Ahab speaks to the corposants, not only the reason why he is in conflict with this creative force, which has earlier revealed itself as being cruelly indifferent to his worship, but also why Ahab believes he is *capable* of a conflict with God:

"Oh! thou clear spirit of clear fire, whom on these seas I as Persian once did worship, till in the sacramental act so burned by thee, that to this hour I bear the scar; I now know thee, thou clear spirit, and I now know that thy right worship is defiance. To neither love nor reverence wilt thou be kind; and e'en for hate thou canst but kill; and all are killed. No fearless fool now fronts thee. I own thy speechless, placeless power; but to the last gasp of my earthquake life will dispute its unconditional, unintegral mastery in me."

Throughout the first part of the novel, Ahab believes that God does not have a mastery over him, that although he can be physically destroyed, his will is free to defy any power that would destroy him. It is this particular belief that makes Ahab feel capable of an indomitable persistence in his search for Moby Dick. "There was an infinity of firmest fortitude, a determinate, unsurrenderable willfulness, in the fixed and fearless, forward dedication of that glance."

Persisting in this attempt to remain willfully independent, even of God, Ahab can be seen turning away again and again from anything that he believes is making him dependent upon God. For this reason, for example, he smashes his quadrant: "Curse thee, thou vain toy; and cursed be all things that cast man's eyes aloft to that heaven, whose live vividness but scorches him, as these old eyes are even now scorched with thy light, O sun!"

However, as Ahab defiantly confronts in the corposants the God that he believes has created him, his concept of God begins to undergo a significant change, resulting in a corresponding change in the nature of Ahab's conflict with Moby Dick. Having earlier worshipped this spirit of fire as the highest supernatural force,

Ahab now learns that it, too, like himself, has its limitations: "There is some unsuffusing thing beyond thee, thou clear spirit, to whom all thy eternity is but time, all thy creativeness mechanical. Through thee, thy flaming self, my scorched eyes do dimly see it. Oh, thou foundling fire, thou hermit immemorial, thou too hast thy incommunicable riddle, thy unparticipated grief."

At this point Ahab's concept of God becomes recollective of the classical concept of Fate, that inscrutable power that overruled gods and men alike and determined the outcome of all events. Hereafter, we can see Ahab's thoughts about the freedom of his own mind undergoing a reversal: he denies now the efficacy of his own thinking with his assertion that "the dead, blind wall butts all inquiring heads at last"; and he comes to accept the idea that Fate, which he apparently equates with necessity, must be in control of everything in his world, including himself:

"Is Ahab, Ahab? Is it I, God, or who, that lifts this arm? But if the great sun move not of himself; but is as an errand-boy in heaven; nor one single star can revolve, but by some invisible power; how then can this one small heart beat; this one small brain think thoughts; unless God does that beating, does that thinking, does that living, and not I. By heaven, man, we are turned round and round in this world, like yonder windlass, and Fate is the Handspike."

We must also note that this conclusion does not prevent Ahab from persisting in his conflict with God, for with his new concept of God as Fate, Ahab no longer sees God as indifferently allowing afflicting forces to exist in man's world. God is now seen by Ahab as being in control of these forces, as he notes when he watches a predatory fish in action: "Look! see yon Albicore! who put it into him to chase and fang that flying-fish? Where do murderers go, man! Who's to doom, when the judge himself is dragged to the bar?" But how, then, does Ahab account for the fact that he has so far been manifesting an "unsurrenderable willfulness"? He now believes that, since Fate is in complete control of everything, his individualizing indomitable will itself is fated. When Starbuck pleads with him as the end approaches to give up his pursuit of Moby Dick, Ahab answers, "Ahab is for ever Ahab, man. The whole act's immutably decreed. 'Twas rehearsed by thee and me a billion years before this ocean rolled. Fool! I am the Fates' lieutenant: I act

under orders." He has no choice now, he says, but to be Ahab, since it was forever fated that he would be so. And he would also say, interestingly enough, that he still holds God completely responsible for whatever disastrous events are brought about by his being Ahab, since it is Fate, he now believes, that will determine the outcome of his assault on Moby Dick.

One further piece of information about Ahab should be noted here. Near the beginning of the novel, Ishmael defines for us his characteristics of "a mighty pageant creature, formed for noble tragedies." By the end of the novel Ahab appears to achieve this tragic stature. He fulfills the role of the classical tragic hero, a man impelled by Fate into committing an act that ends in tragedy. The greater his ensuing grief, the greater his tragic stature. Ahab reaches this realization as he sees Moby Dick destroy his ship. "Oh, now I feel my topmost greatness lies in my topmost grief." But we must not lose sight of the fact that this singular, unqualified view of Ahab nobly fulfilling the tragic hero's role is gained only by limiting ourselves to Ahab's awareness. If we are going to approach the author's vision, we must also consider the other characters placed around Ahab to establish differing views of the same world.

Responding to his world in a manner that leads him into conflict with God, Ahab is well aware that other men do not respond similarly, and yet he persists in seeing his own response as justifiable, for he believes that all other men view their world incorrectly. He illustrates this belief with his attitude toward two other characters whose peculiarities, he asserts, are divergent enough to encompass the natures of all other men. These two are Starbuck and Stubb, for, as Ahab says to them, "Ye two are the opposite poles of one thing . . . ye two are all mankind." Starbuck's and Stubb's different reactions to their world are exemplified by the manner in which each of them, in a moment of calm, looks upon the ocean. Although willing to look into the depths of the ocean, Starbuck desires to see only a "loveliness unfathomable, as ever lover saw in his young bride's eye!—Tell me not of thy teeth-tiered sharks, and thy kidnapping cannibal ways. Let faith oust fact; let fancy oust memory; I look deep down and do believe." Though a man of good intellect, Starbuck lets faith and fancy oust from his mind any irreligious fact or memory about his world, "lest Truth shake me falsely." How can Starbuck maintain a faith that allows him to see in this world the

constant presence of a divine guidance, even when he faces many of those same perplexing hardships that Ahab encounters on the ocean? Melville establishes throughout the novel that one's physical condition plays a major role in shaping one's attitude toward the world: unlike Ahab's body, which is "all aleak," Starbuck's "pure tight skin was an excellent fit"; unlike Ahab, Starbuck is only thirty years old, and "his interior vitality was warranted to do well in all climates." Although he, like all men, will eventually experience man's general mortal plight, he has so far lived a life of such full "inner health and strength" that he sees only God's benevolent hand guiding his world. When he encounters a situation that might suggest the contrary, he prevents any thoughts from entering his mind that would otherwise disturb his belief.

Ahab says that Starbuck and Stubb "are the opposite poles of one thing," that "one thing" apparently being their avoidance of facing the dark side of their world. Unlike Starbuck, Stubb has no consistent beliefs, has, apparently, no thoughts at all about his world or himself, for, as he says, "Think not, is my eleventh commandment." He exists in a state of ignorance, which allows him to be always happy with his life, his mind remaining unaware of the miseries of his world. How is he capable of maintaining such an ignorance? Stubb's "peculiar disposition" arises from his pipe, which keeps him from all but happy thoughts: "I say this continual smoking must have been one cause, at least, of his peculiar disposition; for every one knows that this earthly air, whether ashore or afloat, is terribly infected with the nameless miseries of the numberless mortals who have died exhaling it; . . . against all mortal tribulations, Stubb's tobacco smoke might have operated as a sort of disinfecting agent." Stubb, unlike Starbuck, simply does not look deeply into the ocean. Instead, he leaps up and exclaims, "I am Stubb, and Stubb has his history; but here Stubb takes oaths that he has always been jolly!" Stubb's constant jolliness recalls Ishmael's idea that the ocean, "which is the dark side of this earth . . . is two thirds of this earth. So, therefore, that mortal man who hath more of joy than sorrow in him, that mortal man cannot be true—not true, or undeveloped." Stubb is apparently no more than an undeveloped stub of a man.

Ahab says to Starbuck and Stubb, "Ye two are all mankind; and Ahab stands alone among the millions of the peopled earth, nor

gods nor men his neighbors!" Ahab believes that he is alone among men because he confronts the dark side of his world. He does not hide from it behind his pipe: "What business have I with this pipe? This thing that is meant for sereneness. . . . I'll smoke no more." Nor does he see in his world Starbuck's "portents" and "presentiments," for, as he says, "If the gods think to speak outright to man, they will honorably speak outright; not shake their heads, and give an old wives' darkling hint." And yet Ahab is mistaken when he excludes himself from the full range of mankind's reactions to the world. Although Starbuck and Stubb do respond to their world in separate ways, they are not at opposite poles to each other. They are more accurately to be placed at the opposite pole of Ahab's nature, for, contrary to them, he sees *only* the dark side: "So far gone am I in the dark side of earth, that its other side, the theoretic bright one, seems but uncertain twilight to me." What is needed at this point, therefore, is a character who is capable of looking directly at both sides of his world.

Melville establishes Ishmael as his surrogate narrator to fulfill this role. "With the problems of the universe revolving in me," Ishmael says, his thoughts about his world are sharply distinguished from Ahab's. For example, he feels more identification with his fellowman, for he sees that all men, like himself, experience afflictions: "Well, then, however the old sea-captains may order me about—however they may thump and punch me about, I have the satisfaction of knowing that it is all right; that everybody else is one way or other served in much the same way—either in a physical or metaphysical point of view, that is; and so the universal thump is passed round, and all hands should rub each other's shoulder-blades, and be content."

Ishmael is able to respond positively even to the horrors he finds, again experiencing an identity with them, since both he and they exist within the same world: "Not ignoring what is good, I am quick to perceive a horror, and could still be social with it—would they let me—since it is but well to be on friendly terms with all the inmates of the place one lodges in." Ishmael's ability to maintain such thoughts towards a world in which there are "thumps" and "horrors" results from an eternal calmness he feels existing deep within the turbulence of his mortal life. Unlike Ahab, who has an "overruling morbidness at the bottom of his nature," which causes

him to see only "the dark side of this earth," Ishmael says he has an "inland" calm "amid the tornadoed Atlantic of my being," which allows him to be aware of both the ocean and the land: "Consider them both, the sea and the land; and do you not find a strange analogy to something in yourself? For as this appalling ocean surrounds the verdant land, so in the soul of man there lies one insular Tahiti, full of peace and joy, but encompassed by all the horrors of the half known life."

Because of this greater awareness, Ishmael is able to regard all things in his world with an "equal eye." As a result, he makes a most significant discovery, central to any understanding of his world, which he vividly illustrates with his view of what he believes is "perhaps the grandest sight to be seen in all animated nature," the "peaking of the whale's flukes": "Out of the bottomless profundities the gigantic tail seems spasmodically snatching at the highest heaven. So in dreams, have I seen majestic Satan thrusting forth his tormented colossal claw from the flame Baltic of Hell. But in gazing at such scenes, it is all in all what mood you are in; if in the Dantean, the devils will occur to you; if in that of Isaiah, the archangels." Ishmael realizes that when man relates his thoughts to the world, his mind, being influenced by variable moods, is capable of associating contrary thoughts with the same object. For example, the warm climates of the world, seen earlier as generally suggestive of life, can also be suggestive of death, for, as Ishmael says, "Warmest climes but nurse the cruellest fangs"; and the friendly land, offering "all that's kind to our mortalities," can, for a man on ship-board during a storm, be his "direst jeopardy." And a white whale, suggesting evil, can also suggest good.

For example, Ahab, as we noted earlier, relates the thought of death to Moby Dick's white hump. Ishmael apparently does so, too, for not only does he see the hump as a snow-hill, but he consistently describes the hump as being "pyramidical," an image of one of man's greatest creations having to do with death. However, Ishmael, unlike Ahab, does not stop with this single negative thought of death. He goes on to establish the additional material necessary for us to see in the pyramidical hump a contrastingly positive suggestion: the pyramid as a symbol of the preservation of life in the face of death. When Ishmael, in the bower in the Arsacides, examines the only skeleton of a whale that he ever saw

in its entirety, he concludes: "Yet, as the ever-woven verdant warp and woof intermixed and hummed around him, the mighty idler seemed the cunning weaver; himself all woven over with the vines; every month assuming greener, fresher verdure; but himself a skeleton. Life folded Death; Death trellised Life." For Ishmael, then, "Death trellised Life." Or, as Melville himself later states near the beginning of his next novel, *Pierre*: "the most mighty of Nature's laws is this, that out of Death she brings Life." Each birth of a new generation grows out of the death of an old one, so that all men, as Ishmael says of Ahab, walk "on life and death."

The wrinkled brow, in turn, can also be suggestive of contrasting thoughts. Ahab sees in the brow only the negative implications of grief and tormenting thoughts. But the reader is again made capable of seeing a positive implication because of additional material established by Ishmael. If the hump, being suggestive of death, can also be suggestive of life, since out of death comes life, then the wrinkled brow, suggestive of grief and thought, can also be suggestive of man's greatest knowledge, for out of grief and thought comes man's greatest knowledge. As Ishmael says, "That mortal man who hath more of joy than sorrow in him, that mortal man cannot be true—not true, or undeveloped. With books the same. The truest of all men was the Man of Sorrows, and the truest of all books is Solomon's and Ecclesiastes is the fine hammered steel of woe."

We digress here a moment to see Ahab himself illustrating this point. As a result of his grief and his intense thinking, Ahab *almost* realizes the above-mentioned fundamental truth about life's relationship to death as he watches the carpenter turn a coffin into a life-preserver shortly before the chase for Moby Dick begins: "Here now's the very dreaded symbol of grim death, by a mere hap, made the expressive sign of the help and hope of most endangered life. A life-buoy of a coffin! Does it go further? Can it be that in some spiritual sense a coffin is, after all, but an immortality-preserver?"

Having established the information necessary to illustrate the inadequacy of Ahab's singular thoughts about Moby Dick, Ishmael functions also as the spokesman who attempts to answer a larger question raised by Ahab's limitation. Does a mortal man have the ability to ascertain the "certain significance" of anything he finds existing in his world, including a white whale? Realizing that men's thoughts are dependent on the moods that result from their

peculiar dispositions, Ishmael might well conclude that anything existing will always be suggestive of different thoughts to different men. However, Ishmael does introduce the possibility of a contrary conclusion when he asserts that "some certain significance lurks in all things, else all things are little worth, and the round world itself but an empty cipher." Ishmael, in other words, perceives the need to distinguish between the particular response to the world made by the peculiar mind of an individual, and the "certain significance" that is lurking there.

The desire to clarify this distinction may well be Melville's strongest justification for including all the factual material that pervades Ishmael's narration. Such facts may often appear to be cumbersome—until we realize that Melville, by recounting for the reader all of that objective material from which he has Ishmael draw his conclusions, is attempting to illustrate that Ishmael's beliefs are always "bottomed on the earth." Thus, Ishmael is presented as potentially capable of ascertaining whether his thoughts about a sperm whale are to be associated more closely with his disposition or with the "certain significance" of the whale.

For example, turning from Ahab's mind, with its associative thoughts about Moby Dick, we find Ishmael approaching the sperm whale "as a sensible physiologist, simply." Ishmael thus discovers a fact contrary to the idea of the brow's wrinkled appearance being suggestive of deep thinking: that the "mere handful" of the whale's brain "is at least twenty feet from his apparent forehead in life." Furthermore, Ishmael looks closely and says: "It is as though the forehead of the Sperm Whale were paved with horses hoofs. I do not think that any sensation lurks in it"; neither, apparently, should one associate grief and suffering with the brow. Moving on from the brow, Ishmael notes that the hump "rises over one of the larger vertebrae, and is, therefore, in some sort, the outer convex mould of it." What further thoughts can be accurately related to this physical fact? Leaving the objectivity of his physiological examination, Ishmael applies the "semi-science" of phrenology to the hump and concludes that "from its relative situation, then, I should call this high hump the organ of firmness or indomitableness in the Sperm Whale." But even before reaching this conclusion, he dismisses the certainty of it by stating that all human science "is but a passing fable." Attempting to keep his beliefs

about the whale "bottomed on the earth" by approaching the whale from various viewpoints, as in his physiological, physiognomical, and phrenological examinations, Ishmael is finally led to only one definite conclusion: "Dissect him how I may, then, I but go skin deep; I know him not, and never will."

Not only is he incapable of perceiving the "certain significance" in the whale, but throughout nature he is faced with the same perplexity, as he indicates when he sees the luxuriant natural growth in "A Bower in the Arsacides":

> The industrious earth beneath was as a weaver's loom, with a gorgeous carpet on it. . . . Through the lacings of the leaves, the great sun seemed a flying shuttle weaving the unwearied verdure. Oh, busy weaver! unseen weaver!—pause!—one word!—whither flows the fabric? what palace may it deck? wherefore all these ceaseless toilings? Speak, weaver!—stay thy hand!—but one single word with thee! Nay. . . . The weaver-god, he weaves; and by that weaving is he deafened, that he hears no mortal voice; and by that humming, we, too, who look on the loom are deafened; and only when we escape it shall we hear the thousand voices that speak through it.

Only when we "escape" this world shall we understand its certain significance. Although Ishmael's viewpoint has made obvious the inadequacy of Ahab's thoughts about Moby Dick, Ishmael apparently arrives here at the same perplexing point that Ahab had reached when he asserted, "The dead, blind wall butts all inquiring heads at last." However, even after recognizing this same limitation, Ishmael does not stop functioning as the clarifying spokesman of the novel, for although Ahab has implied that he, too, is incapable of comprehending the certain significance of anything, he nevertheless continues with his attempt to destroy Moby Dick, a persistence that obviously needs further clarification. Having admitted the limitation of his understanding, Ahab dismisses the significance of this admission, along with his belief in the freedom of his will, when he asserts that his thoughts and actions are being controlled by Fate. Again, Melville has Ishmael function to point up the inadequacy of this last assertion.

Like Ahab, Ishmael is not convinced that mortal man has been turned loose to make his own way with his free will through the predominant darkness of his world, for Ishmael states that his life

is being controlled, not by himself, but by "those stage managers, the Fates": "Now that I recall all the circumstances, I think I can see a little into the springs and motives which being cunningly presented to me under various disguises, induced me to set about performing the part I did, besides cajoling me into the delusion that it was a choice resulting from my own unbiased freewill and discriminating judgment." Ishmael would not agree, however, with Ahab's belief that Fate is in control of everything, for Ishmael believes, not in Fate, but in "the Fates."

In the chapter on "The Mat-Maker," as he weaves a sword-mat with Queequeg, Ishmael clarifies his concept of the Fates with his explanation of the loom, an explanation based on Ishmael's idea that one must not choose between contrary thoughts, such as free will and necessity (Ahab's notion of Fate), but must see that *both* can be accepted:

> It seemed as if this were the Loom of Time, and I myself were a shuttle mechanically weaving and weaving away at the Fates. There lay the fixed threads of the warp subject to but one single, ever returning, unchanging vibration, and that vibration merely enough to admit of the crosswise interblending of other threads with its own. This warp seemed necessity; and here, thought I, with my own hand I ply my own shuttle and weave my own destiny into these unalterable threads. Meantime, Queequeg's impulsive, indifferent sword, sometimes hitting the woof slantingly, or crookedly, or strongly, or weakly, as the case might be; and by this difference in the concluding blow producing a corresponding contrast in the final aspect of the completed fabric; this savage's sword, thought I, which thus finally shapes and fashions both warp and woof; this easy, indifferent sword must be chance—aye, chance, free will, and necessity—no wise incompatible—all interweavingly working together. The straight warp of necessity, not to be swerved from its ultimate course—its every alternating vibration, indeed, only tending to that; free will still free to ply her shuttle between given threads; and chance, though restrained in its play within the right lines of necessity, and sideways in its motions directed by free will, though thus prescribed to by both, chance by turns rules either, and has the last featuring blow at events.

It must be stressed here that the "contrast" always to be found "in the final aspect of the completed fabric" is caused by chance, which, with fate, limits man's will. Thus, any individual's life, spun on "the Loom of Time," is ultimately being controlled, not simply by

the individual's free will, nor simply by necessity. Man's will is still free, says Ishmael, but only to the extent that it interblends itself with these forces.

Understanding Ishmael's explanation of the loom is vital to an understanding of the novel. From the bottom of the ocean, where Pip "saw God's foot upon the treadle of the loom," up to the sky, where "the great sun seemed a flying shuttle weaving the unwearied verdure," the loom as an extended metaphor pervades the world of the novel. Melville entitled his opening chapter "Loomings" in part to foreshadow the central role this metaphor would play as he crafted his dramatized answer to the central question that Ahab pondered: Does Fate or free will determine the outcome of events in our world? The forces affecting this world, as Ishmael describes them, are more complex than Ahab ever realized, and their working relationship is more harmonious: "chance, free will, and necessity—no wise incompatible—all interweavingly working together."

Melville had Ishmael, his surrogate narrator, state that these forces interweave. However, as literary craftsman, Melville had yet to *show* his readers that they do. He chose to fulfill that goal by elaborately manipulating the final three chapters of the novel. As Ahab clashes repeatedly with Moby Dick, Melville has Ahab unknowingly assert his will within a sequence of events that are woven into a pattern upon "the Loom of Time." Noting the correlations that Melville draws between these events and Ishmael's concept of the loom enables us to see this pattern.

Or does it? Melville wanted to end his novel with a dramatic experience, the fiction writer's ultimate illusion of making us believe that we are seeing things for ourselves. By compelling us to focus our attention upon the intensifying drama of the concluding events, he dims our awareness of Ishmael, his surrogate narrator, until we assume that we are looking for ourselves directly into the fictional world of the novel. Without question, Melville attained his literary illusion. But in doing so, did he encourage us to overlook his controlling presence? Do we perceive the culminating experience of the novel as Melville crafted it: the final events being woven into a pattern upon "the Loom of Time"?

We must recall here the basic design of the loom: "There lay the fixed threads of the warp. . . . and here, thought I, with my own hand I ply my own shuttle and weave my own destiny into these unalterable threads." Within the final events of the novel, the description of the warp, as necessity, correlates with various descriptions of the trade winds, "that in the clear heavens blow straight on, in strong and steadfast, vigorous mildness; and veer not from their mark." Melville suggestively establishes that whenever anything travels to leeward (with the wind), it may be considered as moving in accordance with necessity, and that free will is operating when anything moves across or against the wind. We find this correlation being repetitively illustrated by the movements of the Pequod and Moby Dick, as can be seen when Moby Dick is first sighted: "He is heading straight to leeward, Sir," cried Stubb, "right away from us." At the beginning of this first encounter, therefore, Moby Dick may be viewed as moving in accordance with necessity, and Ahab as asserting his free will. After Moby Dick destroys Ahab's whaleboat, Ahab returns to his ship, looks for the whale, and sees him "going to leeward still"; and so at the end of the first day's encounter, the last command he gives concerning the ship's direction is to "keep her full before the wind." Now both the Pequod and Moby Dick are travelling to leeward.

The second day's encounter begins when Moby Dick is seen breaching. Ishmael says that "in some cases, this breaching is his act of defiance," not only against man, we might add, but apparently also against necessity, for now it is Moby Dick who turns against the wind to assert *his* free will. "As if to strike a quick terror into them, by this time being the first assailant himself, Moby Dick had turned, and was now coming for the three crews." Again, he destroys Ahab's boat, and then, "as if satisfied that his work for that time was done, he . . . continued his leeward way at a traveler's methodic pace." Once more Ahab returns to his ship to continue his pursuit, and the second day ends with Ishmael noting that "the whale was still in sight to leeward." Thus, it becomes obvious that, after temporary movements made by both ship and whale against the wind, the movement to leeward always prevails, a situation that recalls the "ever returning, unchanging vibration" of the warp of necessity on Ishmael's loom, "and that vibration merely enough to admit of the crosswise interblendings of other threads with its own."

On the third and final day, Ahab and Moby Dick both take turns in traveling against the wind. The day is half over when Ahab discovers that he has oversailed Moby Dick, and so he is the first to change his direction. When the three whaleboats go against the wind to confront Moby Dick again, the whale smashes two of them, leaving only Ahab's intact, and then continues "steadily swimming forward" until he "had almost passed the ship,—which thus far had been sailing in the contrary direction to him." At this point Ahab hails Starbuck, telling him to turn the Pequod around and follow Ahab's whaleboat to leeward. Ahab then manages to harpoon the whale, but the line breaks, and so his whaleboat rushes forward for another try. The noise of the boat approaching causes Moby Dick to turn once more into the wind, to catch sight, not of the whaleboat, but of the Pequod, and so to charge the Pequod, again manifesting his free will. Moby Dick smashes in the bow of the Pequod, Ahab throws his last harpoon and is dragged to his death, and the Pequod sinks—as Tashtego, with hammer in hand, is in the act of nailing up Ahab's red flag to the main masthead.

To conclude these events, Melville writes a long penultimate paragraph, the happenings within which can be viewed as the clearest visual representation of the third member of Ishmael's "Fates": chance. Being interwoven with free will and necessity, chance "by turns rules either, and has the last featuring blow at events." We must first note that just before the ship completely submerges, we see "a few inches of the erect spar yet visible, together with long streaming yards of the flag, which calmly undulated, with ironical coincidings, over the destroying billows they almost touched." Ishmael referred earlier to the masts of the ship as "spines" and to the mast-*head* as "a thought-engendering altitude." Ahab's flag, flying from that suggestive height, might thus be considered as a visible signal of Ahab's purposeful will; the "billows," as their name establishes, are caused by the leeward wind; the "ironical coincidings" of Ahab's flag and the billows might therefore be looked upon as another dramatic illustration of will and necessity interblending. We must further note that "at that instant, a red arm and a hammer hovered backwardly uplifted in the open air, in the act of nailing the flag faster and yet faster to the subsiding spar." Melville calls attention to a sky-hawk that has flown down "from its natural home among the stars" to peck at the

flag, and then concludes his description as follows: "this bird now chanced to intercept its broad fluttering wing between the hammer and the wood; and simultaneously feeling that etherial thrill, the submerged savage beneath, in his death-gasp, kept his hammer frozen there; and so the bird of heaven, with archangelic shrieks, and his imperial beak thrust upwards, and his whole captive form folded in the flag of Ahab, went down with his ship." Ishmael saw chance operating in Queequeg's sword striking the woof. We find the presence of chance in these closing events by noting any similarly described blow, such as when "the head-beat waves hammered and hammered against the opposing bow" of Ahab's whaleboat as he pursued Moby Dick. The "last featuring blow" at these events occurs when Tashtego's hammer strikes against the wing of the sky-hawk, who, it must be stressed, *"chanced* to intercept its broad fluttering wing between the hammer and the wood." When the bird and the flag and the last whelmings of the billows coincide, Melville shows us "chance, free will, and necessity . . . all interweavingly working together."

Melville thus leads us to the following conclusions concerning Ahab's conflict with God. Because of his limited view, Ahab never realized that the willfulness he manifested in his attempt to defy God was, ironically, not in conflict but in harmony with necessity, the force in this world that Ahab attributed to God. Nor did Ahab ever see that God is not to be held solely responsible for the tormenting events that occurred to him, for necessity was only one of three forces that determined the events of his life. Ahab needed to recognize, further, his own free will, and Moby Dick's free will, and, most of all, chance; for, in this mortal world, it is chance that by turns rules all other forces "and has the last featuring blow at events," always creating within "the completed fabric" a perplexing "contrast," seen in these concluding events when Tashtego's final blow causes "the ship of this base treacherous world" and "the bird of heaven" to sink together.

Finally, however, it must be stressed that Ishmael's clarifying view of his world, as he himself realizes, is a limited one. His greater awareness functions primarily to point up the inadequacy of other men's views, especially Ahab's; but it does not lead one to discover the "certain significance" of anything in his world—including these interblended forces, for although man may be capa-

ble of perceiving them, he is still incapable of hearing any immortal voices behind them. Regardless of how persistently man seeks within his world or his mind to understand the nature of God, and so to understand the nature of his own flawed existence within his predominantly dark world, he discovers only that higher truths remain "indefinite." He is unable finally to explain why his world is two-thirds dark, why the complete man experiences more grief than joy, why even "the bird of heaven" experiences affliction. In a dark world, where chance has the final featuring blow at all events, God remains, as Ishmael says, "inscrutable."

Melville may well have established this perplexing human limitation to leave us pondering a final contrast concerning Ahab. Although Ahab has been viewed negatively because his morbid nature compels him to see only the dark side of his world—the ocean—we must also remember, as Ishmael says, that "in landlessness alone resides the highest truth, shoreless, indefinite as God— so, better is it to perish in that howling infinite, than be ingloriously dashed upon the lee, even if that were safety." As a result of his attempt to reach beyond this oceanic world of indefinite truths, Ahab, even when at the very depths of his error, must still be viewed as a rare individual, a "mighty pageant creature."

Whatever lingering questions we may have concerning Ahab or Moby Dick, we can recognize that any adequate comprehension of the novel must include an awareness of the correlation that Melville worked out so meticulously between Ishmael's description of the loom and the closing events. And yet for well over a hundred years this analogy has remained in obscurity. What caused this failure in communication? Did Melville's surrogate narrator, Ishmael, convey the analogy clearly enough? If not, we may readily excuse Ishmael, for his reason seems to have been, simply, that he was never fully aware that the final events were occurring in accordance with his earlier description of the loom. At only one point in the last three chapters does Ishmael allude to the analogy. While describing the reactions of the crew on the second day of the chase, he states: "The hand of Fate had snatched all their souls. . . . The wind that made great bellies of their sails, and rushed the vessel on by arms invisible as irresistible; this seemed the symbol of that unseen agency which so enslaved them to the race." And so he correlates wind and Fate. But where is the rest of the

analogy? Apparently not wishing to have Ishmael explain it to us again, Melville chose instead to dramatize the workings of the loom within a carefully ordered set of details involving the movements of man and whale among the forces of wind and water. Melville attempted to offer us, in other words, not another expository statement such as Ishmael made earlier on the loom—not simply a symbolic construct imposed upon the world as an "explanation"—but a dramatic presentation of an immediate experience possessing an intrinsic significance.

In the chapter preceding "The Chase—First Day," Ishmael utters his final "I" and does not appear again as a character until the "Epilogue." During each of the last three chapters, the stage once more appears to be set directly before our eyes, and our attention focuses on what is happening. If we succumb to this illusion and are carried forward by the stream of intensely exciting events, we will tend to lose sight, not only of Ishmael, the narrator, but of Melville, the craftsman. The happenings will simply occur before us, one after the other. And the significance of the happenings, as defined by the author, will elude us. Our central task as teachers of this challenging novel is to extend the awareness of our students beyond the illusory limits of the story line to the more inclusive view of the unfolding events achieved through the eyes of the author.

A FAREWELL TO ARMS

Having explored a novel in which the author usurps his narrator's role, we look now at a work in which the narrator may have usurped the author's role. Unlike Melville, who revealed his presence at various times in *Moby-Dick*, Hemingway attempted to efface himself from *A Farewell to Arms*. It is possible that he succeeded too well, for most of his readers appear to have limited their vision of the novel to the viewpoint of its narrator, Frederic Henry.

Beginning with the appearance of Robert Penn Warren's article on Ernest Hemingway in the Winter 1947 issue of *The Kenyon Review*, Hemingway criticism has been dominated by Warren's concept of the Hemingway hero, the "initiate," a kind of noble pagan man attempting to live in an essentially hostile pagan world: "When they confront defeat," Warren states, "they realize that the stance they take, the stoic endurance, the stiff upper lip mean a kind

of victory. . . . They represent some notion of a code, some notion of honor, that makes a man a man, and that distinguishes him from people who merely follow their random impulse and who are, by consequence, 'messy.' "[11] To illustrate his concept, Warren praises as initiates "men like Rinaldi or Frederic Henry of *A Farewell to Arms*," and women like Catherine Barkley, who "most nearly approximate the men; that is, they embody the masculine virtues."[12] If we look closely at the novel, however, we will discover that, contrary to Warren's reading, Hemingway has sharply differentiated the viewpoints and life-styles of his major characters. We must question, therefore, the authority of every perspective established within the novel. Hemingway presents Frederic as an individual recalling incidents from his own life and talking directly to us about them. In the manner of a traditional storyteller, Frederic attempts to confine his account to what he thought and felt at the time of the incidents, although there are a few intrusions that allow us to distinguish that earlier period from the time of his narration. For example, at one point he mentions three villages, names two of them, Chernex and Fontanivent, and then remarks that he has forgotten the other. Generally, however, we are kept at the time of the events, for Frederic is not simply recalling. He also relives his memories, brings them to mind so vividly as he tells us about them that the past is once again experienced by him as "now."

We must keep in mind, however, that Frederic is not offering us the experience itself. His account is our experience. Are we to assume, as a result, that Frederic's sensibilities have ultimately controlled the selection and arrangement of the materials comprising his account? Are we to credit him with the artistic handling of these materials—cast him, in other words, into the role of novelist? To do so, we must determine that Frederic, a fictional character, is aware of those techniques employed by Hemingway to control our responses to the narration. We might ask, for example, if Frederic is aware of the following extended metaphor developed within his own narration.

The four seasons may be viewed in a traditionally symbolic manner: spring as the time of birth, the beginning of life; summer, a time of flourishing life; fall, of waning life; winter, of death. In *A Farewell to Arms* nature is portrayed as continuing on through her traditional seasons—but we can also find an interesting contrast:

directly opposed to the activities of nature are the activities and thoughts of man. In the opening pages of the novel, Hemingway quickly establishes that man, his wars, his love, his life, is completely out of harmony with nature. Opposed to the natural beginning of life, spring is now presented as the beginning of war, of death—man renewing his preparations, not to live, but either to kill or to die. Summer then becomes the time of greatest death. Hemingway notes that the green forest has been destroyed by the summer battles, and that the Italians in one summer had lost a total of one hundred ninety thousand men on the Bainsizza plateau, San Gabriele, and the Carso. Fall becomes a time of the waning of death since the fighting will soon have to stop, and winter, ironically, becomes a time of life, a lull in the war, a temporary truce—but only until the spring. Hemingway skillfully manipulates the first few pages of his novel to establish this contrast of man's activities completely out of harmony with nature's—a contrast that Hemingway maintains throughout his book. We can predict, therefore, how the love affair of Frederic and Catherine *must* end, since Hemingway is so careful to present their love unfolding within certain seasons. Catherine becomes pregnant probably near the beginning of July, for she remarks that she has been pregnant for almost three months as October nears. She conceived in summer, the natural time of life, but the seed was one of death. Hemingway repeatedly establishes that Frederic returned to Catherine some time in November. He carries the reader along for many pages, stopping occasionally to keep alive thoughts of the war, and to further contrast the war to nature. Frederic, for example, remarks that he knows there is still fighting in the mountains, for the snow has not yet arrived. When the snow finally falls a few days before Christmas, snow images dominate the next few pages to establish the presence of winter, nature's time of death, but man's time of life. Frederic tells us how he and Catherine lived a good life and were happy during the months of January and February, but then ominous signs begin to appear as Frederic notices that March brings the first break in the winter weather, with rain falling in the night. The approaching birth of the child is now about a month away. If Catherine conceived near the beginning of July, the child should be born around the end of March or the first of April, in spring—nature's time of beginning life, but man's time of death. Frederic

tells us that with the arrival of March 1918, the Germans had begun their offensive in France. Catherine, like the world around her, can bear only death in spring.

Hemingway further qualifies the meaning of winter: man's time of life. The snow does not allow man to live truly, for only until the spring comes again does it act as a temporary anaesthetic for the war, the killing, the pain, as Frederic unconsciously notes when his leg is wounded and the doctor gives him a local anaesthetic with a name that Frederic says sounds like "snow," which deadens the pain by freezing the tissue around the wound. Just as the growing vines appear to be dead for the winter, with their life dulled in them, so too is man alive for the winter, but with death only dulled in him.

Hemingway, then, shows man as being no longer a part of nature, for in man's chaotic world of war and love, his life is in sharp opposition to the natural world around him: his spring becomes the beginning of death; his summer, a flourishing death; his fall, a waning death; his winter, a dulled, anaesthetized life, waiting for the renewal of death.

Was Frederic aware of this extended metaphor within his own narration? If so, then Frederic is indeed Hemingway's surrogate, and we may accept his viewpoint as the most comprehensive—and fall in with the majority of Hemingway's readers, as the following critical readings illustrate.

Robert Penn Warren: In the end, with the death of Catherine, Frederic discovers that the attempt to find a substitute for universal meaning in the limited meaning of the personal relationship is doomed to failure.[13]

Philip Young: Henry is left, at the end, with nothing.[14]

Ray B. West, Jr.: . . . death is the end of life. After death there is only the lifeless statue.[15]

Carlos Baker: Catherine's suffering and death prove nothing except that she should not have become pregnant.[16]

Michael F. Moloney: there is no profound tragic appeal in the main plot. . . . There is a poignancy in the famous conclusion of the book . . . but But what if Frederic is unaware of how Hemingway crafted his material? What if Frederic has kept our attention diverted from Hemingway's viewpoint?poignancy is not to be identified with the tragic vision itself.[17]

But what if Frederic is unaware of how Hemingway crafted his material? What if Frederic has kept our attention diverted from Hemingway's viewpoint?

In the Spring 1958 issue of *The Paris Review*, George Plimpton quotes Hemingway as saying: "I rewrote the ending to *Farewell to Arms*, the last page of it, thirty-nine times before I was satisfied."[18] Is Hemingway saying that to convey the almost literal meaning the critics find in the ending he had to rewrite that ending thirty-nine times? Or might he be suggesting that much more is to be found there, that behind the facade of Frederic's words there is a depth of meaning yet to be seen? If Hemingway had wanted us to experience Frederic's total defeat through Catherine's death, he might well have had Frederic simply walk back to the hotel in the rain immediately after her death occurs. But he chose instead to write a separate, final scene, to take Frederic back into the room where Catherine was lying dead, obviously to have Frederic realize something more than he had yet seen in Catherine's death.

At this crucial moment, we are again confronted with our literary dilemma. Hemingway wished to remain effaced throughout his novel. As a result, he chose to conclude his work, not with a distracting authorial intrusion, but with the hidden art of a literary craftsman. Hemingway established a number of key passages earlier in the novel that he thought he could cause his readers to recollect and associate with Frederick's final perception of Catherine's dead body: "It was like saying good-by to a statue." Using this approach, Hemingway expanded the scope of Frederic's perception well beyond Frederic's immediate words. He was thus able to offer his readers a startling revelation, a dramatic moment of ultimate awareness that resolved the central conflict of Frederic's life. But Hemingway, the effaced author, conveyed that revelation through the crafting of his materials, not solely by the words or deeds of Frederic, and so we are forced to ask if Frederic himself, or any reader caught up in Frederic's narration, was fully aware of what Hemingway conveyed. The answer is to be found in the closing scene of the novel. But since the closing scene is the culmination of the entire work, and since its significance is conveyed to us through the author's craft, we will not be able to grasp it adequately unless we return to the house of fiction and uncover the elusive presence of the author in the act of artistically manipulating his material.

Only Hemingway can reveal to us whether he has kept his own controlling viewpoint limited to Frederic's perspective. Hemingway, in other words, has either cast Frederic in the role of his surrogate narrator, or he has portrayed Frederic as a man of limited awareness, ultimately unable to grasp the profound significance of Catherine's death.

As we reenter the house of fiction, we can raise an important question of technique: Why did Hemingway choose to narrate *A Farewell to Arms* from Frederic's point of view? The essential weakness of the first-person viewpoint is its limitation: everything must be presented through one character's senses and interpreted by him. But this weakness can be turned into an advantage if it is the author's intention to show a limited mind, a mind not fully aware of the meanings of the events it experiences. Recognizing this possibility, we must not simply take Frederic at his own word. To understand his character, we must first define his limitations and the specific role they play by using those standards or sounding-boards that Hemingway has established for us within the world of the novel, the perspectives of the other main characters: Rinaldi, the priest, and Catherine.

Robert Penn Warren considers Rinaldi to be another "initiate" living stoically up to his code of life, a man to be admired, because "He has the discipline of his profession, and, as we have seen, in the Hemingway world, the discipline that seems to be merely technical, the style of the artist or the form of the athlete or bull fighter, may be an index to a moral value. 'Already,' Rinaldi says, 'I am only happy when I am working.' "[19] Hemingway, though, may have conveyed through these words of Rinaldi's a thought of greater complexity, not yet seen because Rinaldi has been viewed simply as another "initiate."

Hemingway portrays Rinaldi and the priest as representative of two forces affecting Frederic's life: Rinaldi as the sensualist, the man of the body; the priest as the man of the soul. Rinaldi, as one force, is presented not only as the sensualist, but also as the surgeon, the man who expertly cuts open the body and looks inside, but in so doing sees nothing of the soul. Robert Penn Warren believes that Rinaldi is an "initiate" because of the code he follows in being a surgeon. But if Rinaldi's role is to represent the man of the body, the sensualist and the skilled surgeon who believes only in the senses,

then might not Hemingway be trying to express the restrictions of such a man?

"No, no," said Rinaldi. "You can't do it. You can't do it. I say you can't do it. You're dry and you're empty and there's nothing else. There's nothing else I tell you. Not a damned thing. I know, when I stop working."
The priest shook his head.[20]

The other force acting in Frederic's life is represented by the priest, the man of the soul, and his symbolically spiritual home in Abruzzi. After Frederic's furlough at the opening of the novel, not having gone to Abruzzi but having overindulged instead in sensuality, Frederic thinks of the priest: "He had always known what I did not know and what, when I learned it, I was always able to forget. But I did not know that then, although I learned it later."[21] The obvious question yet to be answered is, What did Frederic later learn that the priest had always known? The priest's role, then, until the end of the book, will remain a subordinate one simply because the book is being told from Frederic's point of view, and Frederic, throughout most of the book, shows only a vague understanding of what the priest represents until he "learns it later." For the present, though, the priest's most significant act is to offer another standard by which Frederic can be judged: his definition of love. The priest says: "What you tell me about in the nights. That is not love. That is only passion and lust. When you love you wish to do things for. You wish to sacrifice for. You wish to serve."[22] Frederic asks if he would experience that sense of love if he truly loved a woman, and the priest, the man of the soul, not of the body, living another kind of restricted life, replies that he does not know, for he has never loved a woman. The subject is left as a question yet to be answered by Frederic's love for Catherine.

With Rinaldi on the one side and the priest on the other, if Frederic is going to be influenced by one, he must turn away from the other. But with Catherine Barkley he is exposed to both the body and the soul. Catherine is the embodiment of the two forces in Frederic's life. (One is tempted to see her dual nature in her name: *Catherine*, pure, unsullied, and suggestive of the Christian martyr; *Barkley*, because she is English, suggestive of Berkeleianism, the philosophy that holds that physical objects exist only in

being perceived.) Her love for Frederic fulfills the priest's definition—"When you love you wish to do things for. You wish to sacrifice for. You wish to serve."—as she acts out her feelings for him, telling him that she no longer thinks of herself as a separate person, that she exists now completely for his sake, to do whatever he wants. What must be stressed at this point is that she fulfills the priest's definition of love by offering herself *completely* to Frederic, not only physically, and in doing so she presents him with a choice: What is it that Frederic wants from her? What has he always taken? When Catherine finishes tending to his medical needs in the hospital and she asks him what else he would like her to do, Frederic answers, "Come to the bed again."[23] Catherine wishes to give herself completely to Frederic. With his mind narrowed to what Robert Penn Warren would refer to as the "cult of sensation," Frederic takes only what she physically has to offer.

Hemingway portrays Frederic as a selfish sensualist, not only in the beginning, but throughout the book, almost to the very end, as the following examples illustrate. In the beginning of the novel Catherine is little more than a convenience for the satisfaction of Frederic's lust, as he admits when he says that he feels no love for her, that she is simply a better choice than having to go to the local bordello for officers.

In the hospital at Milan, Frederic supposedly declares his love for Catherine at his first sight of her. He tells us that he had not intended to fall in love with Catherine, "But God knows I had."[24] Is Hemingway encouraging us to ask what, in truth, "God knows" about Frederic's declaration of love, or what God's representative, the priest, knows? The nature of Frederic's "love" may be misunderstood at this point if we simply accept as true what the limited first-person narrator, Frederic, says. We must look more closely at how Hemingway shows the feeling arising in Frederic, and then decide if the feeling fulfills the priest's definition of love. When Catherine first appears in the doorway of Frederic's hospital room, he tells us how beautiful she looked to him, more beautiful, he thought, than any other woman he had known. And then he tells us, "When I saw her I was in love with her. Everything turned over inside of me." Frederic's feeling, which *he* labels "love," seems to be based on the physical sight of Catherine—"When I saw her I was in love with her"—enforced by a bodily reaction—"Everything turned

over inside of me." As the priest himself might say, "That is not love. That is only passion and lust."

Hemingway continues to enforce the idea that Frederic's "love" is simply bodily lust. Catherine, asked by Frederic to come back to his room the night of his operation, tells him that he will be sick and he will lose his longing for her. After his operation Frederic admits that Catherine was indeed right. He was sick, and it made no difference to him whether she was there or not. Frederic appears at times to be more anxious than Catherine about their not being married, and yet we find under Frederic's seeming concern his admitting to himself that he enjoyed, really, staying single. Catherine does not want to tell him she is pregnant because she is afraid she will worry him or cause him to be unhappy. His feelings for her, as she sits there beside him pregnant with his child, are best revealed when he tells her that *he* feels trapped. When he takes her to the whorish hotel room for a final round of physical love and she tells him that the room makes her feel like a whore, what are his feelings for her then? He is upset with her for expressing her feelings, since they might detract from his immediate intentions. After he satisfies his various bodily desires, when the time draws near for him to leave Catherine, pregnant with his child, surely at this time it is not unreasonable to expect his feelings for her to be seen, and yet after two brief questions about where she will have the baby and how she will arrange it, questions which she obviously quickly dismisses since she does not want him to worry, he then tells her that it is time to depart. And so the subject is changed, and Frederic, once again, is not too impressively revealing of his concern for Catherine.

When Frederic deserts from the army and meets Catherine at the hotel on the lake they will cross into Switzerland, Hemingway changes the way Frederic expresses his feelings to Catherine, for he tells her now that, without her, he would have nothing left in the world, that he is so in love with her that nothing else exists for him. His expressions of love are similar to Catherine's earlier expressions of no longer having an existence separate from his, of her living now to do whatever he wants. But there is still a lack of balance to be seen: Catherine's statements place the emphasis on Frederic's feelings; Frederic's statements place the emphasis on Frederic's feelings. When is he going to wish to do things for *her*, to sacrifice for *her*, to serve *her*?

When Frederic plays billiards at the hotel with the elderly Count Greffi, they talk about the soul, their becoming devout, and the presence or lack of a religious feeling in each of their lives. Catherine had earlier told Frederic that he is her religion. When Count Greffi tells Frederic that his being in love is a religious experience, does Frederic accept this idea as simply as Catherine would? His answer to the Count, questioning whether love is indeed a religion experience, implies not.

In *The Wound and the Bow*, Edmund Wilson says of their relationship at this point in the novel that, "As soon as we are brought into real intimacy with the lovers, as soon as the author is obliged to see them through a searching personal experience, we find merely an idealized relationship, the abstractions of a lyric emotion."[25] It is true that when Frederic and Catherine reach the house in the mountains of Switzerland, so similar to the setting of the priest's home in Abruzzi, Hemingway does place them within an ideal setting. But we should consider this section of the novel carefully before deciding whether or not Hemingway portrays the relationship between Frederic and Catherine as also ideal. In Switzerland Frederic continues to state his love, but with the emphasis still misplaced upon himself and his own feelings. Does Frederic yet act out his love? Does he exhibit that constant concern for her wants that she does for his? We might expect to see him doing so when he awakens in the night to find Catherine experiencing pains from the impending birth. He asks her if the pains are coming regularly, and when she answers somewhat vaguely, he tells us that he was very sleepy and that he went back to sleep. And so we can find, almost to the end of the novel, diminishing but persisting traces of Frederic's selfish character. He does not, then, possess merely the traits of the "initiate," the typical Hemingway hero, a man, as Warren says, "not obviously given to emotional display or sensitive shrinking."[26] Through his pursuit of sensuality, Frederic is also being presented as a man whose mind is narrowed to an awareness of little but his own desires.

Hemingway clearly contrasts Frederic's character to Catherine's goodness in Frederic's thoughts of her as being one of those people in this world who are exceptionally good, or gentle, or brave, individuals that this world can break only by killing them. Just before her death Catherine says to Frederic that she no longer feels

brave, that she's been broken, and she now knows it. Because Catherine had to be killed to be broken, she can be included among that exceptional group of individuals. Frederic, though, is excluded from this group, for although he is broken by the end of the novel, it is not accomplished by his being killed.

Attempting to keep our attention more focused on the author's craftsmanship, we have thus far been tracing how Hemingway portrayed the sensual, selfish side of Frederic through his relationship with Catherine. But Hemingway also develops another part of Frederic's character. Although his sensuality is maintained, Frederic does undergo a slow and subtle development throughout the entire novel, one that allows him to achieve a greater awareness, not only of Catherine and his relation to her, but of life itself. In the beginning, as a sensualist, Frederic attempts to satisfy his lust in the whorehouse. When he meets Catherine, he narrows his lust to her, but with no thoughts of love. After he is wounded—the first time he is *nearly* defeated, one might say (Frederic states at one point that we do not become Christian until we are defeated. Is it in near defeat, then, that one moves *toward* becoming Christian?)— he experiences feelings of love for Catherine, but they are feelings that still arise from his own physical desires, so when he leaves her again to return to the war he shows little concern for her future. The retreat, his narrow escape from the battle police, and his almost drowning in the river might be seen as the second time he is *nearly* defeated. He comes out of the river to experience another change within himself, a change involving his relationship both to the war and to Catherine. The river, he says, washed his anger away, and his obligation is now shifted to Catherine, for he returns to her as to the only desirable thing left in his life. But the desire is nevertheless a physical one; he is still the sensualist, as he confirms when he explicitly tells us at this point that the only reason he is in this world is to eat and to drink and to go to bed with Catherine.

After he reaches Catherine and they are settled in the hotel, Frederic plays billiards with Count Greffi. During their conversation, Frederic tells him that he might become devout and that he will pray for the Count—a strange remark, coming from Frederic, but suggesting a development to come, for when he later takes Catherine to the hospital, he actually does pray for her. In the face of his possible defeat through the death of Catherine, his "Chris-

tian" awareness of life can be seen slowly broadening: first, to Catherine, as seen in his prayer for her; then to the dead child (Frederic says that, even though he had no religion, he recognized that the child should have been baptised); and finally to his own feelings of love for Catherine. In his prayers for Catherine, Frederic now tells God that he will do anything to save her, and when he speaks to Catherine, he repeatedly asks her what he can do for her. Now, when it is too late, Frederic wishes to sacrifice for, to serve; he is truly in love with Catherine Barkley, when it is too late. Catherine loved Frederic completely but was accepted only physically; Frederic did not achieve that same love for Catherine until her death. The idea of their two loves never quite coming together may well have been what Hemingway meant when he referred to the novel as a *Romeo and Juliet*.

What remains for Frederic to attain is a truer awareness of himself and the role he has played throughout the novel. Hemingway appears to have reserved this attainment for the final scene, for at this point, just before the end, although Frederic achieves a love for Catherine, he still does not feel any responsibility for the consequences of his actions, either with Catherine or in the war. He has earlier said that he did not believe that he would be killed in the war, for it did not have anything to do with him. And now as he views the dead child, he expresses essentially the same feeling, that the child did not seem to have anything to do with him. The child was conceived in the war and is a product of the war, and Frederic is as much responsible for the dead child as he is for the deaths of many within the war. Therefore, this last aspect, Frederic's relation to the war, should be briefly reviewed first, for the final scene must be examined as the culmination of the entire novel.

When Frederic is asked by one of the nurses what his reasons were for entering the war, he answers that he did so because he was in Italy at the time and he spoke Italian. Since it is not a very substantial reason for involving oneself in the deaths of many thousands of men, it raises two significant questions. What compels men, once involved in war, to stop fighting? The answer is given when Frederic tells the priest that armies do not stop fighting so long as they are victorious, that they will continue to wage war, to bring death into the world, until they are defeated. The man who has become Christian by being defeated is the one who stops

fighting. But Frederic, not yet having been defeated, does not comprehend the full meaning of his remark, for he might further ask, *Why* does the Christian stop fighting? Frederic is defeated at the end of the novel. If he becomes Christian because of his defeat, we must look for the answer there.

If *A Farewell to Arms* were meant to end with Catherine's death, then the novel would have stopped at the break on the last page before the last scene. But Hemingway obviously had something more to say, something vital to the novel, for it is this last page that Hemingway himself said he rewrote thirty-nine times. And yet if Frederic's words are literally accepted, the scene remains a shallow one, poignant, as Moloney would say, but surely possessing nothing of a tragic vision.

A Farewell to Arms, however, may be read as a tragedy. Although Frederic Henry has been accepted as admirable for many years now because of his attitude toward life, the admiration seems unwarranted if it is conceded that his attitude results from the very flaw of his character that warps his judgment: his narrowed awareness, a mind restricted to the perception of only sensual experiences, a restriction that causes him to see Catherine as only a physical object. The last step of this tragedy, then, must in some way be the ending that all great tragedy exhibits, the final awareness within the tragic hero of his fault and how it led to the tragedy, and the betterment, not of the circumstances, but of the man himself—a vast amount of meaning to elicit in one image.

> But after I had got them out and shut the door and turned off the light it wasn't any good. It was like saying good-by to a statue. After a while I went out and left the hospital and walked back to the hotel in the rain.[27]

Much has been said by critics about the statement "It was like saying good-by to a statue." To begin to comprehend its meaning, we can look back to two associative passages that Hemingway established earlier in the novel. The first occurs near the beginning of the novel, when Frederic is waiting for Catherine in the office of the hospital: "There were many marble busts on painted wooden pillars along the walls. . . . They had the complete marble quality of all looking alike."[28] If Frederic feels that Catherine's dead body is like a statue, might he not now realize that her physical body, by

itself, that which he thought he loved, is essentially no different from anyone else's body? Rinaldi helps enforce this meaning when he reveals to Frederic a truth he has learned as a man of the body:

> "I tell you something about your good women. Your goddesses. There is only one difference between taking a girl who has always been good and a woman. With a girl it is painful. That's all I know." He slapped the bed with his glove. "And you never know if the girl will really like it."
> "Don't get angry."
> "I'm not angry. I just tell you, baby, for your own good. To save you trouble."
> "That's the only difference?"
> "Yes. But millions of fools like you don't know it."[29]

Hemingway's problem in the final scene of the novel was one of showing the modern, sensual man becoming aware of the soul. Caught within a mind that has been narrowed to experience only the sensuality of his world, Frederic himself has clearly said that he does not know about the soul, for as a sensualist he would have to see the soul to accept its existence. But immediately before Catherine's death he attains a real love for her, not simply for her body, a love that allows him to experience two sights of Catherine—one, when she is alive as the woman he loves; the other, her dead body—and by subtracting the second from the first, Frederic is able to realize his loss. Catherine died as a result of Frederic's wanting and possessing her body, but she also had to die, her final sacrifice for Frederic, for the circumstances to materialize from which he could learn the difference between the body and the soul, to learn that what he finally came to love, and now feels the loss of, has left her body. It was only in his sense of Catherine's having become like a statue that Frederic, being a man of the senses, could possibly realize the difference and learn about the soul.

The child that caused Catherine's death remains as an excellent symbol of Frederic's tragic error: a child of beautiful body, as the doctor who has delivered the child says while holding him up to view: "He's magnificent. He'll weigh five kilos."[30] But it is a body having no breath, possessing no soul.

If we accept as Hemingway's sought-after "third dimension" of prose the extended meaning that Frederic in his two sights of Catherine finally does become aware of the soul, then we might also

realize a fourth dimension: Frederic can now know why the man who becomes Christian stops fighting, no longer wanting to continue killing, for death is no longer simply a physical happening. And perhaps there is even a fifth dimension in a final tragic vision that wars are begun and maintained by men who are ignorant of the soul.

A Farewell to Arms, then, is not simply a love story, nor is it simply a story of war, for these two topics are subordinated to the development of Frederic's growing awareness of life. Throughout the novel, Frederic moves slowly toward becoming Christian. When he deserts from the army, not yet having been defeated, he is not yet Christian, and so he cannot at that point complete his rejection of the war. Only in Catherine's death, if he becomes aware of the consequences of his acts by finally experiencing an understanding of the soul, can he attain a farewell to arms.

How certain can we be that we have grasped the novel as Hemingway conceived it? At the crucial moment, the final scene, where Frederic's awareness should expand to the point of coinciding with Hemingway's, we are faced with a basic problem of craft. We look in vain at the ending for any clear indication from Frederic that he comprehends the significance of his perception that Catherine's body has become like a statue. Certainly we feel the depth of his sadness and can readily admit to his loss being inexpressible. But how are we to know that he comprehends that loss as fully as Hemingway has allowed us to do? With his limited awareness being persistently manifested until the final page, there is little direct evidence that Frederic really knows Catherine's nature.

If Frederic's limitations persist beyond the ending to the time of his narration, if he does not comprehend the nature of his tragedy even as he dramatizes it for us, then we would have to consider him a pathetic figure. However, after Catherine dies and Frederic returns to her room, after he remarks that her body has become like a statue, we can assume that he understands the significance of his remark if we attribute to him at that moment a memory that includes his response to the statues in the hospital and Rinaldi's advice to him about women and sex. Because the final image is Frederic's, we can accept it as having occurred in his mind as a result of such materials established earlier. We can therefore conclude that Hemingway portrayed Frederic as having finally at-

tained an awareness of the soul. Frederic's cryptic statement about the priest seems to support such a conclusion: "He had always known what I did not know and what, when I learned it, I was always able to forget. But I did not know that then, although I learned it later." Frederic makes that comment at the time of his narration, sometime after the events of the novel. Whatever he knows, it is implied, he has learned from those events. And certainly in his language—if we regard it as characterizing Frederic and not Hemingway—and in many of his responses, we see him as an individual possessing the sensitivity needed to experience the full depth of his tragedy. We have also seen him avoid consciously thinking about anything upsetting, an avoidance that would lead him to suppress his verbal responses to his loss of Catherine, but would not rule out his understanding that loss. As he once said to the priest, he never consciously thinks about anything, and yet when he talks to people, he learns that he has discovered things in his own mind without having thought about them. And so we can conclude that on the final page, and afterwards at the time of his narration, Frederic has developed to the point of becoming Hemingway's surrogate, and speaks with the awareness and authority of Hemingway, as he dramatizes his own earlier limitations and the tragedy that results from them.

But then we look again at the concluding sentences of the novel: "It was like saying good-by to a statue. After a while I went out and left the hospital and walked back to the hotel in the rain." We have to surmise that Hemingway took a great chance. Hemingway decided that Frederic would not offer us any explanation of what Frederic had finally experienced. We were to experience the significance of the ending for ourselves within a brief moment that would elicit a single image, which Hemingway assumed would be controlled and clarified by materials he had established in advance. But what if we do not bring the earlier materials to bear on the ending? What if we end the novel by listening solely to the immediate words of the narrator, and the author's more complexly crafted experience remains beyond the boundaries of our awareness? Has Frederic, the narrator, then succeeded in usurping Hemingway's role?

Narrator as Author:
The Separate "I"

ADVENTURES OF HUCKLEBERRY FINN

Each of the authors we have explored thus far established a surrogate narrator who fulfilled his role at the moment he perceived the author's ultimate vision of the world within the novel. We come now to a work in which the author purposefully created a separate narrator who would never develop as a character to the extent of sharing the author's viewpoint. In *Adventures of Huckleberry Finn*, Huck appears as a separate "I" who speaks directly to "you" the reader. Huck is established in the opening lines of the novel as a narrator whose identity is to be distinguished from Twain's: "You don't know about me, without you have read a book by the name of 'The Adventures of Tom Sawyer,' but that ain't no matter. That book was made by Mr. Mark Twain, and he told the truth mainly." Huck does not reveal until the closing lines of the novel that we are reading words supposedly written down at an earlier time by Huck himself: "there ain't nothing more to write about, and I am rotten glad of it, because if I'd a knowed what a trouble it was to make a book I wouldn't a tackled it and ain't agoing to no more." This small gesture by the author toward verisimilitude—we are, after all, reading a book—does not undercut Twain's accomplishment of creating a voice that is dramatically alive. We *listen* to Huck as he

speaks to us about happenings that often seem to be occurring at the very moment he is relating them.

This sense of immediacy in Huck's voice is a beguiling literary creation, effectively diverting our attention away from the author, whose presence as a craftsman in this novel has generally been seen only in his seemingly awkward manipulations of Huck and his world. As a result of this apparent awkwardness, which has raised basic questions among Twain's readers about the novel's integrity, two main critical camps have emerged: those who highlight the novel's apparent flaws, and those who attempt to explain them away. Their critical differences center on the final, long episode of the novel, Huck's and Tom's elaborate, farcical attempt to free Jim from captivity at the Phelps's farm. This episode has repeatedly been judged to be the major structural flaw of the novel, a deviation from the themes and tensions established throughout the former episodes. In response to this charge, defenders of the novel have traced a variety of unifying threads tying the episode to earlier parts of the work—Huck's desire for a family, his apparent death and rebirth, his increasing sense of moral responsibility, his and Jim's search for freedom from society and slavery. Nevertheless, we must admit, along with a host of readers, to being left with the impression that, even after these threads have all been pulled together, the concluding episode still seems to be an awkward ending to the materials that have preceded it.

We can, however, pose a craftsman's question at this point. Was the episode designed to function as a conventional "ending" to the novel? If it is assigned the traditional function of an ending, that of resolving a main conflict established and developed earlier in the work, then it may be judged a failure. However, Twain might not have composed the episode primarily as an "ending," especially since the conflict predominating in Huck's nature throughout the preceding portion of the novel is resolved just before the opening of this incident. Twain says of the novel in one of his notebooks, "a sound heart & a deformed conscience come into collision & conscience suffers defeat."[1] Since the final episode commences immediately after this defeat, we must consider the possibility that Twain decided to extend the novel beyond this point by presenting a new topic of concern: a second major conflict in Huck's nature, which

would be established, developed, and resolved by the farcical happenings at the Phelps's farm.

 Three preliminary steps need to be taken before we can catch sight of Twain in the act of crafting the final episode: we must first examine how he characterized the society which has instilled in Huck his "deformed conscience"; next, we must define, from Twain's perspective, what having a "sound heart" means within this society; and finally we must note the moment in which Huck's sound heart defeats his conscience. Only then will we be ready to walk with Huck up the road to the Phelps's farm.

Twain populates his world with people of widely varying character traits—who nevertheless have disturbing similarities. At one extreme might be placed the "good" people, such as the Widow Douglas, who takes in the son of the town drunk and attempts to raise him in a "regular and decent" manner; or the Wilks girls, who unreservedly give their trust and compassion to everyone seemingly in need of these virtues; or the Phelpses, in whom the above good qualities are combined. At the other extreme are the "bad" people, such as Huck's father, who accepts no responsibility for any existence but his own, and barely accepts that. He believes, on the contrary, that the world should be responsible for him, and so feels that he has a perfect right to leech upon its inhabitants; or, most obviously, the king and the duke, who not only leech but prey upon everyone they meet, including each other, because their life-styles have been fashioned entirely by the strongest motivating force in their natures: an insatiable greed.

However, when the "regular and decent" ways of the "good" people are more closely examined, we discover that these people begin to move toward the other extreme. For example, all aspects of the Widow Douglas's daily life have been regulated by socially accepted conventions. One of these conventions is slavery, which the good Widow shares, without exception, with every "bad" member of her community. Based on the simple premise that "niggers" are merchandise, this particular social code is so pervasive that all consciousness of its dehumanizing effects has been lost even by the best people who appear in this world. Thus, when Mrs. Phelps asks Huck if anyone was hurt by the riverboat accident, and Huck answers, "No'm. Killed a nigger," her response upholds society's unquestioned assumption that human beings are white:

"Well, it's lucky; because sometimes people do get hurt." As the raft proceeds down the river, Twain increasingly contrasts Jim's unfolding humanity with the attitudes held towards "niggers" by the people encountered along the way. The accumulating irony of this contrast culminates at the Phelps's farm after Jim has sacrificed his freedom to help the doctor treat Tom's wound. At the beginning of the novel, the good Miss Watson was tempted to sell Jim to a slave trader for the sum of eight hundred dollars. By the end of the novel, after Jim has shown that he is a man of many human virtues, his greater worth is defined by the old doctor for the people who have gathered to help a neighbor: "I tell you, gentlemen, a nigger like that is worth a thousand dollars—and kind treatment, too." In the terms of this respectable society, Jim's virtues are first listed as merchandise, increasing his market price by two hundred dollars—and the "kind treatment" he receives from these people, who have placed heavy chains on his arms and legs and have put him on a bread-and-water diet, is that "every one of them promised, right out and hearty, that they wouldn't cuss him no more." Thus, we need not consider very seriously Tom's delayed revelation that Miss Watson, on her deathbed, had already made Jim "free," for Jim's paper freedom remains essentially meaningless within all the levels of society presented by Twain. As Huck's father has earlier illustrated, even if Jim were well-dressed, educated, and cultured, society would still allow people like Pap to push him into the gutter as something less than human. And with God's approval, too. For social conventions are also looked upon as being part of God's divine plan. (As Twain mentions of his own upbringing in his *Autobiography*, "In my school-boy days I had no aversion to slavery. . . . the local pulpit taught us that God approved it, that it was a holy thing, and that the doubter need only look in the Bible if he wished to settle his mind—and then the texts were read aloud to us to make the matter sure."2) The ways of society are not only "regular" but "decent," as defined by those prevailing religious attitudes that have been fashioned in society by the teachings of the church. These teachings are accepted in the "sivilized" world in a variety of manners. Some people are more than willing to live their lives in accordance with their religious training—whenever it proves practical to do so. Thus, on the sinking *Walter Scott*, Jake Packard insists on moral grounds that instead of shooting Jim

Turner, he should be left to drown: "I'm unfavorable to killin' a man as long as you can get around it; it ain't good sense, it ain't good morals." Others give verbal assent to their religious training, but manage to overlook its obvious applicability to their own lives. The Grangerfords and Shepherdsons sit in church with their guns and listen to the "preaching—all about brotherly love"; they recognize the value of such teaching: "everybody said it was a good sermon"; and then the next day they go out and slaughter each other as dutiful members of feuding families. Some individuals, through experience, come to recognize the discrepancy between the teachings of the pulpit and the world as it is. Jim tells Huck about the time he gave his last dime to "a nigger name' Balum," who was supposed to be lucky: "Well, Balum he tuck de money, en when he wuz in church he hear de preacher say dat whoever give to de po' len' to de Lord, en boun' to git his money back a hund'd times. So Balum he tuck en give de ten cents to de po' en laid low to see what wuz gwyne to come of it." Huck asks, "Well, what did come of it, Jim?" And Jim's simple but irrefutable answer points up the lie in religious lessons concerning the actual world: "Nuffn' never come of it."

A few individuals who have recognized these incongruities between religion and life make use of religion as an effective aid in preying upon those who have faith in its appearances. We need only recall the king at the camp-meeting, or the king and the duke manipulating the Wilks girls and their townspeople: "Then one of them got on one side of the coffin, and t'other on t'other side, and they kneeled down and rested their foreheads on the coffin, and let on to pray all to theirselves. Well, when it come to that, it worked the crowd like you never see anything like it, and so everybody broke down and went to sobbing right out loud—the poor girls, too." The king's experience has taught him that prevailing religious beliefs, such as God's rewarding the good and punishing the wicked, are actually contrary to the workings of the world as it is. Thus, before entering the town where the Wilks girls live, the king chooses to depart from the raft with Huck, with no plan in mind for his next escapade, and "just trust to Providence." When he runs into "a nice innocent-looking young country jake," who unexpectedly supplies him in conversation with all the information he needs to bilk the Wilks girls and their townspeople, the king draws the

obvious moral he has learned during the course of his long and varied life of deception: "Thish-yer comes of trust'n to Providence. It's the best way, in the long run. I've tried 'em all, and ther' ain't no better way."

A closer look at the social conventions of this world reveals that they are generally based on distortions of reality, regulated lies that society instills into each of its members. For example, we might list with those pervasive distortions wrought by slavery and religion the lie fostered by all conventions of social behavior and dress: that a man's clothing and manners are reflective of his true nature. As Huck watches the king put on his "store clothes," he learns how totally deceiving one's appearance can be: "The king's duds was all black, and he did look real swell and starchy. I never knowed how clothes could change a body before. Why, before, he looked like the orneriest old rip that ever was; but now, when he'd take off his new white beaver and make a bow and do a smile, he looked that grand and good and pious that you'd say he had walked right out of the ark, and maybe was old Leviticus himself." In various ways Twain dramatizes that the average member of society unquestioningly tries to live out these lies. When Colonel Sherburn faces the lynch-mob after shooting down Boggs, he tells them, "Your newspapers call you a brave people so much that you think you *are* braver than any other people—"; then he reveals the truth they are attempting to gloss over by clinging to such a distorted view of their own natures: he has learned from his experiences in the North and the South that "The average man's a coward." And to substantiate his statement, he scatters the mob simply by standing up to them and calling their bluff. Thus, society fosters hypocrisy among its members, which they practice among themselves, and so make the "normal" social relationship one that is based on lies.

As Huck makes his way down the river through various social settings, his most effective defense against people who live falsely with themselves and with others proves to be his capacity to lie. Having reached the age of twelve or thirteen, Huck uses lying as his "regular" manner for coping with people "in a tight place," for his experiences thus far in life have taught him no other approach. Not until he arrives at the Wilks girls' house, over halfway through the novel, and decides to expose the king and the duke to Mary Jane does he realize that there are circumstances in which telling

the truth can be a more efficient means of dealing with trouble: "I says to myself, I reckon a body that ups and tells the truth when he is in a tight place, is taking considerable many resks, though I ain't had no experience, and can't say for certain; but it looks so to me, anyway; and yet here's a case where I'm blest if it don't look to me like the truth is better, and actuly *safer*, than a lie. I must lay it by in my mind, and think it over some time or other, it's so kind of strange and unregular. I never see nothin like it."

We begin to perceive how Twain defined the nature of Huck's "sound heart" as we observe how Huck uses lying and telling the truth, not simply to insure his own survival within a generally false society, but also in sympathetic response to the feelings of others. For example, when Huck first arrives at the Wilks girls' house and watches the king and the duke act out their deception, he plays his own deceptive role to help them, with little concern for the newly met girls, of whose good natures he as yet has no awareness. However, by the time Huck overhears the duke suggest to the king that they depart in the night with the bag of money, Huck's attitude towards the girls has changed: "That made me feel pretty bad. About an hour or two ago, it would a been a little different, but now it made me feel bad and disappointed." This change was obviously brought about within the previous "hour or two" as Huck watched Mary Jane and Susan, with kindness and consideration for his feelings, make Joanna apologize to him for doubting his lies about his life in England: "And when she got through, they all jest laid theirselves out to make me feel at home and know I was amongst friends. I felt so ornery and low down and mean, that I says to myself, My mind's made up; I'll hive that money for them or bust."

When he later sees Mary Jane crying in her room as she is packing to go to England, he goes in to comfort her because, as he says, "I felt awful bad to see it; of course anybody would." But of course anybody would not—we need only imagine the king passing her door. When Huck discovers that she is crying about the slaves having been separated, he blurts out that they will be returned in two weeks—"Laws it was out before I could think!"—since his first consideration at this moment is for her feelings, not for any thoughts about the possible consequences of telling her.

One of the most dramatic responses Huck makes to another person's feelings occurs on the raft after he tricks Jim into thinking

that their separation in the fog had all been a dream. Jim accepts the lie until the sky clears up enough for him to see "the leaves and rubbish on the raft, and the smashed oar." Turning then and looking at Huck "steady, without ever smiling," Jim tells him what he had been feeling as he was alone in the fog: "my heart wuz mos' broke bekase you wuz los', en I didn' k'yer no mo' what become er me en de raf'." His concern for Huck had been so intensely upsetting that when he awoke and found Huck on the raft, "all safe en soun', de tears come en I could a got down on my knees en kiss yo' foot I's so thankful." Jim's concern, however, was not returned by Huck, who simply did not conceive of Jim as having such emotions. "En all you wuz thinkin 'bout wuz how you could make a fool uv ole Jim wid a lie." Having earlier lived with the assumption fostered by society that slaves, as merchandise, are by nature different from people, Huck now experiences the astonishing dignity of Jim's humanity as Jim tells him what he thinks of Huck's trick: "Dat truck dah is *trash*; en trash is what people is dat puts dirt on de head er dey fren's en makes 'em ashamed." As soon as he is aware of Jim's emotions, however, Huck reacts accordingly: "It made me feel so mean I could almost kissed *his* foot to get him to take it back." And then, in contradiction to every value upheld by his world, Huck follows the urging of his young, uncivilized heart and chooses to seek Jim's forgiveness. "It was fifteen minutes before I could work myself up to go and humble myself to a nigger—but I done it, and I warn't ever sorry for it afterwards, neither. I didn't do him no more mean tricks, and I wouldn't done that one," Huck concludes, revealing once again his natural sympathy for others, "if I'd a knowed it would make him feel that way."

The depth of Huck's natural sympathy is manifested in his final response to the king and the duke. Of all the characters who appear in the world of the novel, they have the greatest capacity for arousing vindictiveness in others. Even "sweet and lovely" Mary Jane Wilks, upon hearing of their fraudulent behavior, blurts out to Huck, "Come—don't waste a minute—not a second—we'll have them tarred and feathered, and flung in the river!" We might expect their vicious treatment of Huck and Jim to make Huck equally spiteful toward them, for their provocation is indeed extreme. As Huck says, when he hears they have sold Jim, "After all this long journey, and after all we'd done for them scoundrels, here was it all

come to nothing, everything all busted up and ruined, because they could have the heart to serve Jim such a trick as that, and make him a slave again all his life, and amongst strangers, too, for forty dirty dollars." And yet, as he watches the king and the duke, tarred and feathered, being carried out of town on a rail, his reaction is, not the socially acceptable one of a cruel satisfaction at seeing them get the punishment they have long deserved, but one of personally sympathizing with them in their present plight, and of forgiving them for all the past deeds of their distorted lives: "Well, it made me sick to see it; and I was sorry for them poor pitiful rascals, it seemed like I couldn't ever feel any hardness against them any more in the world. It was a dreadful thing to see. Human beings *can* be awful cruel to one another."

Thus, after examining Huck's responses to the variety of individuals he encounters in his world, we can see how Twain gave the following characteristics to Huck's "sound heart": first, Huck's capability of recognizing that everyone has feelings, from an aristocractic Southerner to a runaway slave; second, his natural sympathy toward everyone's feelings, which fortunately proves to be stronger than the discriminating teachings of society; third, and perhaps his rarest quality, considering the generally deplorable state of humanity, his inability to maintain within himself a negative feeling toward any other human being, including the most vicious and unprincipled representatives of the civilized world.

Because Huck is essentially different in nature from the people who live as members of society, he is faced throughout the novel with an apparently insoluble problem, which Twain illustrates most clearly whenever Huck is by himself. While living at the Widow Douglas's, for example, as he sits alone at night in his room, he looks out the window and tries "to think of something cheerful, but it warn't no use. I felt so lonesome I most wished I was dead." Later in the book, as he approaches the Phelps's farmhouse, with Jim having been sold by the king and the duke, who have also left Huck to himself, he hears "the dim hum of a spinning-wheel wailing along up and sinking along down again; and then I knowed for certain I wished I was dead—for that *is* the lonesomest sound in the whole world." Huck's almost unbearable sense of loneliness impels him to seek the society of others, until he confronts the dire consequences of their living according to regulated lies, and is repelled once more

to loneliness. This pendulum movement between these alternatives illustrates the principal dilemma experienced by Huck within the world of the novel: whether to become a part of society by allowing its conventions to prevail within him, or to live according to his own "sound heart" in an essentially lonely existence. During the course of the novel, Huck does manage at times to avoid this dilemma with the companionship of one other person. After he makes his way by himself to Jackson's Island and discovers that Jim is also there, his immediate reaction is, "I was ever so glad to see Jim. I warn't lonesome now." As the only other good-natured individual in the novel who is also compelled to separate himself from society, Jim offers Huck his one means of escaping from both society and loneliness—until, with his paper freedom, Jim is accepted back into society at the end of the novel.

Throughout most of the novel, from the beginning until the time Huck meets Tom Sawyer at the Phelps's farm, Twain develops the conflict existing in Huck's nature between the natural urgings of Huck's "sound heart" and the voice of his "conscience," which asserts the lies that society has instilled in him. It is important to note that, even though Huck has been raised by Pap in a relatively uncivilized manner, his life has nevertheless been partly shaped by the conventions of his society. Twain introduces Huck as a totally naive boy, who readily accepts whatever he is told as true until his experience proves otherwise. When Tom, for example, calls his gang together at the opening of the novel and "said he had got secret news by his spies that next day a whole parcel of Spanish merchants and rich A-rabs was going to camp in Cave Hollow with two hundred elephants, and six hundred camels, and over a thousand 'sumter' mules, all loaded down with di'monds, and they didn't have only a guard of four hundred soldiers," Huck's reaction is: "I didn't believe we could lick such a crowd of Spaniards and A-rabs, but I wanted to see the camels and elephants, so I was on hand next day," at which time he learns "that all that stuff was only just one of Tom Sawyer's lies."

Huck's attitude toward slavery at the opening of the novel is no different from that of any civilized member of his town. And his moving in with the Widow quickly compounds society's effects upon him. The degree to which he has been influenced is established dramatically when Pap first appears in Huck's room. Pap is

disdainful of the changes that he immediately sees have occurred in Huck as a result of his living within such a house. He ridicules Huck's "starchy clothes," his "bed, and bed-clothes; and a look'n-glass; and a piece of carpet on the floor"; he is disturbed that Huck has been "educated," and particularly that Huck has been taught to read; and he predicts a corruption to come if Huck continues in these "hifalut'n" ways, not knowing that Huck has already experienced it: "First you know you'll get religion, too. I never see such a son." Huck's early life with Pap and his present stay at the Widow Douglas's have resulted, in varying degrees, in his being instilled with the conventions generally upheld by members of society regarding slavery, clothes, household furnishings, education, and religion. Keeping these conventions in mind, we can see definite changes occurring in Huck as he lives in his new "home" on the raft with Jim. Their "wigwam" is barely furnished, with two beds, "a straw tick" and "a corn-shuck tick," and a small spot for a fire. Their clothes are easily put aside: "we was always naked, day and night, whenever the mosquitoes would let us. . . . I didn't go much on clothes, nohow." After Huck later realizes, by watching the king dress, that clothes can be used to deceive others, he displays a new ability to manipulate this societal lie, just as he uses his own lies, to accomplish his own ends. Thus, before going to the Phelps's farm to determine if he can steal Jim once more, he first puts on his "store clothes," as the king might do, to disguise his intended deception with a more socially acceptable appearance.

Although Huck never rejects society's attitude toward slavery, his experiences do qualify his conception of it considerably by increasing his awareness of Jim's humanity, illustrated by such earlier examined incidents as Huck's response to Jim when he tricks him after the fog, and by Huck's discovery that Jim is longing deeply for his wife and children: "I do believe he cared just as much for his people as white folks does for their'n. It don't seem natural, but I reckon it's so." Thus, by the time the king and the duke sell Jim back into slavery, Huck has come to realize that although Jim may still be merchandise, he is also a man: "I said to myself it would be a thousand times better for Jim to he a slave at home where his family was, as long as he'd *got* to be a slave." The religious training Huck received while at the Widow Douglas's exerts its strongest influence upon him just before he goes to the Phelps's farm.

When, as Huck says, "my conscience went to grinding me" about helping Jim escape, Huck realizes "all of a sudden that here was the plain hand of Providence slapping me in the face and letting me know my wickedness was being watched all the time from up there in heaven," for Huck has been taught by society to believe "that people that acts as I's been acting about that nigger goes to everlasting fire." To still his conscience, he writes a letter to Miss Watson, telling her where Jim is, and is relieved to find that he feels "good and all washed clean of sin." But then he begins thinking of his experiences on the raft with Jim, "and I see Jim before me, all the time, in the day, and in the night-time, sometimes moonlight, sometimes storms, and we a floating along, talking, and singing, and laughing. . . . I's see him standing my watch on top of his'n, stead of calling me, so I could go on sleeping; and see him how glad he was when I come back out of the fog; and when I come to him again in the swamp, up there where the feud was: and such like times."

Then, after remembering that he is the only friend that Jim now has, he happens to look at the letter he has written. At this crucial moment Huck's "sound heart" once again prevails over the voice of his "conscience": "It was a close place. I took it up, and held it in my hand. I was a trembling, because I'd got to decide, forever, betwixt two things, and I knowed it. I studied a minute, sort of holding my breath, and then says to myself: 'All right, then, I'll *go* to hell'—and tore it up." Even though Huck accepts society's assertion that slavery is a convention upheld by God, his nature fortunately will not allow him to deny or to distort the stronger emotional truths of his own experience.

Shortly after Huck reaches this decision, and immediately before Huck and Tom begin to plan a way to free Jim, Twain has Huck completely reject his conscience, thus resolving the first main conflict that has persisted within his nature from the beginning of the novel. After arriving too late to prevent the king and the duke from being ridden out of town on a rail, and then feeling his conscience begin to bother him again for no apparent reason, Huck finally realizes the worthlessness of this part of his nature: "it don't make no difference whether you do right or wrong, a person's conscience ain't got no sense, and just goes for him *anyway*. If I had a yaller dog that didn't know no more than a person's conscience does, I

would pison him. It takes up more room than all the rest of a person's insides, and yet ain't no good, nohow."

Contrary to the usual critical charges that this book is only roughly structured, we can perceive by this point that the incidents have been carefully selected and arranged: Twain begins by introducing Huck as a totally naive boy who accepts whatever he is told as true until his own experiences confirm or deny it. Twain next illustrates the degree to which society has succeeded in influencing Huck because of his naïveté. He then takes Huck through a sequence of experiences fashioned to show how Huck, as he learns of the discrepancies in society's teachings, qualifies or overcomes all of society's pernicious effects upon him, both those already accomplished within him and those confronted anew during his adventures down the river. By the time he reaches the Phelps's farm, Huck has shown that he possesses the capacity to turn away easily from a conventional life of comfortable furnishings and starchy clothes; he has learned how clothes, manners, and religious training can all be used as effective aids to deceive oneself and others; and, in spite of prevailing attitudes toward slavery and religion, he has learned that Jim is such a good human being that he would rather go to hell than betray Jim's friendship. Furthermore, he has gained the additional capacity to remain unaffected by newly encountered conventions, such as the pride of the Southern aristocracy, which compels Colonel Sherburn to shoot down a harmless old fool like Boggs, or the family duty maintained by the Grangerfords as they unquestioningly carry on their senseless feud.

Having successfully resolved Huck's conflict with his conscience, Twain commences the final, long episode. As a craftsman concerned with the integrity of his novel, Twain now chooses to extend his work by developing a second major conflict within Huck's nature that was foreshadowed early in the novel: Huck's "sound heart" is now threatened by the only convention remaining from those earlier listed as having already influenced him—his "education." Within Huck's education lurks another dangerous potential for distorting his nature, for society is capable, not only of instilling in Huck a deformed conscience, but also of distorting his intellect. When Huck finally rejects his conscience as worthless, saying it "ain't no good, nohow," his next sentence, which concludes the chapter is, "Tom Sawyer he says the same." Twain now

has Tom Sawyer reenter the novel to offer Huck another alternative to living his life according to the dictates of his conscience: that of following his head rather than his heart.

At the beginning of the next chapter (34), after Huck hears Tom figure out "detective fashion" where Jim is being held prisoner, Huck praises what he believes is the most admirable part of Tom's nature: "What a head for just a boy to have! If I had Tom Sawyer's head, I wouldn't trade it off to be a duke, nor mate of a steamboat, nor clown in a circus, nor nothing I can think of." Twain repeatedly refers to Tom's head throughout the final portion of the novel. For example, Tom thinks that if there are no "difficulties and dangers" to their plan, it is more honorable "to contrive them out of your own head"; after the plan appears to be moving along well, "He said it was the best fun he ever had in his life, and the most intellectural"; after he awakens from the delirium caused by his wound, excited about the outcome of their adventure, and Aunt Sally thinks he is "out of his head again," Tom blurts out, "No, I ain't out of my HEAD"; later, he reveals to Huck "what he had planned in his head" if the escape had succeeded without his being wounded. As mentioned above, Tom, like Huck, has rejected his conscience as being worthless—but their natures have nevertheless remained basically different. Huck's "sound heart" has thus far predominated within him, even over his capacity to think (for example, as stated earlier, when Huck comforts Mary Jane Wilks by telling her the truth about the slaves, he says: "Laws it was out before I could think!") Tom, on the other hand, as a result of having been "educated," has chosen to follow, above all else, the "intellectural" dictates of his head. In the final episode, Twain dramatizes the ways in which Tom's nature has been deformed by such an approach to life, and the dangerous degree to which Tom influences Huck to follow his lead.

The deformed aspects of Tom's ability to think are manifested in two particular ways. When Huck questions the need for making Jim a rope ladder, Tom says, "Huck, you don't ever seem to want to do anything that's regular; you want to be starting something fresh all the time." Tom defines what "regular" means to him when Huck objects to using case-knives to dig a hole under the cabin in which Jim is a prisoner: "It don't make no difference how foolish it is, it's the *right* way—and it's the regular way. And there ain't no

other way, that ever *I* heard of, and I've read all the books that gives any information about these things." Tom accepts completely the authority of the printed word. Making no apparent distinction between fiction and nonfiction, in fact showing a propensity for romantic novels, Tom attempts to regulate his existence by enforcing the past conventions he discovers in books upon present circumstances, whether they are applicable or not. And when the circumstances do not permit him to conform to the rules, such as when he realizes that they do not have thirty-seven years to dig through to Jim, he solves the problem by using his head again in another distorted manner: "Things being so uncertain, what I recommend is this: that we really dig right in, as quick as we can; and after that, we can let on, to ourselves, that we was at it thirty-seven years."

Huck agrees to go along with Tom's suggestion: " 'Now, there's *sense* in that,' I says. 'Letting on don't cost nothing; letting on ain't no trouble.' " When Tom admits that the case-knives will not work for digging and suggests they use picks "and *let on* its case-knives," Huck once again agrees, with the mistaken belief that Tom is using his head to come closer to a fresh and practical approach to their problem: " '*Now* you're *talking*!' I says; 'your head gets leveler and leveler all the time, Tom Sawyer,' I says. 'Picks is the thing, moral or no moral; and as for me, I don't care shucks for the morality of it, nohow. When I start in to steal a nigger. . . . if a pick's the handiest thing, that's the thing I's agoing to dig that nigger . . . out with; and I don't give a dead rat what the authorities thinks about it nuther.' "

But Tom is incapable of accepting Huck's attitude, for his life is not directed, as Huck's is, by the lessons of his own experience; nor does he ever realize that Huck's common sense is indicative of a less distorted ability to think than he displays. Tom now opposes Huck's way of living by asserting the responsibility that he believes results from possessing an educated head: "right is right, and wrong is wrong, and a body ain't got no business doing wrong when he ain't ignorant and knows better. It might answer for *you* to dig Jim out with a pick, *without* any letting-on, because you don't know no better; but it wouldn't for me, because I do know better." Huck gives in and follows Tom because he, too, thinks that Tom knows "better" than he. Considering the almost overwhelming number of exciting escapes that Huck has already experienced—

from Pap's cabin, Jackson's Island, the sinking steamboat, the Grangerford feud, the Royal Nonesuch, the Wilks girls' townspeople—ironically, Huck submits to Tom with the belief that Tom's reading of books has given him more knowledge of the "right" way to bring off an adventurous escape.

Jim adopts a similar attitude. By nature Jim is as practical as Huck: when the boys first dig in to him, he "was for having us hunt up a cold chisel to cut the chain off of his leg with, right away, and clearing out without losing any time." To an even greater degree than Huck, however, because of his having lived his life as a slave, Jim has been influenced by society to subordinate his own thoughts and feelings to what appears to him to be superior knowledge: "But Tom he showed him how unregular it would be, and set down and told him all about our plans. . . . Jim he couldn't see no sense in the most of it, but he allowed we was white folks and knowed better than him; so he was satisfied, and said he would do it all just as Tom said."

Twain is often criticized for changing Huck's relationship to Jim in this final section. Readers have questioned how Huck, after the emotional depth of his earlier experiences with Jim, could allow Tom to take Jim through such a farcical situation. We must not, however, overlook the fact that Huck himself is made into a similarly farcical figure. We need only recall Huck dressed in the "yaller girl's frock" delivering the first "nonnamous letter"; or Huck, with blistered hands, helping Jim roll along the "gaudy big grindstone" onto which they will both scratch Tom's "mournful inscription"—while, as Huck says, "Tom superintended. He could out-superintend any boy I ever see. He knowed how to do everything." We can argue, therefore, that Twain presents Huck and Jim as being equally responsible for the ridiculous circumstances into which they allow themselves to be led, for both submit to the "rules" and "regulations" that Tom has learned "in his head" from books, while ignoring the more comprehensive knowledge attained from the experiences and the emotions of their own lives. Thus, part of Twain's intention in writing this long concluding episode appears to be that of comically illustrating how any individual, even someone as fresh and practical as Huck or Jim, can make a farce of his own existence by willingly allowing his entire nature to be subordinated by a socially deformed intellect.

By submitting to Tom's influence, Huck actually moves closer to the ways of society. Tom's kind of "education," which fosters the unquestioning acceptance of all information passed on by "authorities," carried to the point where one would rather lie to himself by "letting on" than admit to any discrepancy, typifies the means by which every socially regulated lie illustrated earlier has been promulgated by members of society. To suggest the potential danger of their conforming in this manner, Twain likens the two boys and their activities in the final section to characters and events appearing earlier in the work. For example, Tom wants Huck to wear the "yaller girl's frock" the night Huck delivers the letter so that he will look like a servant girl who fulfilled a similar role in one of Tom's books. When Huck objects to wearing the dress, since, as he says, "there won't be nobody to see what I look like, *anyway*," Tom answers: " 'That ain't got nothing to do with it. The thing for us to do, is just to do our duty, and not worry about whether anybody *sees* us do it or not. Hain't you got no principle at all?' " We can recall here a ritual followed by the Grangerfords, where the sons begin each morning by bowing and drinking the same toast to their parents: "Our duty to you, sir, and madame"—an apparently admirable sense of family duty, which they fulfill by continuing their senseless feud with the Shepherdsons without ever knowing, or even questioning, why they are doing so, until the father and all the sons of the family, including young Buck, are shot to death.

The dire direction in which Tom and Huck are heading by following Tom's approach to life is further suggested by Twain's consistent comparison of the boys to the two characters in the novel whose deformed intellects have most grossly distorted their natures: the king and the duke use their heads to live completely deceptive lives based entirely on their ability to "let on." There are numerous parallels that enforce this comparison. For example, Huck's being unexpectedly welcomed in by Mrs. Phelps leads him to a conclusion recollective of the king's philosophy of deception: "Providence had stood by me this fur, all right." Huck's praise for Tom's head is reminiscent of the king's praise for the duke during the Wilks girls episode: "duke—you *have* got a rattlin' clever head on you. . . . You have cert'nly got the most astonishin' head I ever see."

We should consider how well the following description fits the king and the duke: two characters who impersonate distant relatives of a good family for the purpose of stealing from them, who play insensitively on the feelings of that family as they work out their plot, who use clothes, manners, and religion to aid them in their deception, and whose escapade results in their being chased by a band of men. It might also be mentioned that one of the characters is of such a nature that he is not even above deceiving his own partner in their venture. This description, which certainly applies to the king and the duke, also fits Tom and Huck, without exception. Huck plays the role of Tom Sawyer, and Tom plays Sid, distant relatives who have come for a visit, as they act out their deception of the Phelpses with the intention of stealing Jim. Tom, of course, deceives Huck from the beginning in not telling him that Jim has already been freed. To aid them in their plot, they use clothes (Huck's "store clothes" and the dresses they steal at the farm), manners (when Tom, playing a stranger, first arrives at the Phelps's, for example, and is asked to dinner, "he thanked them very hearty and handsome . . . and he made another bow"), and religion (when the boys write the second "nonnamous letter," they give the message an air of sincerity with the method used by the king at the camp-meeting: "I am one of the gang, but have got religion and wish to quit it and lead a honest life again"). And their plot results in an armed band of men chasing them to the river, where, like the king and the duke upon their first appearance in the novel, they escape in a canoe and make their way to the safety of the raft.

Furthermore, although they appear to be only boys engaged in generally comic activities, we discover in them, as they pursue Tom's "intellectural" ways, a dangerous potential, reminiscent of the most corrupted adults in society, for remaining insensitive to the feelings of other human beings. When the boys begin to steal things from around the farm and the losses are called to Aunt Sally's attention, the method they choose to hide their thefts from her is to anger and confuse her, such as when they keep switching the spoons and the sheets as she tries to count them, until she is "just a trembling all over, she was so mad," and "she didn't *care*" how many there were "and warn't agoing to bullyrag the rest of her soul out about it, and wouldn't count them again not to save

her life, she druther die first." After the first "nonnamous letter" is delivered and pictures of a skull and crossbones and of a coffin are stuck on the doors, Huck remarks:

> I never see a family in such a sweat. They couldn't a been worse scared if the place had a been full of ghosts laying for them behind everything.... If a door banged, Aunt Sally she jumped, and said "ouch!" ... she couldn't face noway and be satisfied, because she allowed there was something behind her every time ... and she was afraid to go to bed, but she dasn't set up. So the thing was working very well, Tom said; he said he never see a thing work more satisfactory. He said it showed it was done right.

By having Tom consider the deeply disturbed feelings of the family simply as a means of indicating how "well" his plan is working, Twain illustrates the degree to which Tom's head has distorted his nature by predominating over his heart.

And by having Huck follow Tom to this point, Twain also illustrates that Huck's "sound heart," which earlier would have responded naturally and sympathetically to Aunt Sally's feelings, is dangerously submissive to the "intellectural" ways Huck has adopted under Tom's tutelage. Fortunately, however, as events proceed, Twain shows Huck's own nature reasserting itself over Tom's influence. This reversal begins when Aunt Sally makes Huck go into the sitting room and he discovers "Fifteen farmers, and every one of them had a gun." Huck wants immediately to "get away and tell Tom how we'd overdone this thing, and what a thundering hornet's nest we'd got ourselves into, so we could stop fooling around, straight off, and clear out with Jim before these rips got out of patience and come for us." When he reaches the cabin and tells Tom that the house is full of armed men, Tom reacts in his usual manner: "Why, Huck, if it was to do over again, I bet I could fetch two hundred! If we could put it off till—" But Huck interrupts him with "Hurry! *hurry*!" for he is no longer interested in how grand they can make the escape. Shocked into a new awareness by this latest development in their plans, he realizes now that their "letting on," contrary to his original belief that it "don't cost nothing," could possibly cost all of them their lives. After they make their hazardous escape to the raft and discover that Tom has been shot, both Huck and Jim refuse to follow Tom's order to "man the sweeps, and set her loose!" After "consulting—and thinking" together—using their

own heads again, one might say, to make a practical response to their immediate situation—Huck and Jim decide that a doctor must be brought to the raft, in spite of Tom's repeated insistence to the contrary. Nor do they subsequently pay any attention to Tom's elaborate method for bringing the doctor. When Huck arrives at the doctor's house, his explanation of how Tom received his wound reflects the lesson this latest experience has taught him—that dire consequences can result from "letting on" about one's world: "He had a dream, and it shot him."

Huck's naturally sympathetic response to the feelings of others is restored once again after Mr. Phelps finds him in town and takes him back to the farm. When he goes to bed that night, Aunt Sally "come up with me and fetched her candle, and tucked me in, and mothered me so good I felt mean, and like I couldn't look her in the face." As he watches her tears "drip down, silent," he sees how deeply grieved she is over Tom's disappearance. "And when she was going away," Huck says, "she looked down in my eyes, so steady and gentle," and she asks him to be good and not to run away again that night. We can imagine how Tom Sawyer would have reacted to her request: her emotions would have had little or no effect upon his desire to continue his adventure. Huck, however, responds differently. With thoughts of both Aunt Sally and Tom troubling him through the night, his "sound heart" finally prevails once more within his nature: "But she was on my mind, and Tom was on my mind; so I slept very restless. And twice I went down the rod, away in the night, and slipped around front, and see her setting there by her candle in the window with her eyes towards the road and the tears in them; and I wished I could do something for her, but I couldn't, only to swear that I wouldn't never do nothing to grieve her any more."

Huck's resolve never to grieve Aunt Sally again does not, however, imply that he will hereafter be willing to accommodate his life to her civilized existence as a member of society, for although she and her townspeople are generally good individuals, they still regulate their lives according to society's conventional lies. For example, even though the doctor, as Huck says, "had a good heart in him and was a good man," he nevertheless has been distorted by society's values to the point where he places his responsibility to uphold slavery above his responsibility as a doctor. He explains

to the townspeople the problem he faced when Jim appeared on the raft to help him care for Tom's wound: "Of course I judged he must be a runaway nigger, and there I *was*! . . . It was a fix, I tell you! I had a couple of patients with the chills, and of course I'd of liked to run up to town and see them, but I dasn't, because the nigger might get away, and then I'd be to blame."

We conclude, therefore, by stressing that Twain uses Huck's consistent nature to unify the seemingly disparate parts of the novel: all of the episodes comprising this work, whatever else they may illustrate individually, establish in common the resilience of Huck's "sound heart" among the many deforming influences of his world. By the end of his adventures, Huck has managed, on his own, to reject his worthless conscience and to turn from Tom's "intellectural" ways back to his own common sense. Twain continues Huck's pendulum movement between the alternatives of a distorted life in society and an unbearably lonely existence to emphasize that Huck has persisted thus far in not submitting to a conventional life. After trying unsuccessfully to remain isolated from society on the raft with Jim, and after experiencing the dangerous inadequacy of Tom's approach to life, Huck is left by Twain, in the closing lines of the novel, with a final alternative: "But I reckon I got to light out for the Territory ahead of the rest, because Aunt Sally she's going to adopt me and sivilize me and I can't stand it. I been there before." Still refusing to be subordinated to "sivilized" ways, and with Jim having been accepted back into society, Huck prefers to make his own way to the uncivilized "Territory," where, if we may surmise from the variety of experiences Huck has already undergone in life, his naturally good heart will continue to prevail.

Adventures of Huckleberry Finn, in the judgment of most critics, is a seriously flawed classic. Hosts of readers have reluctantly expressed their discomfort with the final episode, viewing it as the unfortunate result of Twain's back-sliding into cruder forms of folk humor and farce. Certainly we cannot ignore that the novel has its rough spots. But are we willing therefore to agree that Twain was not a competent craftsman? Did he simply move Huck along through a number of loosely strung episodes until he had accumulated enough pages to offer his readers another book, for whatever it was worth? Or did he select and arrange his materials according

to some organizational principle that would ultimately allow him to integrate the entire work before he released it for publication?

We have attempted to follow Twain's footsteps through the novel, with each step representing a craftsman's final choice. We should be left at the end with a clear sense of resolution: Huck's "sound heart" prevails over the distorting forces of society wrought within his own nature, first primarily in his "conscience" and then in his "head." And we should remember that Huck is still a boy, and so should not expect him to share Twain's vision by the end. Huck's "sound heart" may prevail, but he is still affected by society to varying degrees, as seen in his persisting acceptance of slavery. He may choose to go to hell himself for violating society's conventions regarding slavery, but as a boy he has not yet developed the capacity to refute and reject those conventions.

Thus, our challenge as teachers is to encourage our students to experience fully Huck's remarkable existence within the troubled, episodic world of the novel, while having them further view the unifying features of the work from Twain's larger perspective. As Huck himself has so often illustrated in his own adventures, the greatness of the novel will never be established by the insistent assertions of authority. It is experienced, or lost, in each student's reading of the work.

THE CATCHER IN THE RYE

Adventures of Huckleberry Finn and *The Catcher in the Rye* have obvious similarities—and profound differences. Each has a young and naive narrator whose natural goodness is tested as he makes his way through the distorting influences of his world. Huck and Holden both experience an unbearable loneliness that impels them to seek the society of others; the others generally turn out to be deformed individuals who repel Huck and Holden back into loneliness. Each boy grows as a result of his experiences during the course of the novel, but never to the extent of sharing the author's ultimate viewpoint.

Huck and Holden both have distinctive and appealing voices. They each speak as "I" directly to "you," the reader, about happenings that appear to be occurring at the moment of their narration. This sense of immediacy, as we noted earlier, allowed Twain to

divert our attention away from himself as craftsman—to the point where his readers may have overlooked Twain's careful handling of the materials in his final episode. Holden's voice has proven to be even more beguiling, for readers have apparently remained unaware that Salinger has crafted one of the most elaborately constructed sets of symbols to be found within an American novel.

Twain established the two central conflicts of his novel within Huck's nature: heart versus deformed conscience, and heart versus distorted head. Huck's naturally "sound heart" finally prevailed over both. Salinger has a different view of human nature, more complex, more difficult to dramatize, and as old as mankind's philosophical musings. Salinger focuses on the dangerous division existing between Holden's "heart" and "head," and on the need for Holden to integrate the two if he is to develop into a complete human being.

Salinger opens his novel by having Holden state his intention of telling about the "madman stuff" that happened to him around the previous Christmas. Throughout the novel, whenever he acts in an apparently inexplicable manner, Holden repeatedly asserts that he is a "madman" or that he is "crazy." For example, after telephoning Sally Hayes and making a date, Holden says, when she finally appears, that although he didn't really even care for her, he felt as though he were in love and wanted to marry her. "I swear to God I'm a madman."[3]

Salinger has Holden frequently refer to himself as a madman, but without having Holden realize the basis of the comparison: that his nature, which should be developing toward maturity, has stalled within an early state of childhood. A child, at birth, is able to perceive and to feel, but is not yet capable of thinking rationally. He remains an essentially irrational creature—like a madman—until he develops the capability of exerting his rational thought over his random feelings. Although he is a boy of uncommonly deep sensibilities, his nature is still childishly one-sided, for his feelings, like a child's, still predominate over his inadequately developed intellect. Thus, we consistently find Holden's thoughts being either suppressed by, or occurring as a result of, his feelings. For example, after he arrives in New York and checks into a hotel, his sense of loneliness urges him to consider telephoning Jane at her college. After figuring out the excuse he would use to get her to the phone

so late at night, he doesn't call her. The reason he gives is that he wasn't in the right mood—a "reason" that he offers repeatedly throughout his narrative. Later, when he accepts the elevator boy's proposition to send a whore to his room, Holden remarks that his emotional state stopped him from thinking. "When you're feeling very depressed, you can't even think."[4]

Salinger also has Holden's feelings predominate over Holden's experiences of things outside himself. Each of his experiences generally arouses within him an immediate emotional response, over which he exerts no rational control, as is illustrated, for example, by his reaction to Stradlater's statement that his ex-date is too old for Holden: "All of a sudden—for no good reason, really,"[5] he grabs Stradlater in a wrestling hold. Because Holden generally reacts to things outside himself in this manner, with no conscious awareness of the causal relationship between his experiences and his emotional responses, he views his world as a place where things usually *happen* to him *all of a sudden* as immediate occurrences—or, we might stress, they *hap*pen to him as though by *chance*: "Then all of a sudden, something very spooky started happening"[6]; "Then something terrible happened just as I got in the park."[7] It is important to realize that the sense of immediacy accompanying everything that happens to Holden divides his existence into a temporal sequence of seemingly isolated instances occurring one after the other, as is manifested on almost every page of the novel as both his thoughts and his actions repeatedly occur "all of a sudden."

Salinger establishes this sense of immediacy within each thing that happens to Holden to dramatize Holden's sense of transciency. Because he experiences his world temporally, with the present moment always becoming a segment of the past, Holden views his life as being in a state of continual change. Since a developed intellect is needed to realize immutable conceptions, and since Holden's "thinking" is limited to his sense of the mutability of life, Holden remains trapped within time, unable to recognize anything permanent in human existence. For example, as he walks through the park, he recalls the Museum of Natural History from his grammar-school days as a place in which everything displayed in the glass cases stays the same, and mentions how he and the other children, by contrast, changed from visit to visit. Then he remem-

bers Phoebe and wishes he could place her in one of the glass cases to keep her from changing.

Holden would like to keep Phoebe a child because he is troubled by the differences he sees between children and adults, both in their physical appearances and in their personalities. Holden finds children physically acceptable under any conditions, but not adults. Adults become more physically repulsive to Holden the older they get, as his reaction to old Spencer, his history teacher, illustrates. Spencer, as Holden notes, has a terribly stooped posture, ugly chest and legs, and everything in Spencer's room smells like Vicks Nose Drops.

The personality of a child is also preferable to Holden. Phoebe typifies all that Holden likes about a child's nature. For example, she is very affectionate toward him. She is also able to converse with him. And she is capable of discriminating between the good and the lousy things existing in her world, such as the movies they see together.

Salinger, however, moves beyond Holden's limited comprehension to offer his readers a more complex dramatization of human nature. Salinger illustrates, through the crafting of his materials, that as the child grows toward adulthood, its nature undergoes elemental changes. This inevitable consequence of existence is caused, not simply by aging, but by the child's accumulated experiences of its world—as Holden tries to explain when talking about the museum, where everything stays the same except the children visiting, who continue to take in daily experiences of their world, such as wearing a different coat, or having a substitute teacher, or listening to their parents arguing, or seeing a rain puddle with "gasoline rainbows" in it.

This change occurring within the developing child as he experiences his world proves to be, in part, a corrupting one—as is manifested throughout the novel in a variety of ways, but most consistently, perhaps, by the change occurring in the state of one's breath as he matures. Holden remarks in particular whenever anyone has bad breath, such as an aunt of his who has halitosis, or Ackley, who has both halitosis and sinus trouble, causing him to breathe with difficulty when he sleeps, or the Cuban man with bad breath who asks Holden where the subway is and then keeps breathing in Holden's face as Holden gives him directions. The

significance of these recurrent references to breath may at first remain elusive, for, as is often the case in this novel, a symbol that Salinger introduces early in the work may not be understood until he offers a later clarifying passage. In this instance, Holden comments as he is waiting in his hotel room for Sunny, the prostitute, that he tested whether his breath smelled from cigarettes and the alcohol he had drunk at Ernie's bar. "All you do is hold your hand under your mouth and blow your breath up towards the old nostrils."[8] We are reminded by this seemingly casual statement of another act of blowing breath into nostrils: "And the Lord God formed man of the dust of the ground, and breathed into his nostrils the breath of life; and man became a living soul." An examination of additional evidence will further substantiate that Salinger has established in the novel this Biblical association of man's breath with his spirit or soul. Holden's act of blowing his own breath up into his nostrils must therefore be looked on as a more meaningful test than simply one of determining if his breath smells. In other words, the extent to which Holden's breath has been tainted, in this case by the adult acts of drinking and smoking, is, by implication, the extent to which Holden's spirit has been corrupted.

After Holden tests his breath, he brushes his teeth. To brush one's teeth, or to make one's breath smell better, thus becomes equivalent, in symbolic terms, to cleansing one's spirit. As a result, spiritual significance is given to bathrooms, where one cleanses not only his body, but also his soul, a view that is emphasized when Phoebe's mother asks her if she has said her prayers, and Phoebe answers that she said them in the bathroom.

Most people in the novel, however, do not keep their breath clean: Ackley, for example, never brushes his teeth. And most people, unconsciously or indifferently, breathe their tainted breath on others, such as the Cuban man mentioned earlier, or Charlene, the Caulfield maid, who, as Phoebe stresses, always breathes on Phoebe, on her food, and on everything else. Unlike these other people, Holden tries to remain conscious of the state his breath is in by blowing it up into his own nostrils; he tries to keep his breath clean whenever he thinks that it may smell bad; and he is deeply upset whenever he breathes his tainted breath on anyone else, especially if he believes that the other person is untainted, as is illustrated at the end of Holden's breakfast with the nuns, when he

accidently blows smoke in their faces, and apologizes like a "mad-man." Holden's earlier references to himself as a "madman" were based on the irrationality he manifested within his life because of his emotions predominating over his thought. In this instance, however, Holden apologizes to the nuns "like a madman" because of the tainted state of his breath. Salinger establishes this additional basis for the comparison by having Holden refer to his next-to-fa-vorite character in the Bible: "that lunatic and all, that lived in the tombs and kept cutting himself with stones."[9] To understand how the term "madman" is also equated with one whose breath is tainted, we must pursue Holden's biblical allusion to the opening verses of St. Mark:

> And they came over unto the other side of the sea, into the country of the Gad-a-renes.
>
> And when he was come out of the ship, immediately there met him out of the tombs a man with an unclean spirit,
>
> Who had his dwelling among the tombs. . . .
>
> And always, day and night, he was in the mountains, and in the tombs, crying, and cutting himself with stones.

This particular madman is described as "a man with an unclean spirit." Holden apparently identifies with this man because he feels himself to be existing in a similar state: his "unclean spirit," as noted above, is manifested by his breath, tainted by cigarettes and alcohol. This correlation of tainted breath-unclean spirit-madman is maintained throughout the novel as Holden repeatedly com-ments on how he smokes and drinks like a madman. Furthermore, the biblical madman, unlike most of the people in the novel, is trying to keep his corrupted spirit isolated from the rest of the world—a point that also appeals to Holden, as will later be discussed.

Salinger also emphasizes another elemental change in a devel-oping human being: as one's breath continues to be tainted, a loss of breath results. Holden repeatedly comments on being out of breath as a result of smoking too much. The older one grows, the more one experiences this loss, as is illustrated by the Pency Prep alumnus who returns for a visit on Veterans Day and loses his breath just from going up the stairs. Apparently, one finally reaches a state of existence similar to that of Holden's history teacher, old

Spencer, who has the grippe, a disease of the lungs, and who must rely on Vicks Nose Drops to get his breath into his nostrils.

Most of the people encountered by Holden in the novel have already experienced, to varying degrees, the corrupting influence of this world, people whose behavior Holden generally labels as *phony*, for they do not even realize that they have been corrupted. For example, after Holden sees Ernie, the snobbish piano player, make his humble bow to the applauding crowd, he notes that Ernie probably no longer realizes any more whether he is playing well or not, since his audience applauds loudly however he plays. Watching the Christmas Show at Radio City, Holden sees nothing religious about a group of actors carrying crucifixes around the stage, for they all look to Holden as though they are just waiting to go out and have a cigarette. Even Mr. Antolini, an adult who has earlier gained Holden's respect, behaves in a way that causes Holden to run from his apartment, thinking of him as a "flit."

Considering his many contacts with spiritually deficient adults, we can see why Holden likes children so much, for the individual most likely still to have breath would be the one who has least experienced this world, or, in other words, the child—a role obviously fulfilled by Phoebe. When Holden sneaks home and dances with Phoebe, he says afterwards that he was out of breath, but that Phoebe was not. Phoebe uses the pseudonym Hazel Weatherfield. Holden says that Phoebe misspells the first name as Hazle, an archaic word meaning "dry," which can be joined with the initial part of the second name to form a meaningful phrase: Hazle Weather. This phrase, which implies, as part of Phoebe's pseudonym, that she is to be associated with "dry weather," helps clarify the meaning of wet weather, or rain, which is used throughout the novel to symbolize what the child has not yet been altered by: the inevitably corrupting experiences of this world. Holden's repeatedly stated preference for weather that is sunny and dry reflects his desire to exist in a climate that, unlike damp weather, would not be detrimental to his already impaired lungs. Phoebe's association with dry weather suggests that she has yet to experience the world to the point where her breath is affected.

Holden can remember when he, too, as a small child, was also out of the rain. He recalls the auditorium in the museum and how he loved the smell it had, as though it were always raining outside,

and the auditorium was the only dry setting in the entire world. But Holden is no longer a small boy. Finding himself now on the brink of adulthood, he will soon be sitting in a pouring rain, as we see him doing at the end of the novel. Holden's dilemma, therefore, throughout the book, is that he is unable to prevent his impending loss of that uncorrupted spirit possessed by children, such as Phoebe, before they have been immersed in the experiences of this world.

Holden's sense of this inevitable loss of childhood spirit is further manifested by his feeling that he might disappear whenever he crosses a street, that he might step from the curb, as though from a cliff, and fall out of sight, as is illustrated by his walk up Fifth Avenue near the end of the novel, where he does not stop until he is "way up in the Sixties" to catch his breath. To understand why childhood might "disappear" in a street, we must realize the symbolic significance of movement. (In this particular instance, the numbers of the streets crossed by Holden are suggestively correlated with chronological stages in an individual's life. For example, old Spencer may be recalled here for an explanation of why Holden does not stop crossing streets until he is "way up in the Sixties." When Holden goes to visit his history teacher, he mentions having seen on an earlier visit an old Navajo blanket that Spencer and his wife had bought in Yellowstone Park. He then adds that someone as old as Spencer can get a great deal of pleasure from simply buying an old blanket. The point he is making is clarified when he arrives at the house and asks Mrs. Spencer if Mr. Spencer is over his grippe yet, and she answers, "Over it! Holden, he's behaving like a perfect—I don't know what."[10] Mr. Spencer is behaving like a perfect—child, we may add, for what Holden finds appealing about old Spencer, and the reason that Holden is able to stop crossing streets when he is "way up in the Sixties," is that a man of old Spencer's age has reached his *second* childhood.)

However strained this last correlation may be, the important idea to be derived from this material is that Salinger has made *movement*, usually in a straight line, symbolic, not only of aging, but of proceeding from one state of existence to another. Salinger uses various colloquial expressions in the novel to strengthen this idea, such as Mrs. Hayes's criticism that Holden has no direction in life, or Mr. Antolini's advice to Holden about the first step he should

take when he knows where he wants to go. This symbolic conception of movement functions consistently throughout the novel to clarify such points as (1) why Holden always wants to feel a goodbye, to *know* he is leaving a place, or a state such as childhood, rather than discovering one day that it is no longer there, or that it has disappeared; (2) why Holden always wants to know where he is going, as seen when he keeps getting up from his seat on the subway to look at the map, and loses all the fencing foils, or when he admits that sex is something he does not understand because "You never know *where* the hell you are"[11]; and (3) why Holden is persistently concerned with taxis, trains, buses, suitcases, hotels—anything suggestive of traveling, of proceeding out of one place or state into another.

Salinger also symbolically develops a second kind of movement, up and down. Any downward movement—toward earth, we might say—suggests a deeper immersion into the experiences of this world. Thus, any kind of fall, from a cliff, into a street, out of a window, implies a loss of childhood spirit, which Holden would prefer to keep up, on a cliff, above any involvement with the world below. Throughout his entire narrative, Holden feels increasingly depressed, until, just before the resolution to the novel, he reaches his lowest state of depression. This word, "depress," denotes both an emotional state: "to lower in spirits," and a physical movement: "to press down; lower." We can understand, therefore, why Holden is "depressed" by such thoughts as having to take suitcases down in elevators, for a combination of depressing movements is suggested in this act: downward in the elevator, and forward on a trip to another place.

Faced with his impending movement into the spiritually impaired state of adulthood, Holden considers various means of escaping from the world's influences to preserve his childhood. For example, he attempts at times to close himself off from these influences. This particular means of escape is reflected in the peculiar name the author has given him: Holden Caulfield. The division noted earlier in Phoebe's pseudonym, Hazle Weather/field, directs our attention to a similar division in the name Holden Caul/field. *Holden* is an archaic past participle of *hold*, and *Caul*, traced back to Old French *cale*, a kind of cap, is a membrane sometimes enveloping the head of a child at birth. Within the limits of Holden's

narrative, that which is "held" by him as a "caul," a kind of cap, is obviously his red hunting hat, which has a peak that Holden pulls down over his eyes and earlaps to cover his ears. Just as a membrane enveloping the head of a child at birth would temporarily keep the child from perceiving the world into which it is born, Holden's red hunting hat functions at times to close him off from his world.

Holden would also like to stop his development toward adulthood by physically preserving his body from change, as is illustrated by his interest in the Egyptian mummies, who were treated in ways that prevented their flesh from rotting, essentially preserving them for long spans of time, and by his interest in what happens to the ducks in the lagoon in Central Park when the lagoon freezes over. The significance of the ducks is clarified when Holden encounters Horwitz, the taxi driver, who turns their conversation away from the ducks to talk about how the fish are able to exist in the ice, not moving, frozen in place for the winter. Horwitz thus establishes that the fish are by nature capable of achieving a complete lack of movement—by a method, however, of no use to Holden, as Horwitz reveals when he adds that if Holden were a fish, Mother Nature would look after him in the same way. Unfortunately, Holden is not a fish. Mother Nature has not fulfilled his need. Being warm-blooded, he shares the plight of the ducks; his getting frozen in the ice for the entire winter is no solution to his dilemma. On the contrary, when Holden, with wet hair, begins to feel ice forming on the back of his head, he realizes that he could catch pneumonia, a disease of the lungs.

Holden also tries to escape the influences of this world by using his imagination to form a fantasy: he attempts to create a "make-believe" substitute for the actual world, one in which, even though he has become "big," he is capable of preserving the state of childhood. Thus, he mentally fashions for himself the role of the catcher in the rye, standing at the edge of a cliff as children play nearby in a rye field, and catching them before they fall off. The peculiar setting of this fantasy is recollective of two actual settings Holden would like to avoid, since they are not as beneficial to the preservation of childhood. The first setting, analogous to the cliff, is any street-curb from which, as noted earlier, a child may step and fall down in the street, possibly ending his childhood. Holden

removes this danger in his fantasy by giving himself the role of the catcher. The second setting, analogous to the big field, is the park. In contrast with the city, with its concentrated gathering of corrupted adults, the park is a setting more often associated, in the context of Holden's experiences, with children. However, unlike the big field in Holden's "make-believe" world, in which children can play without falling from childhood, the park too clearly reflects those corrupting influences of the actual world from which Holden wishes to escape, for Holden finds the actual park to be a lousy setting, full of dog droppings and cigar butts, and the benches looking as though they had just been rained on.

Holden's fantasy, however, proves to be no practical solution to the dilemma he faces in the actual world. And so, in desperation, as the novel nears its conclusion, Holden decides to attempt a compromise withdrawal from the world, a withdrawal similar to the kind he considered early in the novel when he asked Ackley about how to join a monastery. He decides that he will go out West, where it is dry and sunny (an escape from rain), and live there as a deaf-mute (an escape from people).

Shortly after reaching this decision, an incident occurs that illustrates for Holden the futility of attempting any retreat from this world. As he is waiting for Phoebe at the museum to return her Christmas money before starting out West, he meets two small boys who ask where the mummies are. As they near the tomb of the mummies, the two boys become frightened and run off, leaving Holden by himself in a setting recollective of the biblical madman, who withdrew from the world to live "in the tombs." Alone now in the museum tomb of the mummies, Holden experiences a moment of peace, until he notices a familiar obscenity scrawled on the wall: "Fuck you." Holden now recognizes that he will never be able to escape this corrupting world, not even within a tomb or a grave—in other words, in death. He is positive now that his own tombstone will have his name, his dates, and then "Fuck you" on it. The obscenity is particularly meaningful to Holden's dilemma, for not only does it express an adult act that confuses Holden—"You never know *where* the hell you are"—the crude statement also suggests a corruption of that act, another worldly influence to be experienced by growing children, as Holden notes when he first

sees the obscenity on the school wall and worries about Phoebe and the other children seeing it.

Once Holden realizes that he cannot escape the world's corrupting influences, he leaves the tomb, goes into the bathroom in the museum, and falls. This event, we must assume, since it occurs in a bathroom (a place that has earlier been given spiritual significance), is meant to signify the fall of Holden's childhood spirit, as is also suggested by the ensuing change in his relationship with Phoebe after he leaves the bathroom and meets her out in front of the museum. The evening before he fell, Holden went home to see Phoebe, a warm and tenderly sad meeting between a child and a boy who was leaving childhood. Now, when Phoebe arrives and asks Holden if she can go with him out West, he responds to her almost abusively: he tells her to shut up, grabs the suitcase she is carrying, and makes her cry. As a result, Phoebe gets so mad at him that she, in turn, tells him to shut up, and then runs across the street, leaving Holden on the opposite side—an act that strengthens the sense of separation now existing between them. After this crucial moment, however, in which Holden appears to have been defeated in his desire to remain close to childhood, the sequence of events that Salinger develops to end the novel shows the breach between Holden and Phoebe being repaired. And as a result of their moving slowly back together into another warm relationship, Holden finally experiences a resolution to the dilemma he has faced throughout the novel.

Salinger has Holden experience this resolution at the moment that Holden's previously one-sided nature becomes complete. As mentioned earlier, Holden's feelings, like a child's, have predominated over his inadequately developed intellect. Although a variety of happenings contribute to the awakening of Holden's intellect, we might look closely at two in particular. When Holden sneaks home to visit Phoebe, her reaction illustrates, and thus allows Holden to gain a better perspective of, the one-sided nature of the irrational child. When Phoebe tells Holden that their father will be angry about his leaving school, she then hides her head under her pillow in her bed, as, Holden tells us, she often does. Holden pleads with her to take the pillow off her head, but she refuses to do so, and Holden recognizes that "You can't even reason with her sometimes." Holden goes next to Mr. Antolini's apart-

ment, where Mr. Antolini advises him that Holden is by nature a student seeking knowledge, and so in the subsequent direction his life will take, his intellect will play a necessary role. An important point is then clarified by Mr. Antolini. Holden's nature has thus far remained one-sided because, in his responses to his perceptions of the world, his emotions have prevailed within him; but the other side of human nature, the intellect, can be equally delimiting to one's life. We might recall Carl Luce, who had the highest I.Q. at Holden's prep school. The narrow self-satisfaction and the lack of any meaningful feelings for others he manifests during his conversation with Holden at the Wicker Bar dramatically illustrates that intellect, by itself, is as distorting to one's life as irrational emotion. Mr. Antolini now clarifies for Holden that a human being must fulfill both sides of his nature. Thus, says Mr. Antolini, if Holden continues searching for knowledge, "you're going to start getting closer and closer . . . to the kind of *information* that will be very, very dear to your *heart*."[12] (Italics added.) In other words, Mr. Antolini is asserting that within the complete human being, intellect and emotion, which are usually considered opposite and conflicting forces, must exist and work together.

Holden is later awakened by Mr. Antolini patting him on the head, an act Salinger apparently uses to signify the awakening of Holden's intellect, for after Holden flees from the apartment, embarrassed by Mr. Antolini's behavior, Holden reveals that his intellect is no longer subordinated by his emotions. After his immediate emotional rejection of Mr. Antolini, Holden begins to "think" about the incident: "I started thinking that even if he was a flit he certainly'd been very nice to me."[13] Holden now consciously recognizes that he need not totally reject an individual for behaving at times in a phony way, since opposite qualities can exist in the same person at the same time.

If Salinger had earlier characterized Holden as someone who responded to everything he experienced with both sides of his nature, Holden would have recognized the existence of opposite qualities, not only within people, but in every single thing he perceived in his world. For example, the Museum of Natural History would have appeared to him, not only as a number of isolated glass cases in which everything always stayed the same, but as a record of the whole flux of evolutionary development that

has continuously changed everything existing on this earth. Salinger found the solution to Holden's dilemma in Holden's being able to perceive, with both sides of his nature, that everything in reality has two faces: that the ice in the lagoon in Central Park can both preserve and kill; that the "gasoline rainbows" Holden mentions are composed of "gasoline" and "rainbows"; that an old teacher can be like a child, and a child, such as Phoebe, can act at times, as Holden says, like a schoolteacher; that everyone's nature extends, at the same time, back toward childhood and forward toward adulthood. We can see Holden himself, with his hat on backwards, facing in two directions, as typifying the sense of reality that Salinger established in this novel. Therefore, if something that stays the same also conveys a sense of continuous change, then something that Holden earlier saw as continuously changing, such as childhood, should also convey a sense of staying the same.

Holden gains this new awareness as a result of reexperiencing his own childhood. When he decides to leave for the West, he wishes first to return Phoebe's Christmas money. Planning to tell her, in a note, to meet him at the museum, he goes to Phoebe's school, where he experiences the sense of everything being exactly the way it was when he attended the school. Thus, when he sees a boy going toward the bathroom, he notes that the boy is carrying the same kind of wooden pass that Holden used to carry. And when he sits on the stairs to write the note, he remarks that the stairs smell the same now as they did when he went to the school. By reexperiencing his own childhood in relationship to that of Phoebe's generation, Holden is able to associate childhood, not only with the past, as something waning and ending, but also with the future, as something beginning and becoming. Holden has thus far remained trapped in time, unable to recognize anything permanent within human existence, because of his inability to perceive that both the past and the future may be found in the present moment. Continuing now in this new direction, he eventually reaches such a moment: as he watches Phoebe on the carousel, his sense of the past and his sense of the future become completely integrated, and he finally experiences an immutable conception of childhood.

We approach this moment by starting at the point where Holden meets Phoebe in front of the museum. Her appearance at that time is recollective of Holden's earlier in the novel: she is wearing his red

hunting hat and carrying his old suitcase, and, Holden notices, she is out of breath from carrying the suitcase. When she asks to go with him out West, his initial outburst of emotion angers Phoebe and causes her to turn away from him. After he takes the suitcase into the check-room in the museum, he then comes out and tries to *reason* with her: If he lets her skip school that afternoon, will she stop her "crazy" behavior? (We might note here in passing that Holden reacts at this point first with emotion and then with reason, illustrating that though both sides of his nature are now active, they still remain divided from each other.) When he repeats his question, she responds to this apparently adult attempt to keep her in childhood by acting, we might say, "like a child." In a manner reminiscent of Holden's one-sided reactions to his world, she responds irrationally, like a "madman," running across the street away from him without looking either way for oncoming cars. After this moment of separation, Holden and Phoebe slowly move back together again. When they reach the zoo, Phoebe crosses back to Holden's side, but stays behind, following him, until she stops to watch the sea lions. Holden then goes back and stands behind her. As they go through the zoo, she then walks on the opposite side of the sidewalk from him. When they leave the zoo and head for the carousel, Holden remarks that she then walks next to him. Finally, she starts talking to him again, asking him about the carousel, and he asks her if she wants to go for a ride. By the time they reach the carousel and Holden watches her going around on her first ride, he reveals that he has gained a new perspective concerning her movements and her eventual fall. Phoebe, like the other children on the carousel, tries to grab for the gold ring. As he watches her, Holden worries that she might fall, but he recognizes now that it would be wrong to interfere: "The thing with kids is, if they want to grab for the gold ring, you have to let them do it. . . . If they fall off, they fall off, but it's bad if you say anything to them."[14]

Holden has become intellectually capable of giving up his desire to be the catcher in the rye. Holden's hunting hat, at this moment, reenforces the idea that Holden has given up the role of the catcher. Phoebe put the hat back on Holden's head for a while as it began to rain. When Holden says, as he sits in the downpour, that his neck got soaked, he is apparently referring to the now exposed *back* of his neck, the point being made indirectly that Phoebe has put the

hat on him with the peak forward, not backwards as a catcher would wear it.

Holden realizes by this point that it is "bad" to keep a child in childhood. As he has learned from watching Phoebe's anger wane with the passing of time and events, Phoebe must be allowed to experience her world if her one-sided nature is to develop beyond its present state. It is "bad" to interrupt her movement forward, even though it will result in the eventual fall of her inexperienced, innocent spirit, for the only alternative to this process would be to keep her in the same state, unmoving, undeveloping, as though she were in a glass case—an eternal child, but an incomplete and lifeless human being.

Therefore, Holden becomes capable of accepting the necessity for movement within a child's existence. Even though it steadily brings the child into greater contact with corrupting influences, the child will never attain a complete existence unless it continues "becoming" within this world. This change within Holden's outlook is stunningly illustrated at the end on the novel when all of the movements developed symbolically throughout Holden's narrative are brought together in a manner acceptable to Holden: that is, by the movements of Phoebe on the carousel. We must first recall, as presented earlier, that a *forward* movement is suggestive of proceeding from one state of being to another, and that a movement *up* suggests the uncorrupting isolation of spiritual heights, and *down*, a deeper immersion into worldly experiences. As Phoebe rides upon her horse, her actions illustrate every one of these symbolic movements: she goes forward, a suggestion of her nature changing, but in a circular motion, which keeps her essentially in the same place; and, at the same time, the horse she sits on continues moving her up and down. As a result, all of these characteristic motions, with all of their opposite qualities, are harmoniously blended within the immediate moment for Holden's perception as he watches Phoebe on the carousel riding her horse around and around.

As the various aspects of Phoebe's ride are more closely examined, we discover that Salinger has fashioned the carousel into a symbol embodying such a host of opposite qualities that it approaches, as a literary creation, the inexhaustible complexity of reality. Having noted the interplay of opposite motions established

above, we can look now at a sampling of the other ambiguities associated with the carousel. For example, as Holden approaches the carousel with Phoebe, he remarks that it is playing the same music that it played when he was a child, that the little children now riding it were having the same experience he had. Within Holden's immediate perception of the carousel, we find a sense of the past—in Holden's remembrance and reexperience of his own particular childhood—and of the future, as suggested by the presence of the little kids—childhood, in other words, as a general state, continuously beginning.

Salinger uses two colloquial phrases throughout the novel to establish an additional ambiguity associated with the carousel. At different times throughout his narration Holden mentions "horsing around. . . . It was very childish." In other words, "horsing around" is equivalent to acting "childish." Phoebe, on the carousel, is literally "horsing around." As noted earlier, her going "around," if contrasted with movement in a straight line, suggests a permanence in the childhood state she is experiencing at that moment. But a second phrase used in the novel implies a limitation to that experience, for although she may be "horsing around," she is also, at the same time, "riding for a fall."

The song that the carousel plays for the children as Phoebe first rides is "Smoke Gets in Your Eyes," a title that brings to mind those earlier references to the debilitating effect of cigarette smoke upon one's breath, or spirit. Thus, the carousel, as a symbol of enduring childhood, plays a song suggestive of its eventual corruption.

As noted before, Phoebe's going "around," rather than straight ahead, suggests that she exists, while on the carousel, within an unchanging, timeless state. However, as her name establishes, Phoebe may be associated with the moon—and as the moon goes "around and around," it constantly changes, moving through phases that have been used for ages as a standard of time. Furthermore, as Hazle Weatherfield, she was associated with dry weather; as Phoebe, however, she is also related to wet weather, again through her connection with the moon, which has been traditionally viewed as having control over the rain.

We might also consider placing the following surmise within this sampling of ambiguities. Two colors are brought together as Phoebe rides the carousel: blue and brown. Since she is still an

unfallen child, the blue of her coat might possibly suggest the height at which she exists in spirit: above the earth, in the sky, or the heavens—where one would also see the moon; the horse she rides is brown, a color we may associate with the earth. If these two colors are, indeed, suggestive of the heavens and the earth, then they might be viewed together as another effective illustration of the dependency of human existence upon a blending of spirit and matter.

The carousel, therefore, as a symbol composed of a complexity of opposite qualities and tenuous ambiguities, all existing together within a harmony of music and motion, typifies the sense of reality Holden finally perceives. As a result, the dilemma that he has faced throughout his narration is resolved, for he is capable now, as he sits in the rain, of accepting the world as it is. Furthermore, as is revealed by his concluding response to Phoebe on the carousel, the divisive aspects of his nature, his emotions and his intellect, are finally integrated: "I felt so damn happy all of a sudden, the way old Phoebe kept going around and around. . . . I don't know why. It was just that she looked so damn *nice*, the way she kept going around and around in her blue coat and all."[15]

By means of these seemingly simple statements, Salinger establishes that Holden's response at this moment is an *aesthetic* one: he "felt so damn happy" because "she looked so damn *nice*." An aesthetic response is, by nature, a blending of sense perception, emotion, and intellect. It is not dependent on one's being conscious of a reason for responding so—as Holden says, "I don't know why." It is elicited only when one perceives something that gives pleasure to every aspect of one's nature at the same moment—a pleasure manifested in this case when Holden, by simply watching Phoebe on the carousel, feels "so damn happy."

Where, then, is Holden at the end of the novel? Critics have seen him as narrating his story to an analyst in a mental institution, Holden's concluding retreat from his world. But why would Holden talk *about* the psychoanalyst if he were supposedly talking *to* the analyst? And certainly at least one psychoanalyst is often found on the staff of various kinds of institutions. Furthermore, why would Holden have been placed in a mental institution in the West rather than near his home? We need not surmise in this manner to determine where Holden is. Salinger gives us enough

information in the novel to place Holden exactly: within a particular state of existence. On the final page, Holden refers to his becoming sick after he went home. The nature of Holden's sickness was clarified at the beginning of the novel, for when Holden introduced his narrative from the unidentified place he is in, he refers again to his loss of breath from smoking too much and to his having grown considerably in height during the previous year: "That's also how I practically got t.b. and came out here for all these goddam checkups and stuff."[16] Having finally attained a solution to his dilemma, Holden is now attempting to recover, at least partially, from the particular physical impairment caused by his experience of growing up within a corrupting world. He is out West—but no longer wishing to isolate himself from people—because the dry and sunny climate is beneficial to his immediate condition. Avoiding the rain temporarily, apparently in a sanitarium for lung diseases, Holden is recovering from his loss of breath.

We conclude by stressing that Holden is talking, not to an analyst, but to "you," the reader. Holden's reason for doing so was established earlier by Mr. Antolini, when he described for Holden "the kind of information that will be very, very dear to your heart." Holden will discover, Mr. Antolini says, that many people before him have also been troubled and confused by human behavior and by the corruption of the human spirit from experiencing this world. Fortunately, Mr. Antolini tells him, some of them wrote down their troubled thoughts and feelings: "You'll learn from them—if you want to. Just as someday, if you have something to offer, someone will learn something from you."[17] Holden is talking directly to anyone who might be as troubled as Holden was about the nature of this world in which everyone exists. He offers his narration of *The Catcher in the Rye* as a record of his troubles for anyone who might wish to learn from his experiences. As Mr. Antolini says, "It's a beautiful reciprocal arrangement. And it isn't education. It's history. It's poetry."[18]

In writing *The Catcher in the Rye*, Salinger may have been influenced by the writings of Carl Jung, especially *The Integration of the Personality*, as is suggested by the many parallels existing between these two works. For example, in reporting the dreams of a particular individual whose personality has yet to become integrated, Jung notes a dream in which the dreamer makes a statement that

might serve as a fitting description of Holden Caulfield's dilemma: "The existence of the left does not contradict that of the right. Both are in every man. . . . there are *symmetrical* and *crooked* persons. The crooked ones are those who can realize only the *one* side in themselves, the left *or* the right. They are still in a childhood state."[19] The course to be taken by such a one-sided individual, as described by Jung, parallels the direction Holden finally takes, which leads to the integration of his divided nature: "No one can free himself from his childhood without first generously occupying himself with it. . . . Nor is this freedom accomplished through mere intellectual knowledge; it can be effected only by a re-remembering, which is also a *re-experiencing*."[20]

The carousel, which plays such a central role in the completion of Holden's development, fits Jung's description of a "mandala," a symbol of integration or wholeness: " 'Mandala' . . . means circle or magic circle. Its symbolism embraces all concentrically arranged figures, all circular or square circumferences having a centre, and all radial or spherical arrangements."[21] As a mandala figure, the carousel would also be included by Jung within a particular class of archtypes, which he labels *archtypes of transformation*: "these archtypes are genuine and true symbols. . . . just in so far as they are ambiguous, full of intimations, and, in the last analysis, inexhaustible. . . . Our intellectual judgement, of course, keeps trying to establish their singleness of meaning, and so misses the essential point; for what we should above all establish . . . is their manifold meaning, their almost unbounded fullness of reference."[22]

Such symbols of man's developing nature will always include ambiguities and contrarieties, but as Jung categorically states, and as Holden finally experiences: "in human life there is no totality that is not based upon the conflict of opposites."[23] Jung further describes this central truth about human life by recalling a paradoxical remark attributed to Thales, that only rust gives a coin its value. In a passage that may be suitably applied to Holden's existence, Jung states that the remark "simply means that there is no light without shadow and no psychic completeness without imperfection. To round itself out, life calls, not for *perfection*, but for *completeness*."[24] Those persisting ambiguities within Holden's state of existence at the end of the novel may illustrate one of the most strongly emphasized ideas of Jung's work: "*For in the adult there is*

hidden a child—an eternal child, something that is always becoming, is never completed. . . . This is the part of human personality that wishes to develop and to complete itself."[25]

If Salinger was indeed influenced by Jung's *The Integration of the Personality*, he would have found it difficult not to go on to Friedrich Schiller's letters on aesthetic education. As Jung nears the end of his book, he refers his readers to Schiller's work in a most enticing manner: "The yearning for personality has become a real problem that occupies many minds today, whereas earlier there was only one man who foresaw this question—Friedrich Schiller—and his letters on aesthetic education have lain dormant like a Sleeping Beauty of literature while more than a century has passed."[26] Within Schiller's letters we discover a concern with the opposing demands made upon man by each aspect of his "sensuous-rational nature" and a method for harmonizing these contrarieties: that of making man "aesthetic." Schiller defines this term as follows:

For readers to whom the pure significance of this word—so often misused through ignorance—is not entirely familiar, what follows may serve as an explanation. Every phenomenon whatsoever may be thought of in four different connections. A thing may relate directly to our sensuous condition (our being and well-being); that is its *physical* character. Or it can relate to our reason, and furnish us with knowledge; that is its *logical* character. Or it can relate to our will, and be regarded as an object of choice for a rational being; that is its *moral* character. Or finally, it can relate to the totality of our various powers, without being a specific object for any single one of them; that is its *aesthetic* character. A man can be pleasant to us through his readiness to oblige; he can cause us to think by means of his transactions; he can instil respect into us by his high moral standards; but finally, independently of all these and without our taking into consideration any law or any design in our own judgement of him, but simply contemplating him, simply by his manifesting himself—he can please us. In this last-named character we are judging him aesthetically.[27]

At the end of *The Catcher in the Rye*, Holden "felt so damn happy" because Phoebe "looked so damn *nice*, the way she kept going around and around in her blue coat and all." Salinger uses Holden's aesthetic response to Phoebe on the carousel to dramatize the resolution of Holden's dilemma: the finally achieved integration of Holden's divided nature.

Can we be convinced by this point that two main viewpoints exist in *The Catcher in the Rye*: Holden's and Salinger's? Holden's sense of his world is available to us directly through his words and actions. But he has the limited awareness and sensibilities of a teenager, however sensitive and perceptive we consider him. Salinger's viewpoint is revealed by means of his craftsmanship, including his elaborate symbolism, which deepens and enriches the significance of Holden's narrative far beyond Holden's comprehension. Salinger controlled the selection and arrangement of every detail in his novel, without exception. The unity he achieves out of such intricately planned diversity is a remarkable accomplishment, both in itself as a work of art, and in the opportunity it offers us, as teachers, of sharing such a work with our students.

5

Author or Narrator?

THE RED BADGE OF COURAGE

We have thus far examined novels in which there was little doubt about the distinction or correlation being drawn between the viewpoint of the main character and that of the author. We come now to a work in which the author continually shifts back and forth between these viewpoints—and loses his readers by doing so.

Why did Stephen Crane choose a third-person voice to narrate *The Red Badge of Courage*? The only character in the novel whose thoughts and feelings are revealed is Henry Fleming, the main character. Crane could easily have achieved this focus by making Henry Fleming a first-person narrator and limiting us to the extent of Henry's awareness. But what if Crane wished, at his artistic discretion, to transcend the awareness of his main character? What if Crane wanted, at whatever moments he chose, to offer his readers a larger, more perceptive, and thus essentially ironic viewpoint of Henry's thoughts and feelings? Such a significant dramatic addition would require the author to manipulate the narrative voice with greater dexterity. If Crane did not wish to confuse his readers, he would have to maintain a clear distinction every step of the way between the two viewpoints he had established.

Henry Fleming enters the novel as a naive youth about to face his first combat. After an initial skirmish, he runs from the battle

in terror, and then later returns and lives through a variety of war experiences that develop him into a seasoned veteran. Throughout this progression of events, Crane obviously alters the narrative viewpoint repeatedly. At times, as in the following passage, which occurs after Henry returns to his regiment and discovers that his desertion has remained "in the dark," Crane restricts the narrator's description solely to Henry's consciousness: "He remembered how some of the men had run from the battle. As he recalled their terror-struck faces he felt a scorn for them. They had surely been more fleet and more wild than was absolutely necessary. They were weak mortals. As for himself, he had fled with discretion and dignity."

At other times, however, Crane extends the narrator's viewpoint beyond the limits of Henry's awareness. Note, for example, the following presentation of Henry's growing desire to enlist: "One night, as he lay in bed, the wind had carried to him the clangoring of the church bell as some enthusiast jerked the rope frantically to tell the twisted news of a great battle. This voice of the people rejoicing in the night had made him shiver in a prolonged ecstasy of excitement." In addition to his description of Henry's experience, the narrator simply states for the reader's information that the news is "twisted."

If the narrator does indeed repeatedly establish that Henry's awareness is confined within boundaries narrower than those that are opened to the reader, then a fundamental level of dramatic irony exists throughout the novel. However, the ironic viewpoint is not always immediately apparent. Within the second passage cited above, as noted, Henry's "prolonged ecstasy of excitement" is being caused, the narrator states, by the sounds of people rejoicing over "twisted" news—an obvious irony. In the first passage, however, although we seem to be restricted to Henry's thoughts, the more extensive viewpoint needed to perceive their ironic limitations has to be carried forward by the reader, for it has been supplied earlier by the narrator in his description of Henry at the time he ran: "He, too, threw down his gun and fled. . . . He ran like a rabbit. . . . he was like a proverbial chicken. . . . He ran like a blind man." Henry's subsequent assertion to himself that, unlike the others who had run so frantically, "he had fled with discretion and

dignity" is fashioned by Crane so that no further word from the narrator is necessary for the reader to realize its ironic implications.

Because the entire story, including the workings of Henry's mind, is conveyed to the reader in the narrator's third-person voice, readers may find it difficult at times to distinguish if the viewpoint is restricted to Henry's consciousness or expanded to the narrator's larger vision. Consider, for example, in the final sentence of the following passage, if the narrator continues to limit his description solely to Henry's impressions: "When the sunrays at last struck full and mellowingly upon the earth, the youth saw that the landscape was streaked with two long, thin, black columns which disappeared on the brow of a hill in front and rearward vanished in a wood. They were like two serpents crawling from the cavern of the night."

Regardless of the difficulty, this distinction between viewpoints must be maintained wherever possible; if it is not, our comprehension of Henry's nature will be drastically distorted, as may be illustrated with the closing lines of the novel:

He had rid himself of the red sickness of battle. The sultry nightmare was in the past. He had been an animal blistered and sweating in the heat and pain of war. He turned now with a lover's thirst to images of tranquil skies, fresh meadows, cool brooks—an existence of soft and eternal peace.

Over the river a golden ray of sun came through the hosts of leaden rain clouds.

Since the narrator's voice does not appear to intrude here to comment ironically, we might be led to conclude that these impressions are being given the authority of the narrator's most extensive viewpoint. In other words, we might assume that by the end of the novel Crane has expanded Henry's awareness to the point where it is equal to the narrator's, and thus is no longer to be viewed ironically. How can we, as readers, determine if such a correlation has taken place within the world of the novel? Has Crane supplied us with the means to measure accurately the boundaries of Henry's developing awareness as we proceed through the novel?

We can begin to answer this question by noting the specific characteristics that Crane has given to Henry's mind. These characteristics may be introduced by means of a particularly revealing incident. After Henry has deserted and is wandering in the forest,

"a tremendous clangor of sounds," which arouses his curiosity, sends him running back toward the battle: "As he hastened, there passed through his mind pictures of stupendous conflicts. His accumulated thought upon such subjects was used to form scenes." We discover that the images that occur within Henry's mind, here and throughout the rest of the novel, are formed, as we would naturally expect, out of materials derived from his "accumulated thought." Although Henry is certainly a naive and inexperienced farm-boy at the time he enlists, we must not make the error of concluding that he is therefore empty-headed. If we recognize the content of Henry's "accumulated thought," we will realize that none of the words and images used by the narrator in telling the story is beyond the scope of Henry's knowledge. His speech, for example, is reflective of an early training not shared by everyone in his regiment. The morning after Henry has returned from flee-ing, he loudly condemns the general to his comrades until "A sarcastic man" speaks up: "Mebbe yeh think yeh fit th' hull battle yestirday, Fleming." Henry responds with a pronunciation that calls attention to their different backgrounds: "Why, no . . . I don't think I fought the whole battle yesterday." As Crane reveals near the opening of the novel, Henry has been educated at a "seminary," where he goes just after enlisting "to bid adieu to many school-mates." The formal subjects with which his education has ac-quainted him are presented indirectly throughout the novel. "He had read of marches, sieges, conflicts, and he longed to see it all." He is attributed with "thought-images of heavy crowns and high castles," with "visions of broken-bladed glory," with a knowledge of "Greeklike struggles" and "Homeric" battles. "There was a portion of the world's history which he had regarded as the time of wars." When he flees into the forest, he views the landscape as "A fair field holding life. It was the religion of peace." The din of conflict resuming shortly thereafter suggests to him "a celestial battle; it was tumbling hordes a-struggle in the air." A column of infantry heading toward the battle makes him feel "that he was regarding a procession of chosen beings. The separation was as great to him as if they had marched with weapons of flame and banners of sunlight." Later, as he himself charges into battle, the enemy flag appears to him "as a craved treasure of mythology, hung amid tasks and contrivances of danger." We may conclude

from such indirect evidence that Henry's "accumulated thought" is composed in great part of a "secular and religious education" consisting of at least an acquaintance with the world's history, and with Homeric, religious, and mythological literature.

Thus, when the "two long, thin, black columns" of troops that Henry sees just after sunrise are figuratively described as being "like two serpents crawling from the cavern of the night," the mythological cast of this image suggests that, even though it is conveyed in the narrator's voice, the image should not be excluded from that category of "pictures" drawn from Henry's "accumulated thought." In this particular instance, as in others, Crane takes care to establish the validity of such a suggestion. We may notice, in the following series of passages, how Crane moves from having the narrator openly state that Henry perceives the image to expecting the reader to realize that Henry does so, with no further indication from the narrator:

From off in the darkness came the trampling of feet. The youth could occasionally see dark shadows that moved like monsters.

A moment later the regiment went swinging off into the darkness. It was now like one of those moving monsters wending with many feet.

When the sunrays at last struck full and mellowingly upon the earth, the youth saw that the landscape was streaked with two long, thin, black columns. . . . They were like two serpents crawling from the cavern of the night.

Additional evidence will substantiate that the figurative language appearing in the description of Henry's sensory perceptions is, indeed, to be included within the boundaries of Henry's consciousness: all such words and images, as will be seen, express Henry's personalized views of himself and his world, emotionally colored according to his varying moods.

To illustrate, we can note how Henry distorts his views of the natural world. When he runs into the forest, for example, while fleeing from the battle, his escape is slowed by the trees and the undergrowth. Henry thus characterizes the landscape as follows: "The creepers, catching against his legs, cried out harshly as their sprays were torn from the barks of trees. The swishing saplings

tried to make known his presence to the world. He could not conciliate the forest. As he made his way, it was always calling out protestations." However, when new sounds of fighting arouse Henry's curiosity and he tries to hasten back toward the battle, the same impediments to his movements are given another characterization appropriate to his altered state of mind: "Sometimes the brambles formed chains and tried to hold him back. Trees, confronting him, stretched out their arms and forbade him to pass. After its previous hostility this new resistance of the forest filled him with a fine bitterness. It seemed that Nature could not be quite ready to kill him."

While deep within the forest, after the noises of battle have dimmed with distance, Henry thinks of the landscape as a place suggestive of "the religion of peace." As he walks on, he reaches a spot where the natural growth is seen by him within this mental frame: "At length he reached a place where the high, arching boughs made a chapel. He softly pushed the green doors aside and entered. Pine needles were a gentle brown carpet. There was a religious half light."

It must be stressed again that the figurative language in this passage manifests the present mood of Henry's mind, that such words and images are indicative of how Henry alters his sensory impressions according to his varying mental states. (In passing, it should also be noted that because Crane has characterized Henry as someone who colors his impressions with religious significance, it does not necessarily follow that Crane is thus giving religious significance to his novel.)

Following the night that Henry returns to his regiment with a head wound and a story that he learns will allow him to keep his desertion "in the dark," and so to avoid the disgrace and the deep sense of shame he had anticipated, his view of the dawn reflects his "unexpected" pleasure at being able to take his place again among his comrades: "When the youth awoke it seemed to him that he had been asleep for a thousand years, and he felt sure that he opened his eyes upon an unexpected world. Gray mists were slowly shifting before the first efforts of the sun rays. An impending splendor could be seen in the eastern sky."

Perhaps the most dramatic instance of Henry's mental state influencing his perception occurs immediately after he watches Jim

Conklin fall dead. Looking down on Jim Conklin's "paste-like face" and at the death-wound in his side, Henry realizes that the life of his friend has departed from the dead body lying before him. Henry had earlier personified Nature as alive and vital, as possessing the moods and passions of a human being who was responsively conscious of Henry's individual existence. As he now turns, with rage, toward the battlefield to shake his fist, his deeply impressionable experience of Jim Conklin's loss of life forcefully molds his perception of what appears before him into a single, stunning image of Nature cold and devoid of life: "The red sun was pasted in the sky like a wafer." (A "pasted" wafer, in Crane's day, was a small adhesive disk used as a seal on letters, documents, etc.) Henry's emotionally distorted mind is evident to the very end of the novel, where, in the closing line, he looks with another mood upon Nature: "Over the river a golden ray of sun came through the hosts of leaden rain clouds." The ironic implications of such impressions, even though they clearly appear to have been colored by Henry's varying moods, are not manifested, however, until we comprehend the larger perspective opened by the narrator. This perspective is often established in advance and thus will not be apparent in later passages, such as the closing line above, unless it is carried forward by the reader. Therefore, to delineate the boundaries of Henry's mind, and so to perceive the dramatic irony resulting from his limited awareness, we must take two further steps: first, we must trace the greatest extent to which Henry's consciousness is expanded by his battle experiences, as revealed in his final impressions in the novel; and then these impressions must be considered within the larger scope of the narrator's vision.

Henry's reaction to his first battle is presented in carefully graduated steps suggesting someone going to sleep and then awakening. At first sight of the enemy, his "intellect" wavers: "As he caught sight of them the youth was momentarily startled by a thought that perhaps his gun was not loaded. He stood trying to rally his faltering intellect so that he might recollect the moment when he had loaded, but he could not."

During the enemy's charge, Henry lapses into a "battle sleep" while fighting. His thoughts are suppressed now below his consciousness, occurring only as hazy dreams never clearly remembered afterwards: "He, in his thought, was careering off in other

places, even as the carpenter who as he works whistles and thinks of his friend or his enemy, his home or a saloon. And these jolted dreams were never perfect to him afterward, but remained a mass of blurred shapes." When the charge is repulsed and the emotional crisis has passed, "The youth awakened slowly. He came gradually back to a position from which he could regard himself. . . . He thoughtfully mopped his reeking features."

The enemy's second charge occurs when Henry is mentally off-guard. The fear now aroused within him floods his conscious mind and once again submerges his "intellect," causing him to run from the battle "like a rabbit." During his desertion, after he has learned that his comrades have held their position, he encounters an advancing column of infantry. Henry enviously views them as "a procession of chosen beings" because their present circumstances suggest to him that these seemingly worthy individuals have been "chosen" for acts of glory by some higher power that has apparently, and hostilely, not found him deserving of the same benevolence. He therefore longs for different circumstances that would extenuate his shameful situation. He even wishes for the defeat of his entire army, for if this desired course of events actually occurred, it would allow him to believe that, instead of having existed out of grace, he had acted as a "prophet" aware of the workings of the higher powers that cause such happenings on earth, as a "seer" existing in harmony with these powers. Thus, his suspicion that the powers, with hostile intentions, have brought about his present disgrace would be allayed:

In a defeat there would be a roundabout vindication of himself. He thought it would prove, in a manner, that he had fled early because of his superior powers of perception. A serious prophet upon predicting a flood should be the first man to climb a tree. This would demonstrate that he was indeed a seer.

A moral vindication was regarded by the youth as a very important thing.

Henry subsequently receives his head wound from a Union soldier, is led back to his regiment by an unidentified companion, and finds that his story of being wounded by the enemy is readily accepted. When such new circumstances allow him to return to his comrades without being disgraced, he is able to adopt a different

attitude toward the higher powers: "In the present, he declared to himself that it was only the doomed and the damned who roared with sincerity at circumstance." He no longer suspects that something hostile is lurking behind the events he experiences. On the contrary, because he was able to roam among various conflicts during his wanderings, and then to return with his desertion undetected, he is now convinced that he has become not only "a man of experience" but also a "chosen" being: contemplating the "dragons" of battle he will face again, he asks himself, "how could they kill him who was the chosen of gods and doomed to greatness?"

Therefore, during his second fight, he undergoes a different reaction to battle: his rage is no longer turned toward unassailable abstractions, but is channeled now specifically toward the enemy: "He had a wild hate for the relentless foe. Yesterday when he had imagined the universe to be against him, he had hated it, little gods and big gods; today he hated the army of the foe with the same great hatred."

As the enemy charges, Henry's intellect is again submerged, but this time, within "the chaos of his brain;" his "intent hate" predominates and makes him fight like "a war devil." Instead of feeling, as he did earlier, like "a driven beast" being "pestered" by the enemy, Henry now fights aggressively, like an animal naturally equipped for conflict with "teeth and claws." As a result, he awakens from his "battle sleep" to the unexpected admiration of his comrades, which allows him, when he is able to think again, to consider himself in a new light: "These incidents made the youth ponder. It was revealed to him that he had been a barbarian, a beast. He had fought like a pagan who defends his religion. Regarding it, he saw that it was fine, wild, and, in some ways, easy. . . . he was now what he called a hero. And he had not been aware of the process. He had slept and, awakening, found himself a knight."

Henry's image of himself is qualified, however, before his next contact with the enemy. When he goes looking for water with Wilson, he overhears the general and an officer talking. The officer, calling Henry's regiment "a lot 'a mule drivers," offers them for a strategic charge. "I don't believe many of your mule drivers will get back," the general soberly comments. "These happenings had occupied an incredibly short time, yet the youth felt that in them he had been made aged. New eyes were given to him. And the most

startling thing was to learn suddenly that he was very insignificant." Having "thought of a fine revenge," Henry rushes forward during the charge, apparently in hopes of being gloriously killed so that he might bring "a kind of remorse upon the officer." When the color sergeant is fatally shot, Henry grabs the flag and carries it while his comrades begin to retreat. As he follows them back with a deep sense of shame, a great hatred for the officer arouses within him a strong feeling of pride, which causes him to act with a daring defiance of the enemy as he retreats: "He . . . wrapped his heart in the cloak of his pride and kept the flag erect."

After the withdrawal has ended, and his emotions have waned enough to allow his intellect to function again consciously, Henry has a mixed reaction. He reflects at first upon the charge and is astonished to learn that his mind had drastically distorted certain aspects of his experience: "He discovered that the distances, as compared with the brilliant measurings of his mind, were trivial and ridiculous. . . . The time, too, now that he reflected, he saw to have been short. He wondered at the number of emotions and events that had been crowded into such little spaces. Elfin thoughts must have exaggerated and enlarged everything, he said."

He does not, however, recognize any distortion in his impressions of his own behavior, which, it must be noted, he is now able to recall to consciousness. Although he had at first charged "unconsciously in advance," he had subsequently passed "into a clearer atmosphere," where, for the first time during actual combat, "His mind took a mechanical but firm impression" of everything and everyone around him. As a result, after the battle subsides, he has a new reaction: instead of awakening from a "battle sleep" where events occurred as hazy dreams unable to be remembered afterwards, Henry now consciously recollects impressions of which he had remained unaware during the battle: "However, to the youth there was a considerable joy in musing upon his performances during the charge. He had had very little time previously in which to appreciate himself, so that there was now much satisfaction in quietly thinking of his actions. He recalled bits of color that in the flurry had stamped themselves unawares upon his engaged senses."

When Henry later learns that his deeds had been looked upon with admiration and praise by the colonel and the lieutenant, his

self-satisfaction is intensified enough to place him in a new frame of mind for his next encounter with the foe: "When the woods again began to pour forth the dark-hued masses of the enemy the youth felt serene self-confidence." Henry's new mental state no longer allows such an impending conflict to suppress his intellect completely. He attempts now "to study the distance between him and the enemy. He made vague calculations." As Henry advances against the foe, in his final charge of the novel, instead of his thoughts being submerged beneath the emotional effects of the battle, he discovers that he is now capable of knowing what he is thinking during such an intense period: "He had no time for dissections, but he knew that he thought of the bullets only as things that could prevent him from reaching the place of his endeavor. There were subtle flashings of joy within him that thus should be his mind." Henry does not, of course, determine what he will think at these emotional moments, no more that he decides which sensory impressions will enter his consciousness; he simply *knows* that this thought is occurring in his mind and is pleased to find it there.

Therefore, during the course of the novel, Henry's conscious-ness does indeed expand, as may be seen in the difference between his first and final reactions to combat. Henry went through his initial conflict "as one who dozes," his "battle sleep" keeping his thoughts so well concealed from him that he was prevented upon awakening from recollecting them. Completely lacking in battle experience, and having gained no clear thoughts from his first encounter, Henry at that moment had nothing within his mind to offset the distorting influence of his vanity, which grossly exagger-ated the significance of this first battle:

So it was all over at last! The supreme trial had been passed. The red, formidable difficulties of war had been vanquished.
He went into an ecstasy of self-satisfaction. . . . Standing as if apart from himself, he viewed that last scene. He perceived that the man who had fought thus was magnificent.
He felt that he was a fine fellow.

However, by the time of his final conflict, Henry is capable of a more complex reaction, for his awareness has expanded to the point where he is able to recognize all of the thoughts and the

impressions that have entered his mind during the course of the battle. Thus, because he can later call forth into consciousness the "procession of memory" he has accumulated, he is able "to more closely comprehend himself and circumstance."

Henry "began to study his deeds, his failures, and his achievements." He reviews his past acts now like someone watching a parade: "they marched before him clearly. From this present viewpoint he was enabled to look upon them in spectator fashion and to criticize them with some correctness." As he watches "his procession of memory," his attention is immediately captured by the sight of "his public deeds," which he is gleeful to find "were paraded in great and shining prominence." His self-satisfaction is thus aroused, and his memories take on color: "Those performances which had been witnessed by his fellows marched now in wide purple and gold. . . . He spent delightful minutes viewing the gilded images of memory. He saw that he was good."

His self-satisfaction, however, is then offset "with some correctness" as he discovers, much to his consternation, that his "failures" are also a part of the procession: "Nevertheless, the ghost of his flight from the first engagement appeared to him and danced. . . . For a moment he blushed, and the light of his soul flickered with shame." Henry then undergoes an agonizing period during which he fearfully wonders if "his vivid error . . . would stand before him all his life." With pleasurable and painful memories both occupying his consciousness at the same moment, he is left in a mental turmoil, which prevents him from attaining a satisfactory view of himself.

We must carefully note here the manner in which Henry's inner conflict is resolved: "Yet gradually he mustered force to put the sin at a distance." Having weighed his acts separately, as though he had placed them on each side of a chemist's scale, Henry now mentally forces the scales to tip in his favor. This feat is certainly not a new one to him. Earlier, after returning from his desertion, he had "allowed no thoughts of his own to keep him from an attitude of manfulness. He had performed his mistakes in the dark, so he was still a man." And later, after he was praised by the colonel and the lieutenant for his daring actions, he "speedily forgot many things. The past held no pictures of error and disappointment." This final time, Henry "mustered force to put the sin at a distance" until "at last his eyes seemed to open to some new ways." Crane's

use of "seemed" should signal the reader to consider carefully whether or not the "ways" now opened are indeed ultimately "new." Henry looks again inside himself and is overjoyed to find that his mind has rejected his earlier unfounded beliefs: "He found that he could look back upon the brass and bombast of his earlier gospels and see them truly. He was gleeful when he discovered that he now despised them." And he is able, furthermore, to find within his memory a more solid basis for his new beliefs: "He felt a quiet manhood, nonassertive but of sturdy and strong blood. He knew that he would no more quail before his guides wherever they should point. He had been to touch the great death, and found that after all, it was but the great death. He was a man."

Thus far, we need not contradict the conclusions reached by Henry. Although it may be asserted that he cannot take credit for making himself into this kind of an individual, we nevertheless cannot deny him credit for *being* such a person. He has, indeed, fought heroically, as his final combat illustrated. And he is certainly no longer overwhelmed, as he was earlier, by a fear of death. And there is no indication at the end that he would act otherwise in the future. Therefore, Henry is now able to believe, with a calm "assurance" he had not possessed before, that he has attained his desired state of existence: "He was a man."

However, before assuming that unqualified praise is thus being heaped upon Henry, we must notice what being "a man" signifies within the narrator's larger perspective offered earlier in the novel. As will be seen, the "force" that freed Henry from his sense of failure, and subsequently allowed him to return to personally laudatory perceptions, is composed of *selfishness* and *conceit*, which are established by Crane as the naturally predominant characteristics of every man existing in this world.

After the first charge in which Henry takes a part, he is unable to realize "why he himself was there." The narrator goes beyond the bounds of Henry's comprehension to offer the reason:

The men, pitching forward insanely, had burst into cheerings, moblike and barbaric, but tuned in strange keys that can arouse the dullard and the stoic. . . . There was the delirium that encounters despair and death, and is heedless and blind to the odds. It is a temporary but sublime absence of selfishness. And because it was of this order was the reason, perhaps,

why the youth wondered, afterward, what reasons he could have had for being there.

The narrator then continues on to show why the moment is "temporary": "Presently the straining pace ate up the energies of the men. . . . Since much of their strength and their breath had vanished, they returned to caution. They were become men again."

Having thus asserted that men, by nature, do not characteristically display an "absence of selfishness," the narrator next illustrates, during their subsequent retreat, that their existences as "men" are also bounded in a contrary direction. Withdrawing like a "mass," like "a machine run down . . . . a forceless thing," they lose again their identities as men. As they are about to conclude "that they were impotent," that they "could not fight well," an advancing group of the enemy surprises them into turning and fighting again fiercely enough to repel them. Their "elation" at having accomplished this deed arouses in them a sense of "pride," exaggerated to the point of conceit as it allows them to deny that they had ever felt the debilitating lack of confidence that had just unmanned them: "The impetus of enthusiasm was theirs again. They gazed about them with looks of uplifted pride, feeling new trust in the grim, always confident weapons in their hands. And they were men."

Crane thus reveals in these passages that the traits he considers as generally prevailing within a man, as actually defining the nature of "a man," are selfishness and conceit. Therefore, Henry's conclusion, after his agonizing period of self-doubt, that "He was a man," if appraised now within this larger perspective of man, is one of the most ironic disclosures of the novel: that once again Henry's natural conceit has prevailed. Unhindered now by any offsetting force, it will influence his remaining thoughts and impressions. When the first of his "failures" had earlier appeared before him, "the light of his soul flickered with shame." Immediately after regaining his sense of manhood, however, Henry feels that he attains a new spiritual state of being: "So it came to pass that as he trudged from the place of blood and wrath his soul changed." As noted earlier, Henry discovered after the final battle that "he was enabled to more closely comprehend himself and circumstance." Examining "himself," he found that he would henceforth be able to hold a positive attitude toward his existence.

To ascertain the resulting state of his soul, he now completes his consideration of "circumstance."

With his natural conceit influencing him to give still greater weight to his achievements, Henry now believes that one of his previous assumptions has been firmly substantiated: that the "gods" controlling all events on earth have indeed "chosen" him. His concluding thoughts and impressions are colored by this state of mind:

It rained. The procession of weary soldiers became a bedraggled train, despondent and muttering, marching with churning effort in a trough of liquid brown mud under a low, wretched sky. Yet the youth smiled, for he saw that the world was a world for him, though many discovered it to be made of oaths and walking sticks. . . . He turned now with a lover's thirst to images of tranquil skies, fresh meadows, cool brooks—an existence of soft and eternal peace.

Henry's thoughts of an "eternal" peace reveal that he is anticipating not simply the pleasurable circumstances of his remaining existence on earth, but the spiritual salvation that he believes is forthcoming as a result of his having been so fortunately singled out by the powers above. Thus, although he is existing under "a low, wretched sky" along with his "despondent and muttering" comrades, he does not look up, as he has done before, "with tragic glances at the sky." Now the sky is seen from a positive state of mind, colored by Henry's feeling that the storm of battle has passed, that a time of calm is about to begin. As he turns and looks out across the river, his closing view of Nature is recollective of a familiar quasi-religious landscape painting: streaming down through an overcast sky, a cathedral sunray signals the end of turmoil and the advent of peace, not only in the world, but in the soul of the perceiving man. "Over the river a golden ray of sun came through the hosts of leaden rain clouds."

Thus, to the very end of the novel, Henry never becomes aware of the larger, ironic perspective of himself offered by the narrator: he never perceives that, because he is a "man," his conceit will naturally predominate whenever circumstances permit; nor does he ever realize the strength of his conceit, which impels him to his most colorful conclusion, that he is "the chosen of gods."

However, the quality of Henry's nature will not be defined conclusively until we recognize that Henry's persisting lack of awareness is counter balanced by his increasing capacity to judge himself "with some correctness." After performing his first heroic act, he admits to himself that "he had not been aware of the process," and thus he could not accredit himself with having willfully accomplished the deed. As he gains consciousness of himself during battle, not only does he become aware of how drastically his mind had distorted his impressions of space and time, but he also realizes that during the most intense moments of conflict he has no control over his own thoughts as they pass through his consciousness. Therefore, when Henry afterwards views himself as a hero, he is not making claims to any willful attainments of his own—such an obvious self-deception on his part would surely cause us to reject him with scorn. Henry knows quite clearly that his daring deeds and his heroic thoughts have resulted from an involuntary interaction of his peculiar nature and of the particular circumstances in which he found himself. His ensuing conceit, though, is not to be seen as entirely unfounded: it is based on Henry's realization that his comrades did not all respond in the same manner, that his acts of heroism, however unwillfully accomplished, nevertheless distinguish his existence from those around him: "the youth smiled, for he saw that the world was a world for him, though many discovered it to be made of oaths and walking sticks." Thus, he apparently reasons, the higher powers who control the natures of men and their circumstances must have benevolently singled him out.

We must also note that Henry's human failings are not to be considered solely as negative characteristics: they also function to strengthen his appeal as a character by allowing us to empathize with Henry as he undergoes his sequence of shameful and glorious experiences. As a result, we feel inclined by the end of the novel, when attempting to weigh Henry's resulting nature, to tip the scales in Henry's favor—that is, if we include ourselves within the category that Crane labels "man."

In his introduction to the Riverside Edition of *The Red Badge of Courage*, Richard Chase states that the novel is "certainly one of the best of American fictions, despite its lack of unity and the embarrassment the author seems to feel about the necessity of pointing a moral. The embarrassment is plain enough in the vague and

pretentious language of the last five paragraphs, which surely have nothing to recommend them but the description of the sky."[1]

How could any reader, particularly as noted a critic as Richard Chase, consider "the language of the last five paragraphs" to be "vague and pretentious"? Many readers have recognized that Henry Fleming's nature changes as he proceeds through his war experiences, but the resulting quality of his nature, especially as he is portrayed at the conclusion of the novel, has been widely disputed. Judging from Richard Chase's response, we might wonder whether the confusion arises because readers have not clearly followed the expanding and contracting scope of the narrator's viewpoint, and the ironic perspectives thus established. Considering the possibility of such an oversight, we are left with the task of guiding our students to an adequate awareness of the consummate skill with which Crane handled the narrative voice. Only then will they be able to grasp the novel.

THE TURN OF THE SCREW

Our final choice of works is an old chestnut in the realm of literary criticism. Since it is, at most, a short novel of questionable weight, and since we have already examined one of James's more substantial novels, why are we including it here? Judging from published responses to date, this particular work appears destined to go down in literary annals as an example of an unresolvable critical dispute. Nevertheless, James offers us here a new viewpoint that we cannot ignore. We have been exploring novels thus far that may not have been successfully communicated to readers, even though their authors strove to attain that communication through the most advanced practices of their craft. In *The Turn of the Screw*, however, we encounter an author in the act of consciously and purposefully attempting to mislead his readers. James chooses to create an unreliable narrator "just for the fun of it," as he would say, but with an exquisite and horrifying twist.

The work is about a young woman of limited background who is hired by a man to serve at his country estate as governess to his orphaned niece and nephew, Flora and Miles. The circumstances are somewhat unusual, since the man does not wish to be bothered at all. The children are to be left under her complete care, with the

help of a housekeeper, Mrs. Grose, and her staff. The arrangement appears to be working out satisfactorily, until the governess sees a "trespasser." According to Mrs. Grose, who identifies the governess's description of the trespasser, it is Peter Quint, a valet who had died some time earlier. Shortly afterwards, a second "apparition" appears to the governess: Miss Jessel, the former governess. The governess concludes that the apparitions are after the children. Vowing to resist, she recounts for us the story of her struggle.

James would have been delighted to discover that critics are still arguing over a central question raised by this work: Do, or do not, the apparitions of Peter Quint and Miss Jessel exist? Both sides of the controversy have managed to perpetuate their views by repeatedly citing particular passages from the work. For example, the detailed description of Peter Quint that the governess recounts to Mrs. Grose is consistently pointed to as irrefutable evidence by those critics who assert the reality of the apparitions. The nonapparitionists, in turn, point to any of the obvious errors in the governess's narration as irrefutable evidence of her distorting mind, such as her statement that it was Mrs. Grose who "had instantly recognized and named" Miss Jessel from the governess's description of her. With so much critical attention having been focused on the work, why has the controversy remained unresolved after so prolonged an argument?

We might approach *The Turn of the Screw* with the observation that the work has been carefully fashioned to attain a particular literary effect, that which James calls "pure romance." In his Preface to *The American* James distinguishes the romantic from the real as follows:

The only *general* attribute of projected romance that I can see, the only one that fits all its cases, is the fact of the kind of experience with which it deals—experience liberated, so to speak; experience . . . exempt from the conditions that we usually know to attach to it . . . and operating in a medium which relieves it, in a particular interest, of the inconvenience of a *related*, a measurable state. . . . the balloon of experience is in fact of course tied to the earth, and under that necessity we swing, thanks to a rope of remarkable length, in the more or less commodious car of the imagination; but it is by the rope we know where we are, and from the moment that cable is cut we are at large and unrelated. . . . The art of the romancer is, "for the fun of it," insidiously to cut the cable, to cut it without our detecting him.[2]

In his preface to *The Aspern Papers*, James refers to *The Turn of the Screw* as a "sinister romance."[3] We must, therefore, look closely at this work to discover how its author, fashioning his material with the "art of the romancer," has attempted "insidiously to cut the cable, to cut it without our detecting him."

However, an important question must first be answered. Who *is* the author of this romance, according to James? The experiences narrated in the prologue to the tale are certainly not "romantic" by James's definition. What remains, then, is the tale itself. The author of the tale, as James takes care to establish in the prologue, the writer of the narrative that Douglas will read from the "thin old-fashioned gilt-edged album," is the governess. We must approach the tale, therefore, in hopes of detecting the governess practicing the "art of the romancer."

To do so, we must first realize that all of the governess's "experiences" with the apparitions have been carefully wrought by her into a sequence. She begins with experiences of realistic effect, and then artfully attempts to retain this effect while insidiously moving deeper and deeper into romance. For example, her first experience with Quint, her distant sight of him on the tower, is fashioned by various means to produce a realistic effect, such as her lengthy description, immediately upon sighting the man, of the tower on which he appears, the accuracy of the description giving a sense of reality to everything she sees at that moment, including the man. Furthermore, her complete puzzlement about who this "unknown man" might be is certainly shared by the reader, who can also accept the plausibility of the "inference" she offers after thinking over the matter, that "some unscrupulous traveler, curious in old houses, had made his way in unobserved, enjoyed the prospect from the best point of view, and then stolen out as he came." If the realistic effect is achieved, as James says, by fulfilling the reader's "general sense of the way things happen," then we need not doubt the predominant effect of this first experience with Quint as narrated by the governess.

The realistic effect of the governess's second encounter with Quint, as he peers into the window of the dining room, is strengthened with the added impact of his nearness to offset the *noticeable* romantic effect of elements that begin entering her narration at this time. For example, she tells her reader that she now knows with

"certitude that it was not for me he had come there. He had come for someone else"—a certitude that occurs to her simply because Quint's stare leaves her face "for a moment during which I could still watch it, see it fix successively several other things." She is surprisingly no longer puzzled about what this "unknown man" might be looking for. Instead, she reacts to his averted stare by asserting that there came to her "a sudden vibration of duty," although we are again not sure why, or what the nature of the "duty" is. Furthermore, after going out to the terrace to confront the man and finding him gone, she says, "There were shrubberies and big trees, but I remember the clear assurance I felt that none of them concealed him. He was there or was not there: not there if I didn't see him."

The detailed description of Quint that the governess recounts to Mrs. Grose in the next chapter probably achieves the strongest realistic effect in the entire work—and rightly so, for it is designed to be followed by, and so to alter the effect of, an idea that, by itself, might have been viewed upon its introduction as the most blatantly romantic in the work: that the governess had not seen simply an "unknown man" prowling the grounds, but a full-fledged apparition. Nonapparitionists have attempted to establish the probability that the governess already had the description in mind before Quint's second appearance, noting that her answer to Mrs. Grose's following question about the identity of the man suggests that someone at Bly or in the village might already have supplied her with it. Mrs. Grose asks, "Then nobody about the place? Nobody from the village?" And the governess answers, "Nobody—nobody. I didn't tell you, but I made sure." Nonapparitionists have also attacked Mrs. Grose's identification of the description, showing, for example, how the governess's statements "help" Mrs. Grose toward her answers, and how Mrs. Grose apparently reacts, not to the description, but to the statement that the man looked "like an actor," the specificity of the description seemingly not having reached her, a point strengthened by her need, following the description, to ask, "But he *is* handsome?" And yet from whatever angle the attack comes, and whatever doubts are established, the detailed description of Quint retains its realistic effect, and apparitionists continue pointing to it.

The solution to this particular dilemma may be one of simply realizing that the analyses of critics on *both* sides of the controversy should be accepted: as indications of how successful this early chapter is in fulfilling its function of "insidiously" leading the reader into a carefully wrought romance. The governess's detailed description of the apparition and Mrs. Grose's identification of it achieves, even after a close examination, a convincing realistic effect—and yet there are, indeed, doubts that can be raised. But nothing more decisive than doubts, for if the governess had allowed the reader to determine so early in her narration that her experiences with the apparition were not real but "romantic," then instead of insidiously cutting the cable, she would have blatantly slashed it in two, revealing too quickly that the "car" of her imagination was "at large and unrelated" to that "measurable state" of the real world that produces "our general sense of the way things happen."

The governess, however, is by no means so blatant. Having established her strongest realistic effect, the influence of which will remain with the reader throughout her successive experiences, she then proceeds with a studied slowness to lead the reader deeper into her romance. To illustrate the effectiveness of her art, we should first note how the romantic elements that continue entering her narration become progressively more noticeable when singled out, until, by the end of the work, they appear almost ludicrous. Then we can attempt to determine what means she used to succeed so well, as James says the romancer must do, in having "drugged" in the reader any "reflexion and criticism" concerning these romantic elements, so that "the way things don't happen may be artfully made to pass for the way things do."

Her next "experience" with an apparition occurs as she is with Flora by the pond. "Suddenly, in these circumstances, I became aware that . . . we had an interested spectator." The governess is sitting "on the old stone bench which overlooked the pond; and in this position, I began to take in with certitude, and yet without direct vision, the presence, at a distance, of a third person." It is interesting to note how her thoughts progress toward the unnatural in identifying this appearance of someone across the pond: "an interested spectator. . . . a third person. . . . an alien object. . . . the apparition"—all of these labels being attached before she even

raises her eyes, "with certitude, and yet without direct vision." However, one qualifying implication does remain for the reader, that there might have been at least *indirect* vision, perhaps a peripheral view.

Mrs. Grose is again involved with the identification of this second apparition, but readers are now able to see, as they were not with the first identification, that the governess's assertion of what she thinks has occurred is a distortion of fact. She tells her readers: "I had only to ask her how, if I had "made it up," I came to be able to give, of each of the persons appearing to me, a picture disclosing, to the last detail, their special marks—a portrait on the exhibition of which she had instantly recognized and named them." And yet only a few pages back, we find the detailed "portrait" from which the identification was made: "a woman in black, pale and dreadful"—a rather slim picture compared to the description of Quint. Mrs. Grose's supposed recognition of this picture reveals a further distortion in the governess's account:

> My friend, with an odd impulse, fell back a step. "Was she someone you've never seen?"
> "Yes. But someone the child has. Someone *you* have." Then, to show how I had thought it all out: "My predecessor—the one who died."
> "Miss Jessel?"
> "Miss Jessel. You don't believe me?" I pressed.
> She turned right and left in her distress. "How can you be sure?"

The governess herself had obviously identified the second apparition as being her "predecessor—the one who died" (the knowledge of Miss Jessel's recent death having been given to her by the uncle before she came to Bly), and so she is clearly distorting her narration when she says that Mrs. Grose "had instantly recognized and named" her. And yet the distortion is qualified, if we wish to strain the point, for it could be said that the governess was right in asserting that Mrs. Grose had "named" the apparition, since Mrs. Grose was, indeed, the first actually to speak the name "Miss Jessel."

The governess's next encounter with Quint, which occurs on the staircase, takes us a step deeper into her romance. She has stayed awake all night, reading in bed, until, "though I was deeply interested in my author, I found myself, at the turn of a page and with

his spell all scattered, looking straight up from him and hard at the door of my room," after which she rises "with all the marks of a deliberation that must have seemed magnificent" and proceeds out of her room, along the lobby, and to the staircase, where she finally sees Quint. This particular experience rules out completely the earlier qualification of a possible indirect vision having caused her awareness of the apparition, for all that she looks at here before going out is the door of her room. And yet there is another, but dimmer, qualification in the possibility that she might have *heard* something, for as she stares at her door, she says, "There was a moment during which I listened, reminded of the faint sense I had had, the first night, of there being something undefineably astir in the house."

As we continue through her narration, we discover that her ability to know an apparition is present becomes less and less dependent on her physical senses: from a direct vision of Quint on the tower and at the dining-room window, to a possible indirect vision of Miss Jessel across the pond, to a possible sound of Quint on the staircase. In the next instance, neither sight nor sound is needed by her to be aware of an apparition. Awakening one night, she sees Flora at the window, "peering out into the night." Without looking out herself, she reaches the following conclusion: "She was face to face with the apparition we had met at the lake, and could now communicate with it as she had not then been able to do." But when she goes to another window to see for herself, she, and the reader (with a slight smile?), discover that her "apparition" is none other than "poor little Miles," who is standing out on the lawn. The governess then asserts that she sees Miles looking "at something that was apparently above me. There was clearly another person above me—there was a person on the tower." Without any additional sights or sounds, the "something" that is "apparently" above her becomes, in the very next sentence, a "person" who is "clearly" on the tower—another conclusion that the reader is unable to accept from the governess solely on the basis of her simply asserting that it is true.

This gap between what the governess *says* is true and what the reader is capable of accepting is further widened when the reader compares her next experience, with Miss Jessel in the schoolroom, to the account of the incident she later gives to Mrs. Grose. After

walking to the church with the others, the governess, instead of going in with them, decides to leave Bly, for, as she says, "I might easily put an end to my predicament by getting away altogether." She returns home to pack her things and finds Miss Jessel sitting in the schoolroom. The governess relates the incident as follows: "she had looked at me long enough to appear to say that her right to sit at my table was as good as mine to sit at hers. . . . actually addressing her—'You terrible, miserable woman!'—I heard myself break into a sound that, by the open door, rang through the long passage and the empty house. She looked at me as if she heard me, but I had recovered myself and cleared the air."

On the basis of this one-sided conversation, qualified only by two statements—"she had looked at me long enough to appear to say" and "She looked at me as if she heard me"—the governess tells Mrs. Grose the following blatant lies:

> "I came home, my dear," I went on, "for a talk with Miss Jessel."
> . . . "A Talk! Do you mean she spoke?"
> "It came to that."

The above-mentioned qualifications might make this last answer a plausible one, except for the governess's answer to Mrs. Grose's next question:

> "And what did she say?". . . .
> "That she suffers the torments—!"
> It was this, of a truth, that made her, as she filled out my picture, gape. "Do you mean," she faltered, "—of the lost?"
> "Of the lost. Of the damned. And that's why, to share them—" I faltered myself with the horror of it.
> But my companion, with less imagination, kept me up. "To share them—?"
> "She wants Flora."

Even by straining to recognize the fullest possible meaning that might have been communicated by Miss Jessel's expressive looks, the reader is still unable to accept two of the governess's assertions: the first, because of clear evidence to the contrary, that the reason the governess went home was to have a talk with Miss Jessel; the

second, because of no corroborating evidence having been seen, that Miss Jessel "told" the governess that "She wants Flora."

The difficulty of accepting the governess's assertions, without corroborating evidence or in the face of conflicting evidence, increases continually to the end of her narration. For example, when Miles plays the piano for the governess so that Flora can slip away, the governess, upon realizing that Flora is missing, tells Mrs. Grose, with no apparent basis, "She's with her!" When Mrs. Grose asks where Miles is, the governess answers, "Oh, he's with Quint. They're in the schoolroom." But the reader has just seen the governess leave Miles in the schoolroom, with absolutely no evidence to suggest that Quint is present.

Even more damaging to the authority of her assertions is the incident which occurs when the governess and Mrs. Grose go to the pond and find Flora. When the governess sees Miss Jessel appear, she grabs Mrs. Grose's arm and points to the apparition: "Mrs. Grose's dazed blink across to where I pointed struck me as a sovereign sign that she too at last saw." But on the very next page Mrs. Grose makes "her loud, shocked protest, a burst of high disapproval. 'What a dreadful turn, to be sure, Miss! Where on earth do you see anything?' "

What remains of her "experiences" with the apparitions is the final appearance of Quint, perhaps the most ludicrous incident in the work when the romantic elements are singled out. That such blatant elements have been passed off so insidiously upon the reader attests to the great degree of success that can be attained by "the art of the romancer." Therefore, instead of simply proceeding into her narration of this closing experience and falling under its closely wrought spell, we can approach it from another direction. If the governess is indeed such an unreliable narrator, then the extent to which she distorts the material that passes through her point of view before reaching the reader can perhaps be determined by attempting to look at that same material from a more objective point of view, one that can be corroborated by evidence found in the narration. The difficulty of gathering such evidence, of course, is that it must be arrived at *indirectly*, since the entire account is limited to the governess's awareness.

Before turning to her closing experience, therefore, we might quickly consider certain implications of the narration preceding

this scene in hopes of reestablishing what the governess has so successfully "drugged": "our general sense of the way things happen." First, there is a clear indication, against which there is no conclusive evidence to be found anywhere in her narration, that she is the only person who sees the apparitions. Second, if this implication is accepted, then Miles and Flora, though a bit precocious, can be seen as two normal children. And third, as normal children they surely see the governess differently from the way in which she says they do—as is suggested by the implications of the following account, which brings together some of her own inadvertent statements about her behavior around the children, thus allowing us to consider what the children's reactions must have been to such behavior.

At first she seemed "dazzled by their loveliness," their attractiveness being "a constant joy" for her. But then she began watching them with "a stifled suspense." She appeared with "ugly signs" on her face of having cried. She began to keep them "in constant sight," while revealing a "greater tension." There were moments when, with "an irresistible impulse," she displayed a "sharper passion for them" by "catching them up and pressing them" to her heart. She began roaming through the house late at night, waking Flora with her supposedly "noiseless" wandering, which, said Miles, sounded like "a troup of cavalry." At one point she completely gave up "speaking to them" for "a month." (A month!) She shut herself up "audibly" in her room, where she "flung" herself about and "broke down in the monstrous utterance of names." After these scenes, she "chattered more than ever" and then fell into prolonged "hushes," during which she would "tremble" and sit with "a chill" until they would "kiss" her and end the incident by asking when their uncle would come. But she refused to mail the letters they wrote to their uncle, and her "exasperation" with them increased. With her "inexorable . . . perpetual society," by means of which she "had all but pinned the boy" to her shawl, she treated them "like a goaler with an eye to possible surprises and escapes." When Miles attempted to bring up the question of his future schooling as they walked to church, she tried to laugh, but managed only to look "ugly and queer." Instead of going into church, she returned home by herself; the others returned after church and followed Miles's suggestion, as she learned from Mrs. Grose, that they pass over the incident and

try to "do nothing but what she likes." Visiting Miles at night in his room, where he again tried to discuss his schooling, she "threw" herself "upon him . . . embraced him," and kissed him. He told her, "ever so gently," that he wanted her to leave him alone. She released him, questioned him a bit more, and then dropped on her knees beside the bed to "seize once more the chance of possessing him." The next day, when the governess and Mrs. Grose finally found Flora by the pond, the governess pointed across the pond, crying out, "She's there, she's there!" and "passionately" accused Flora of seeing Miss Jessel. Mrs. Grose was unable to see anyone.

The obvious implications of the above excerpts from the governess's narration lead us to the conclusion that the children must have been conscious all along of her increasingly eccentric behavior. Also, her remaining unaware of this fact would prevent her from seeing that the children's reactions to her behavior are not, as she asserts, unnatural.

One further point needs to be established for a better understanding of the closing scene: that Miles, before being left alone with the governess, had heard about her experiences with Miss Jessel and Quint. Even though the governess most emphatically warns Mrs. Grose against Miles and Flora talking together before Flora leaves—"they mustn't, before she goes, see each other for three seconds"—the governess, with a surprising lack of any reaction, learns the next morning that Miles "had breakfasted—in the presence of a couple of the maids—with Mrs. Grose and his sister." Our "general sense of the way things happen "would suggest that, during this time, Miles must have asked why Flora was being taken away. On the basis of successive evidence, we can plausibly surmise that the upsetting incident at the pond was openly discussed. Mrs. Grose's explanation would have brought out that this incident of the governess's claiming to have seen an apparition was one of many, beginning with the appearance of Quint on the tower. The maids who were present at the breakfast must also have heard, as is suggested by their fitting response to the reappearance of the governess: "What had happened naturally caused them all to stare." More decisively revealing, however, are Miles's succeeding reactions to her, especially near the end of the work, after the governess grabs him and shrieks, supposedly at someone, "No more, no more, no more!" Miles can see no one. When he asks her,

"Is she *here*?" even the governess realizes that Miles has in mind "some sequel to what we had done to Flora," thus upholding the surmise that Miles has already heard about the incident at the pond. When the governess says, "It's not Miss Jessel! But it's at the window—straight before us. It's *there*—the coward horror, there for the last time!" Miles's next question, "It's *he*?" further upholds the surmise that he had also heard about her other experiences, beginning with Quint.

How, then, does the governess manage to convince her readers that Miles can ask such questions only as a result of his secret intercourse with the apparitions? By the same means she has used throughout to drug her readers into accepting her entire narration. To illustrate her "art" of doing so, we look now at the governess's final experience with Quint—but not only from the governess's viewpoint. To see this material more objectively, and thus to learn how unreliable a narrator the governess is, we can employ the same method that James used to create her seeming "authority": the fashioning of a purposeful point of view. If we use a third-person voice and excerpt from the governess's narration only those words that would be presented by an effaced narrator, and then compare this view with what the governess *says* is happening, the immense gap between appearance and reality will become obvious.

The scene should first be set. After Flora and Mrs. Grose had left, the governess spent "the next hour or two" wandering "all over the place" and looking as if she "were ready for any onset." Later, she had dinner served in the dining room for herself and Miles. When the waiter finally left after the meal, Miles was alone with her. Knowing, as was surmised, of her eccentric behavior, he stood before her, trying to converse with her, as she sat on the couch, knitting. At one point during their conversation, her "voice trembled so that [she] felt it impossible to suppress the shake"; at another it became "almost grotesque." Miles, "more and more visibly nervous," felt "the approach of immediate fear." He "picked up his hat, which he had brought in," wanting to leave the room. Before allowing him to do so, she asked him to satisfy one small request.

"Tell me"—her work preoccupied her and she was off-hand!—"if yesterday afternoon, from the table in the hall, you took, you know, my letter."

[Before he could answer] she sprang straight up, getting hold of him, drawing him close while she fell against the nearest piece of furniture.

We should pause here for a moment to appreciate fully how Miles must have felt, standing alone before this troubled woman as she calmly posed her question, and then having her suddenly jump up, grab hold of him, clutch him to her, and fall against a piece of furniture.

The incident is daringly repeated a second time, her leap being even more pronounced because of Miles's attempt to back away from her after she releases him. Miles tries to "avert himself again, and that movement made *her*, with a single bound and an irrepressible cry, spring straight upon him." Miles then "uttered" a "cry" and apparently tried to break away from her, for the governess mentions "the grasp with which I recovered him": "She caught him, yes, she held him—it may be imagined with what a passion—... at the end of a minute.... his little heart... had stopped."

It seems a bit romantic to say that a boy such as Miles would be literally frightened *to death* by these circumstances, especially since there is a good deal of indirect evidence that suggests that the governess, after twice squeezing the breath from the boy's body, manages, the third time, to suffocate him. After the first time she pounced on him, she noticed that "He looked in vague pain all round the top of the room and drew his breath, two or three times over, as if with difficulty." Shortly after, "with a deep-drawn sigh, he turned away from me again.... He was soon at some distance from me, still breathing hard." After she pounced again, she saw that "Miles panted" and that "his head made the movement of a baffled dog's on a scent and then gave a frantic little shake for air." For her final act, she grasps him and squeezes—"it may be imagined with what a passion"—for the length of an entire minute, long enough, considering the already frightening happenings that have kept him breathing with difficulty, to suffocate him.

By what primary means, then, was the governess able to "drug" our "reflexion and criticism" concerning these events to give her distorted narration a persisting realistic effect? As was stated earlier, we can note the difference between the relatively terse account

that an effaced narrator would give of the events and the governess's profusively interpretive account, convincingly strengthened by her emotional commitment to what she is asserting. For example, looking at the first time that the governess pounces on Miles, we find the following (the necessity for this long quotation will become clear afterwards):

"Tell me"—oh, my work preoccupied me, and I was off-hand!—"if, yesterday afternoon, from the table in the hall, you took, you know, my letter."

My sense of how he received this suffered for a minute from something that I can describe only as a fierce split of my attention—a stroke that at first, as I sprang straight up, reduced me to the mere blind movement of getting hold of him, drawing him close, and, while I just fell for support against the nearest piece of furniture, instinctively keeping him with his back to the window. The appearance was full upon us that I had already had to deal with here: Peter Quint had come into view like a sentinel before a prison. The next thing I saw was that, from outside, he had reached the window, and then I knew that, close to the glass and glaring in through it, he offered once more to the room his white face of damnation. It represents but grossly what took place within me at the sight to say that on the second my decision was made; yet I believe that no woman so overwhelmed ever in so short a time recovered her grasp of the *act*. It came to me in the very horror of the immediate presence that the act would be, seeing and facing what I saw and faced, to keep the boy himself unaware. The inspiration—I can call it by no other name—was that I felt how voluntarily, how transcendently, I *might*. It was like fighting with a demon for a human soul, and when I had fairly so appraised it I saw how the human soul—held out, in the tremor of my hands, at arm's length—had a perfect dew of sweat on a lovely childish forehead. The face that was close to mine was as white as the face against the glass.

This passage, which represents, as does her entire narration, the manner in which *she* experiences events, reveals that she pours forth her interpretive thoughts in such a profusion that they flow over and distort, almost completely submerge, reality. She gives her thoughts so fully on every incident, she so engages and occupies our minds, that we are "drugged" by the sheer quantity of her words into accepting everything that she asserts. As she herself says, in a remark that might well include her readers, "I was a screen—I was to stand before them. The more I saw, the less they would."

We might also note here that all of the "realistic" elements throughout her account are placed with care predominantly within subordinate, and thus less emphatically noticeable, portions of each sentence—one of the effective techniques included within the "art of the romancer" for suppressing the reader's sense of the "realistic."

In his preface to *The Aspern Papers*, James refers to *The Turn of the Screw* as a work "of cold artistic calculation, an *amusette* to catch those not easily caught."[4] Later, he adds, "How can I feel my calculation to have failed, my wrought suggestion not to have worked, that is, on my being assailed, as has befallen me, with the charge of a monstrous emphasis, the charge of all indecently expatiating? There is . . . from beginning to end of the matter not an inch of expatiation."[5] James can well assert that there is no expatiation in the work, no unnecessary lengthening of the governess's narration, for, as we saw, he needed every word that the governess utters to enforce the consistent distortion of reality that her viewpoint effects until that very consistency takes on a seeming reality of its own.

Not only, however, for the reader. The horror of the tale results from the fact that James creates the governess as an author who has practiced "the art of the romancer" not only upon her reader, but upon herself. James has her cut the cable with an insidious art of which even she remains unaware. As a result, the governess's state of mind as she commits her closing act conveys a final effect of exquisite horror, for while grasping Miles and squeezing the breath from his body until "his little heart . . . had stopped," she intensely persists in believing, to the very end, that she is courageously protecting him.

James set out to fashion a work "of cold artistic calculation, an *amusette* to catch those not easily caught." We can imagine him wondering how far into the work he would be able to move his readers, to what extremes he could have the governess distort the "reality" of his fictional world, before his readers recognized the game he was playing with them. But the game was based on the premise that his readers would, at some point, awaken to the fact that they had, indeed, been "caught." The controversy that remains concerning *The Turn of the Screw* is, indeed, the best indication of how well James succeeded—beyond his expectations—in imposing upon his readers the governess's distorted view of the world within the work.

6

Afterthoughts

Why does an author craft his work? To what ultimate end? Sensing that our authors had hidden something in their works, readers have been digging for generations to find the buried treasure. In many cases they reconstructed the very nature of the novel, attempting to approach a fictional work as though it were constructed in "levels." Readers have referred to a "symbolic level," as though it had been added by the author to a "literal level," and may therefore be extrapolated, by itself, as the "meaning" of the novel.

After fashioning an interpretation of the "symbolic level," some readers have then displayed a propensity to speak as though they consciously understood the novel with an overall perspective that the author had lacked while writing the work. Thus, if they encountered any character or event that was unrelated to their interpretation, they tended to ignore or to gloss over that aspect of the work as insignificant, or perhaps even to declare it a flaw. To allay any doubts they may have had about passing these judgments on the works of such remarkably perceptive authors, they insisted that their understandings of the novel were based on direct analyses of the text, and so were actually clearer than the author's understanding of his own work. Typically, to support this assumption, they quoted D. H. Lawrence's ubiquitous statement "Never trust the artist. Trust the tale"[1] and then referred to "the Intentional

Fallacy,"[2] and finally, for an illustration, pointed to Richardson's *Clarissa*, noting that the author manifested, not simply his intended respect for virtuous young ladies, but also a latent dislike. And so authors of novels were summarily categorized as intuitive individuals who did not consciously apprehend the nature of their own writings, and the floodgates of interpretation were opened wide.

Responding to the torrential outpouring, another camp of critics began to condemn all interpretive readings of novels. These individuals asked, instead, for a more direct, antisymbolic description of the literal experience conveyed by the novel, devoid of an attempt to show what the experience "means." They developed different approaches to the novel, attempting to refocus primary attention on the work of art, certainly an admirable goal in itself, until they became as restrictive as any interpretive reader, for each camp tended to delimit itself to one aspect of the work, promulgating an illusory distinction between the literal experience and its significance.

In writing *Moby-Dick*, Melville obviously gave his readers the opportunity to experience vicariously, through Ishmael's narration, how it must have been for a man to go whaling. But if the novel is viewed as nothing more than a literal presentation of particular experiences, then the unifying significance of the work as a whole, as conceived and fashioned by Melville, will remain inaccessible—and the experiences themselves will most likely be misunderstood. As has been manifested by the flood of publications that has nearly overwhelmed this novel, there exists in readers a need to see the meaning of the experience presented. Undoubtedly, Melville recognized that need as he meticulously fashioned the overall experience embodied in his novel to illustrate its significance—not, it must be stressed, as a meaning lurking beneath or behind the surface of his novel, but as an inextricable part of the experience itself. Melville's evident intention in writing *Moby-Dick* was not that of constructing his work in "levels." He was concerned with a literal experience that, for him, had deep significance. His intention was to fashion his presentation in such a manner that the experience itself directly and dramatically illustrated that significance for the reader. But we are forced again at this point to raise that troubling question: Did he succeed? If we believe that he did, then how can we account for the multitude of

diverse and often contradictory responses to the novel that loom around it?

We can illustrate the enormous weight of misdirected effort in the critical responses made to our seven classic novels by examining briefly a recent historicist's interpretation of *Moby-Dick*. In *Subversive Geneology* Michael Paul Rogin, with unquestioned intelligence and a vast accumulation of carefully researched historical materials, is determined to prove that Melville wrote *Moby-Dick* as a response to specific political events of the mid-1850s, including the political conflicts that arose over the terms of California's admission to statehood, the expansion of slavery into newly won territories, and the enforcement of the Fugitive Slave Law, all of which "posed, by 1850, the gravest threat to the Union since its founding."[3] Rogin then concludes: "*Moby-Dick* is not a symbolist text which flees history to some deeper, universal pattern. Rather, it embodies the catastrophe prophesied in 1850, explores its source, and comments on the efforts to escape it."[4] By focusing too intently on his own purpose, Rogin manages to overlook Melville's extended metaphor of the loom, culminating in and controlling the events of the last three chapters of the novel. The ending of the novel is now to be viewed as Melville's response to Judge Lemuel Shaw's 1851 decision in the *Sims* case to uphold the Fugitive Slave Law in Massachusetts. "Other evidence in *Moby-Dick* also suggests the impact of Shaw's ruling on the climax of Melville's tale," Rogin asserts, and then defends his position as follows.

According to Rogin, "Melville conceived the final confrontation between Ahab and the white whale sometime in the first half of 1851. He may well have written his last chapters only after returning from a trip to New York in June."[5] Rogin notes that two New York antislavery leaders wrote public letters to protest Judge Shaw's decision, and that on May 12, 1851, the New York *Herald* responded, attacking "The Anti-Slavery Agitators" by comparing the Union to a whale caught in a "terrible current" of "political excitement" caused by abolitionist "fanatics."[6] Rogin then concludes: "In Melville's alternative ending, a whale sinks the fanatic. If one reads the ending of *Moby-Dick* in the light of the *Herald*'s intention, then the white whale sank the *Pequod* and the Union was saved."[7]

Rogin's interpretation of the novel's ending raises a number of troublesome questions. How does Rogin know that "Melville con-

ceived the final confrontation between Ahab and the white whale sometime in the first half of 1851." (Italics added.) The craftsmanship of the novel indicates otherwise. The events of the ending are controlled by the concept of the loom, which pervades the entire novel. Are we to assume that an author does not "conceive" his materials until the moment he actually writes them down, or that he does not perceive the ending toward which he is shaping his novel until he actually reaches the end? Did Melville read the May 12, 1851 issue of the New York *Herald* during a trip he made to New York in June? Can we assert with any conviction that Melville "may well have written his last chapters only after returning from" that trip? If we are to accept Rogin's interpretation, we would have to conclude that Melville, caught up in the political events of his day, remained unaware of his own accomplished craftsmanship, as illustrated by his extended concept of the loom.

Rogin asserts that "*Moby-Dick* is not a symbolist text which flees history to some deeper universal pattern." Melville, however, confronted a much more difficult task than that of embodying certain political events of his day, however important they proved to be historically. He strove to craft a "deeper universal pattern," for he was intent on offering us a clarifying dramatization of the very forces of reality that cause and control all of the happenings of this mortal world.

We have said that it was clearly Melville's *intention* to convey a specifically crafted experience to his readers—although such a statement may not be acceptable among current critics, where a generalized conception of "the Intentional Fallacy" still prevails. Certainly, any statement a novelist makes about his published work must be closely examined in the light of the work itself, for there have been many instances in which such statements have proven to be misleading or inaccurate when applied to the work. Admittedly, the author may not be able to speak accurately, in a critical, expository manner, of his imaginative writings. But we must always distinguish between the novelist's *stated* intention and the novelist's intention as fulfilled within his finished work.

No claim is being made that as novelists compose reams of manuscript they remain in conscious control of every word. Most probably, they will write intuitively to varying degrees throughout their work, and will thus include aspects that have a significance

that may elude their awareness. The point being stressed, however, is that each of our novelists may be attributed with having had a central purpose in mind while writing his work. Although we may accept the obvious qualification that the author's mind is never *really* known, the presence of a meticulously fulfilled intention, worked out over hundreds of pages of crafted text, might lead us to conclude, not unreasonably, that the intention is the author's.

The deconstructionists, however, would strongly disagree, claiming that there is no "final authority" in literary readings, that all readings of a novel are open to "demolition." Colin Campbell asks, "What is deconstruction?" in his article "The Tyranny of the Yale Critics." He continues:

To "deconstruct" a text is pretty much what it sounds like—to pick the thing carefully apart, exposing what deconstructors see as the central fact and tragic little secret of Western philosophy—namely, the circular tendency of language to refer to itself. Because the "language" of a text refers mainly to other "languages" and texts—and not to some hard, extratextual reality—the text tends to have several possible meanings, which usually undermine one another. In fact, the "meaning" of a piece of writing—it doesn't matter whether it's a poem or a novel or a philosophic treatise—is indeterminate.[8]

The weakness of a philosophical position is usually found at the point its premises are established. We turn, in this case, to Robert Moynihan's "Interview with Paul de Man" and note one of de Man's premises about the nature of literature:

Surely there's a priority of the author before the critic, but that's a false model. Within the text itself it's impossible to separate moments of writing from moments of reading in the text, so that it is always possible within the text itself to reverse those priorities. An author doesn't invent something and then start to read it. Any invention is always already a reading, and any reading is an invention, to some extent. . . . When you write the text you are constantly reading. Anyone who writes a text is at that moment reading it, and the production of a text is as much an act of reading as it is writing.[9]

As de Man has stated, the deconstructionist believes that the author's invention is the text he holds before him, that the invention occurs at the moment the language is selected. Therefore, any

creative writing is at the same time also a creative reading. Since the two come into existence at the same moment in time, they can always be exchanged for each other, both by the author and the critic. Accepting that premise, the deconstructionist is then in a position to claim that his variant and contradictory readings are simply facets on the multifaceted diamond of the originally written work—a diamond that is unfortunately viewed as not only fracturing the light passing through it, but causing each facet to reflect back upon the others, thereby confusing the light and losing any clarity. Each diamond is thus judged to be innately defective in its capacity to convey light to the viewer.

Contrary to de Man's textual responses, the reading and writing of a fictional work are not reversible acts. Each reading, if the author achieves his goal, is a recreation of the author's invention, which he has attempted to embody in the form of writing. What a writer of fiction essentially invents is not the language, but an imagined experience. Language is the unfortunately limited means by which the author must attempt to embody and thereby communicate the experience.

Deconstruction arises from a particular attitudinal approach to literature: if we come to the text intent on making multiple localized associations, we can easily do so, for language, to any fertile mind, is always highly suggestive. That simple fact poses to every author what may well be his greatest challenge in communicating his essential creation, for he must employ his craft in a manner sufficient to contain those unfocused associations that will arise within his reader. The author, as craftsman, accepts the responsibility of guiding his reader to more selective associations by establishing a predominant conceptual relationship among his materials that defines which of their many suggestive threads are part of the basic fabric of the work. To encourage any reader to consider a novel as a field of potentially multitudinous responses, each by itself as invalid as the others since each "undoes" the others, is to mislead the reader and to deny the author his exceptional accomplishment.

If we come to the text intent on recreating the author's original creation and so sharing with him the basic imaginative experience he has attempted to communicate through language, we can do so—provided, of course, that the author has adequately controlled his craft. Poorly constructed novels invite multiple readings. Can

we say, therefore, that a finely constructed novel invites a basic reading, with the potential for a multitude of enriching perspectives to be based on that reading?

But what if we are unable to follow the author's footsteps through hundreds of pages of crafted text and we lose our way? Can we say by the end that we have experienced the novel as the author intended? Writers of fiction have long recognized the difficulties that arise from their dependence on a reading audience of highly diversified backgrounds and capacities. Consider, for example, Saul Bellow's comments in the *New York Times Book Review*: "It is never an easy task to take the mental measure of your readers. There are things that people *should* know if they are to read books at all. . . Besides, a certain psychic unity is always taken for granted by writers. 'Others are in essence like me, and I am basically like them, give or take a few minor differences.' "[10]

And therein lies the dilemma. If an author, with his subtle craft, shapes his novel into a significant experience that is unmistakably evident to his own eyes, does he assume that it will also be experienced in that manner by his readers, with whom "a certain psychic unity is always taken for granted"? What a stinging disappointment it must be to authors who discover otherwise. Some are driven afterwards to speak directly to their readers, attempting to lessen the extent of their first failure by offering an explanation of their central purpose in writing a particular novel, as Saul Bellow did for *Herzog* in the article cited. Most others, we suspect, eventually recognize that they have not successfully communicated with their readers, except, perhaps, for an extremely limited audience of individuals capable, by nature and learning, of sharing their works, and they let their novels go, like wayward children, to make their own way in the world.

Why does an author craft his work? Each of our authors wished us to experience the grand illusion of existing within a fictional world, seeing and feeling directly for ourselves. Each of them strove to achieve this goal by hiding his intermediary presence, purposefully masking the choices he made as he selected and manipulated his material. After looking more closely at their works, we are left with the distinct possibility that they all may have succeeded too well. By creating the grand illusion, each author may have lost control over his reader's responses. The

ultimate significance of his crafted experience may have been left to the shaping sensibilities of each reader.

If we are to move our students beyond this paradox of craft, we must encourage them to develop greater capacities to sit enthralled in the house of fiction without losing awareness of the author's presence. Only then will they be able to see through the eyes of the author, who stands alone at the window he has opened for us onto his imagined world.

Notes

THE AUTHOR'S VIEWPOINT

1. Robert Moynihan, "Interview with Paul de Man," *The Yale Review*, Summer 1984, p. 585.

2. E. M. Forster, *Aspects of the Novel* (New York: Harcourt Brace & World, 1927), p. 45.

3. Forster, p. 130.

4. M. H. Abrams, "Forward," *Literature and Belief* (New York: Columbia University Press, 1958), p. xi.

5. Wayne C. Booth, *The Rhetoric of Fiction* (Chicago: University of Chicago Press, 1961), p. 75.

6. Henry James, "Preface," *The Portrait of a Lady* (Boston: Houghton Mifflin, 1956), p. 7.

7. Allan Tate, *The Man of Letters in the Modern World* (New York: Meridian Books, 1957), p. 78.

8. Percy Lubbock, *The Craft of Fiction* (New York: Viking, 1957), p. 1.

9. Jonathan Culler, *On Deconstruction: Theory and Criticism After Structuralism* (Ithaca, N.Y.: Cornell University Press, 1982), p. 32.

10. Culler, pp. 32–33.

11. Culler, p. 38.

12. Culler, p. 38.

13. Christopher Norris, *Deconstruction: Theory and Practice* (London: Routledge, 1988), pp. 4–5.

14. Norris, pp. 22, 24.

15. Moynihan, p. 588.

16. Gary B. Madison, "Coping with Nietzsche's Legacy: Rorty, Derrida, Gadamer," *Philosophy Today*, Spring 1992, p. 10.

17. Edgar Allan Poe, *Selected Writings of Edgar Allan Poe* (Boston: Houghton Mifflin, 1956), p. 454.

18. Booth, p. 388.

AUTHOR AS NARRATOR

1. Arnold Kettle, *An Introduction to the English Novel*, Vol. 2 (London: Hutchinson's University Library, 1953), p. 31.

2. Marjorie Perloff, "Cinderella Becomes the Wicked Stepmother," *Nineteenth Century Fiction*, March 1969, p. 414.

3. Carl van Doren, *The American Novel* (New York: Macmillan, 1940), p. 172.

4. Lyall H. Powers, *Henry James's Major Novels* (East Lansing: Michigan State University Press, 1973), p. 75.

5. William Bysshe Stein, "The Portrait of a Lady: *Vis Inertiae*," *Western Humanities Review*, Spring 1959, pp. 186–87.

6. Rebecca West, *Henry James* (New York: Nisbet & Company, 1916), p. 69.

NARRATOR AS AUTHOR: THE SURROGATE "I"

1. Richard Chase, *Herman Melville: A Critical Study* (New York: Hafner, 1971), p. 49.

2. J.W.N. Sullivan, "Melville's Lonely Journey," in *Moby-Dick As Doubloon*, ed. Hershel Parker and Harrison Hayford (New York: W. W. Norton, 1970), p. 162.

3. Lewis Mumford, *The Golden Day: A Study in American Experience and Culture* (New York: Boni and Liveright, 1926), p. 150.

4. Harry Slochower, *Mythopoesis* (Detroit, Mich.: Wayne State University Press, 1970), p. 235.

5. Edmund Bergler, "A Note on Herman Melville," *American Imago*, Winter 1954, p. 387.

6. D. H. Lawrence, *Studies in Classic American Literature* (New York: Viking, 1923), p. 160.

7. Walter E. Bezanson, "*Moby-Dick*: Work of Art," in *Moby-Dick: Centennial Essays*, ed. Tyrus Hillway and Luther S. Mansfield (Dallas, Tex.: Southern Methodist University Press, 1953), p. 56.

8. Richard Brodhead, *Hawthorne, Melville, and the Novel* (Chicago: University of Chicago Press, 1976), p. 161.

9. Gordon H. Mills, "The Castaway in *Moby-Dick*," *University of Texas Studies in English*, Vol. 29, 1950, pp. 240–41.

10. Bernard DeVoto, *Mark Twain's America* (Chautauqua, N.Y.: Chautauqua Institution, 1932), p. 313.

11. Robert Penn Warren, "Hemingway," *The Kenyon Review*, Winter 1947, p. 2.

12. Warren, p. 17.

13. Warren, p. 22.

14. Philip Young, *Ernest Hemingway* (Minneapolis: University of Minnesota Press, 1965), p. 15.

15. Ray B. West, Jr., "The Biological Trap," *Hemingway* (New Jersey: Prentice-Hall, 1962), p. 148.

16. Carlos Baker, *Hemingway: The Writer As Artist* (Princeton, N.J.: Princeton University Press, 1963), p. 101.

17. Michael F. Moloney, "Ernest Hemingway: The Missing Third Dimension," *Hemingway and His Critics* (New York: Hill and Wang, 1961), p. 183.

18. George Plimpton, "Ernest Hemingway," *The Paris Review*, Spring 1958, p. 66.

19. Warren, p. 23.

20. Ernest Hemingway, *A Farewell to Arms* (New York: Charles Scribner's Sons, 1969), p. 174.

21. Hemingway, p. 14.

22. Hemingway, p. 72.

23. Hemingway, p. 106.

24. Hemingway, p. 93.

25. Edmund Wilson, *The Wound and the Bow* (New York: Oxford University Press, 1947), p. 222.

26. Warren, p. 1.

27. Hemingway, p. 332.

28. Hemingway, p. 28.

29. Hemingway, p. 66.

30. Hemingway, p. 325.

NARRATOR AS AUTHOR: THE SEPARATE "I"

1. Samuel Clemens, Notebook #28a [I], TS, p.35 (1895), Mark Twain Papers, University of California Library, Berkeley. Cited in Henry Nash Smith's "Introduction" to *Adventures of Huckleberry Finn* (Boston: Houghton Mifflin, 1958), p. xvi.

2. Clemens, *The Autobiography of Mark Twain*, ed. Charles Neider (New York: Harper & Brothers, 1959), p. 6.

3. J. D. Salinger, *The Catcher in the Rye* (New York: Bantam Books, 1964), p. 134.

4. Salinger, p. 91.

5. Salinger, p. 30.

6. Salinger, p. 197.

7. Salinger, p. 154.

8. Salinger, p. 91.

9. Salinger, p. 99.

10. Salinger, p. 6.

11. Salinger, p. 63.

12. Salinger, p. 189.

13. Salinger, p. 195.

14. Salinger, p. 211.

15. Salinger, p. 213.

16. Salinger, p. 5.

17. Salinger, p. 189.

18. Salinger, p. 189.

19. Carl Jung, *The Integration of the Personality* (New York: Farrar & Rinehart, 1939), p. 169.

20. Jung, p. 111.

21. Jung, p. 95.

22. Jung, p. 89.

23. Jung, p. 48.

24. Jung, p. 163.

25. Jung, p. 284.

26. Jung, pp. 281–82.

27. Friedrich Schiller, *On the Aesthetic Education of Man*, translated by Reginald Snell (New Haven, Conn.: Yale University Press, 1954), p. 99.

AUTHOR OR NARRATOR?

1. Stephen Crane, *The Red Badge of Courage*, ed. with an Introduction by Richard Chase (Boston: Houghton Mifflin, 1960), p. xv.

2. Henry James, "Preface to *The American*," *The Art of the Novel* (New York: Charles Scribner's Sons, 1934), pp. 33–34.

3. James, "Preface to *The Aspern Papers*," *The Art of the Novel*, p. 170.

4. James, "Preface to *The Aspern Papers*," p. 172.

5. James, "Preface to *The Aspern Papers*," p. 177.

AFTERTHOUGHTS

1. D. H. Lawrence, *Studies in Classic American Literature* (New York: Viking, 1923), p. 2.

2. W. K. Wimsatt, Jr. and M. C. Beardsley, "The Intentional Fallacy," *The Verbal Icon: Studies in the Meaning of Poetry* (Lexington: University of Kentucky Press, 1954).

3. Michael Paul Rogin, *Subversive Geneology* (New York: Alfred A. Knopf, 1983), p. 103.

4. Rogin, p. 107.

5. Rogin, p. 142.

6. Rogin, pp. 142–43.

7. Rogin, p. 143.

8. Colin Campbell, "The Tyranny of the Yale Critics," *New York Times Magazine*, February 9, 1986, p. 23.

9. Robert Moynihan, "Interview with Paul de Man," *The Yale Review*, Summer 1984, p. 592.

10. Saul Bellow, "The Civilized Barbarian Reader," *New York Times Book Review*, March 8, 1987, p. 1.

Bibliography

Abrams, M. H. "Forward." *Literature and Belief*. New York: Columbia University Press, 1958.

Baker, Carlos. *Hemingway: The Writer As Artist*. Princeton, N.J.: Princeton University Press, 1963.

Barthes, Roland, *S/Z An Essay*. Translated by Richard Miller. New York: Hill and Wang, 1974.

Bellow, Saul. "The Civilized Barbarian Reader." *New York Times Book Review*, March 8, 1987, pp. 1, 38.

Bergler, Edmund. "A Note on Herman Melville." *American Imago*, Winter 1954, pp. 385–97.

Bezanson, Walter E. "*Moby-Dick: Work of Art*." In *Moby-Dick: Centennial Essays*, edited by Tyrus Hillway and Luther S. Mansford. Dallas, Tex.: Southern Methodist University Press, 1953.

Booth, Wayne C. *The Rhetoric of Fiction*. Chicago: University of Chicago Press, 1961.

Brodhead, Richard. *Hawthorne, Melville, and the Novel*. Chicago: University of Chicago Press, 1976.

Campbell, Colin. "The Tyranny of the Yale Critics." *New York Times Magazine*, February 9, 1986, pp. 20–26.

Chase, Richard. *Herman Melville: A Critical Study*. New York: Hafner, 1971.

Clemens, Samuel. *The Autobiography of Mark Twain*. Edited by Charles Neider. New York: Harper & Brothers, 1959.

_____ . Notebook #28a [I], TS (1895). Mark Twain Papers. Berkeley: University of California Library.

Crane, Stephen. *The Red Badge of Courage*. Edited with an Introduction by Richard Chase. Boston: Houghton Mifflin, 1960.

Culler, Jonathan. *On Deconstruction: Theory and Criticism After Structuralism*. Ithaca, N.Y.: Cornell University Press, 1982.

Davis, Robert Con and Ronald Schleifer, eds. *Rhetoric and Form: Deconstruction at Yale*. Norman: University of Oklahoma Press, 1985.

de Man, Paul. *Blindness & Insight*. New York: Oxford University Press, 1971.

Derrida, Jacques. *Of Grammatology*. Translated by Gayatri Chakravorty Spivak. Baltimore, Md.: Johns Hopkins University Press, 1976.

DeVoto, Bernard. *Mark Twain's America*. Chautauqua, N.Y.: Chautauqua Institution, 1932.

Forster, E. M. *Aspects of the Novel*. New York: Harcourt Brace & World, 1927.

Hemingway, Ernest. *A Farewell to Arms*. New York: Charles Scribner's Sons, 1969.

James, Henry. "Preface to *The American*." *The Art of the Novel*. New York: Charles Scribner's Sons, 1934.

———. "Preface to *The Aspern Papers*." *The Art of the Novel*. New York: Charles Scribner's Sons, 1934.

———. "Preface." *The Portrait of a Lady*. Boston: Houghton Mifflin, 1956.

Jung, Carl. *The Integration of the Personality*. New York: Farrar & Rinehart, 1939.

Kettle, Arnold. *An Introduction to the English Novel*. Vol. 2. London: Hutchinson's University Library, 1953.

Lawrence, D. H. *Studies in Classic American Literature*. New York: Viking, 1923.

Lubbock, Percy. *The Craft of Fiction*. New York: Viking, 1957.

Madison, Gary B. "Coping with Nietzsche's Legacy: Rorty, Derrida, Gadamer." *Philosophy Today*, Spring 1992, pp. 3–19.

Miller, J. Hillis. Introduction. "Interview with Paul de Man," by Robert Moynihan. *The Yale Review*, Summer 1984, pp. 576–78.

Mills, Gordon H. "The Castaway in *Moby-Dick*." *University of Texas Studies in English*, Vol. 29, 1950.

Moloney, Michael F. "Ernest Hemingway: The Missing Third Dimension." *Hemingway and His Critics*. New York: Hill and Wang, 1961.

Moynihan, Robert. "Interview with Paul de Man." *The Yale Review*, Summer 1984, pp. 576–602.

Mumford, Lewis. *The Golden Day: A Study in American Experience and Culture*. New York: Boni and Liveright, 1926.

Norris, Christopher. *Deconstruction: Theory and Practice*. London: Routledge, 1988.

Perloff, Marjorie. "Cinderella Becomes the Wicked Stepmother." *Nineteenth Century Fiction*. March 1969, pp. 413–33.

Plimpton, George. "Earnest Hemingway." *The Paris Review*. Spring, 1958, pp. 61–89.

Poe, Edgar Allan. *Selected Writings of Edgar Allan Poe*. Boston: Houghton Mifflin, 1956.

Powers, Lyall H. *Henry James's Major Novels*. East Lansing: Michigan State University Press, 1973.

Rogin, Michael Paul. *Subversive Geneology*. New York: Alfred A. Knopf, 1983.

Salinger, J. D. *The Catcher in the Rye*. New York: Bantam Books, 1964.

Schiller, Friedrich. *On the Aesthetic Education of Man*. Translated by Reginald Snell. New Haven, Conn.: Yale University Press, 1954.

Slochower, Harry. *Mythopoesis*. Detroit, Mich.: Wayne State University Press, 1970.

Stein, William Bysshe. "The Portrait of a Lady: *Vis Inertiae*." *Western Humanities Review*, Spring 1959, pp. 177–90.

Sullivan, J.W.N. "Melville's Lonely Journey." In *Moby-Dick As Doubloon*, edited by Hershel Parker and Harrison Hayford. New York: W. W. Norton, 1970.

Tate, Allan. *The Man of Letters in the Modern World*. New York: Meridian Books, 1957.

Van Doren, Carl. *The American Novel*. New York: Macmillan, 1940.

Warren, Robert Penn. "Hemingway." *The Kenyon Review*, Winter 1947, pp. 1–28.

West, Ray B., Jr. "The Biological Trap." *Hemingway*. Englewood Cliffs, New Jersey: Prentice-Hall, 1962.

West, Rebecca. *Henry James*. New York: Nisbet & Company, 1916.

Wilson, Edmund. *The Wound and the Bow*. New York: Oxford University Press, 1947.

Wimsatt, W. K., Jr. and M. C. Beardsley. "The Intentional Fallacy." *The Verbal Icon: Studies in the Meaning of Poetry*. Lexington: University of Kentucky Press, 1954.

Young, Philip. *Ernest Hemingway*. Minneapolis: University of Minnesota Press, 1965.

Index

About the Author

WILLIAM A. GLASSER is President of Southern Vermont College. He has taught American literature and creative writing for most of his professional career. He has published short stories, poetry, and critical articles in a variety of scholarly and popular magazines, and he has won national awards for innovative administrative systems he developed for higher education.

ISBN 0-275-94959-1

90000>

EAN

9 780275 949594

HARDCOVER BAR CODE

Understanding the Male
Hustler
Steward, Sam

DATE DUE			